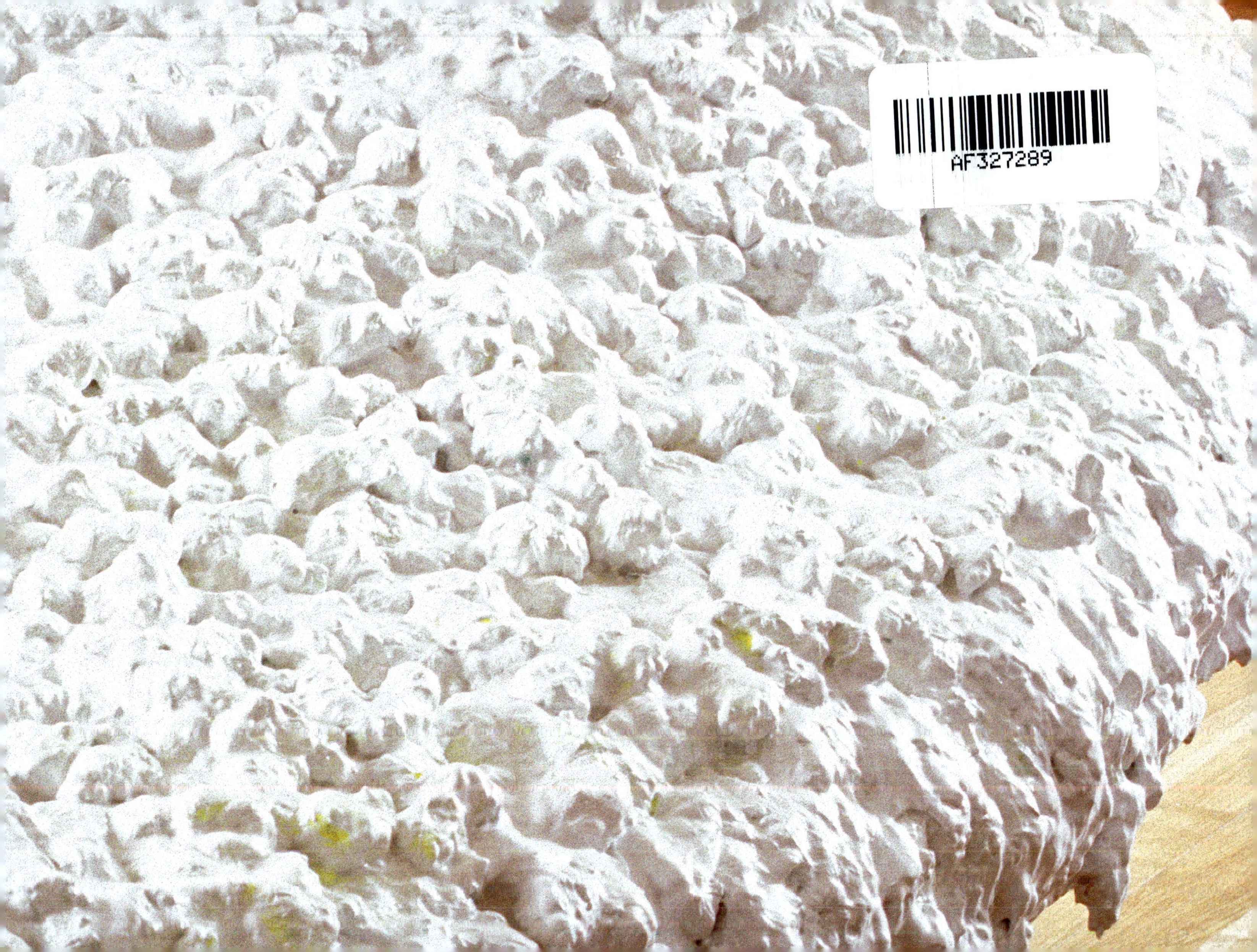

Gereon Krebber
Sorrysorrysosorry

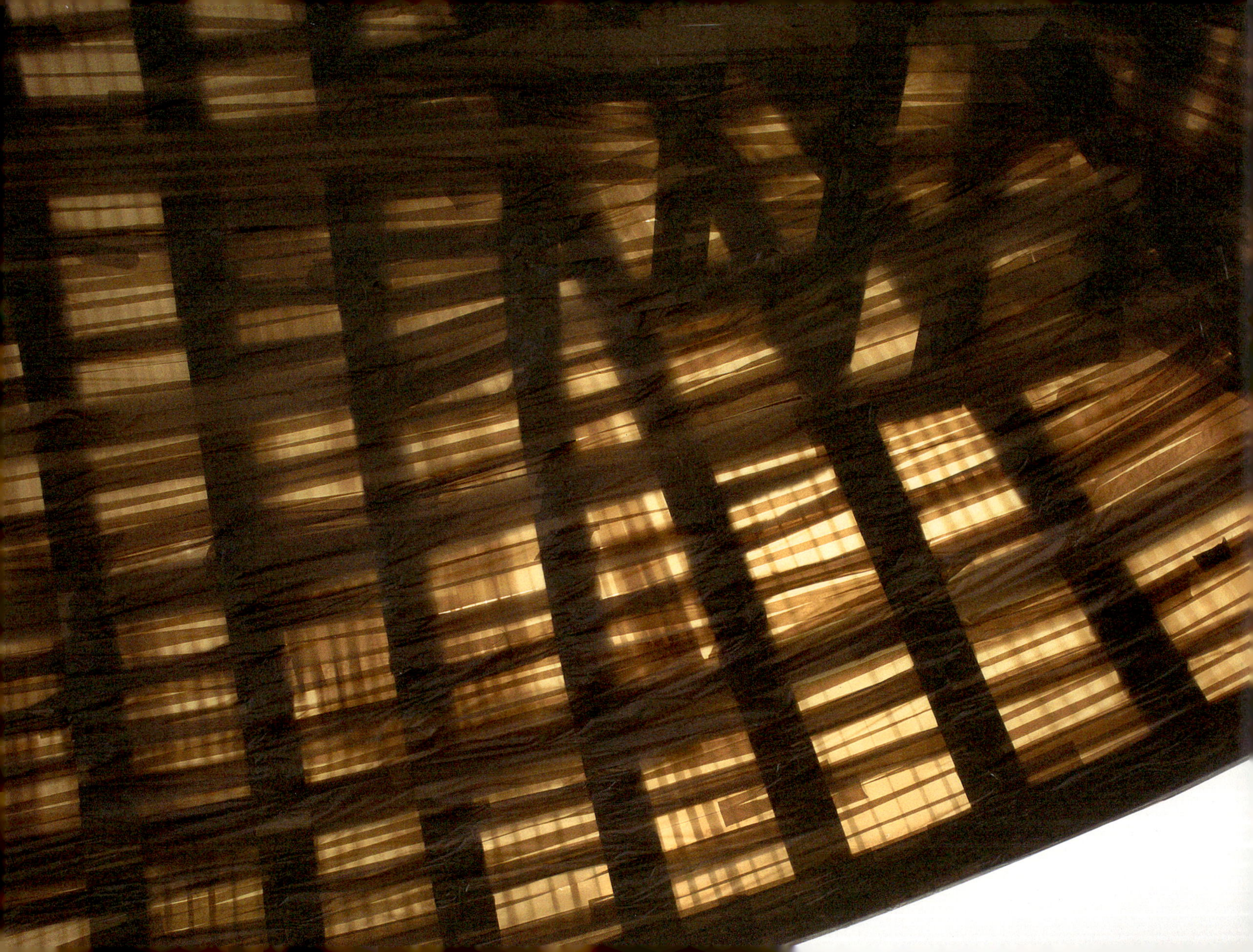

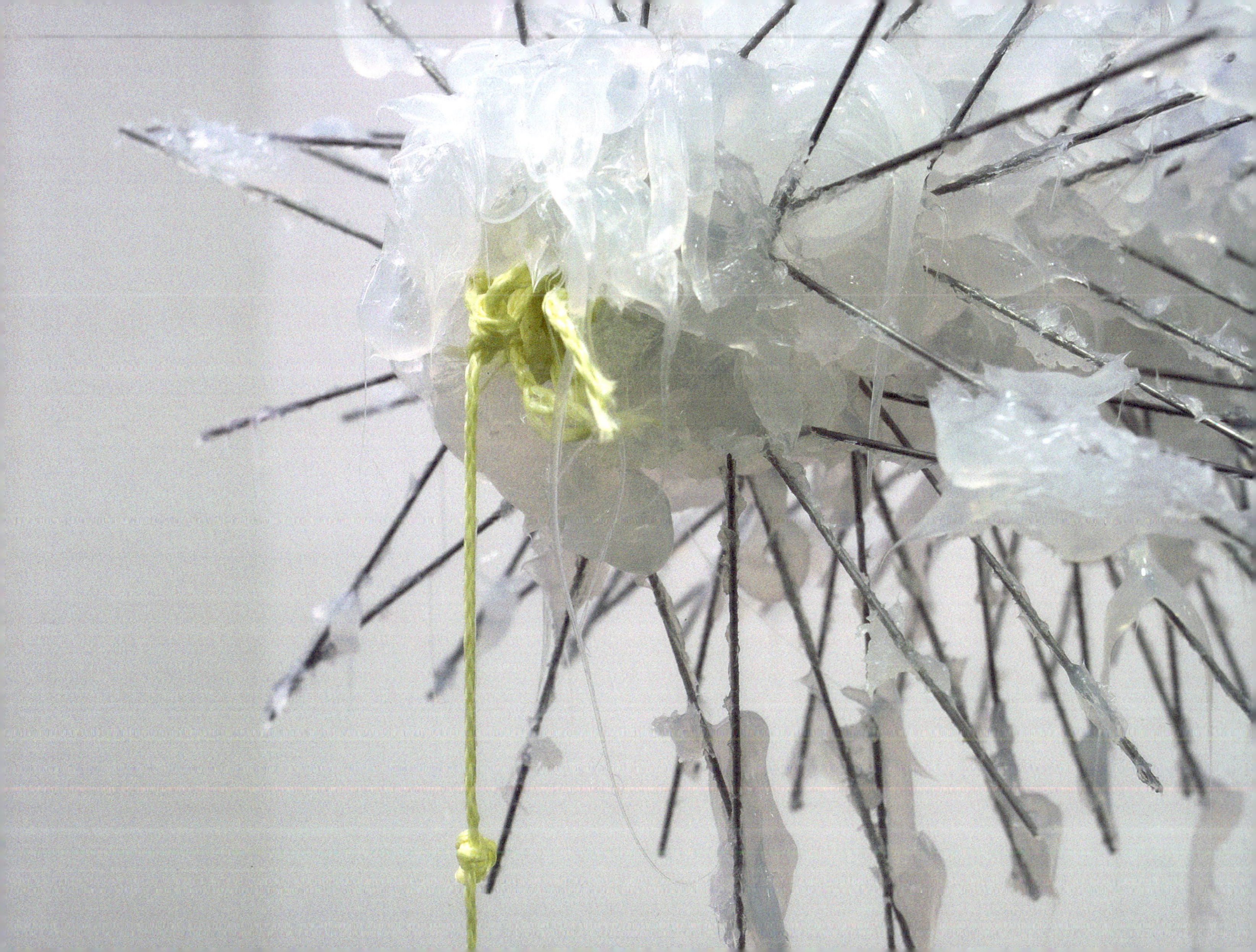

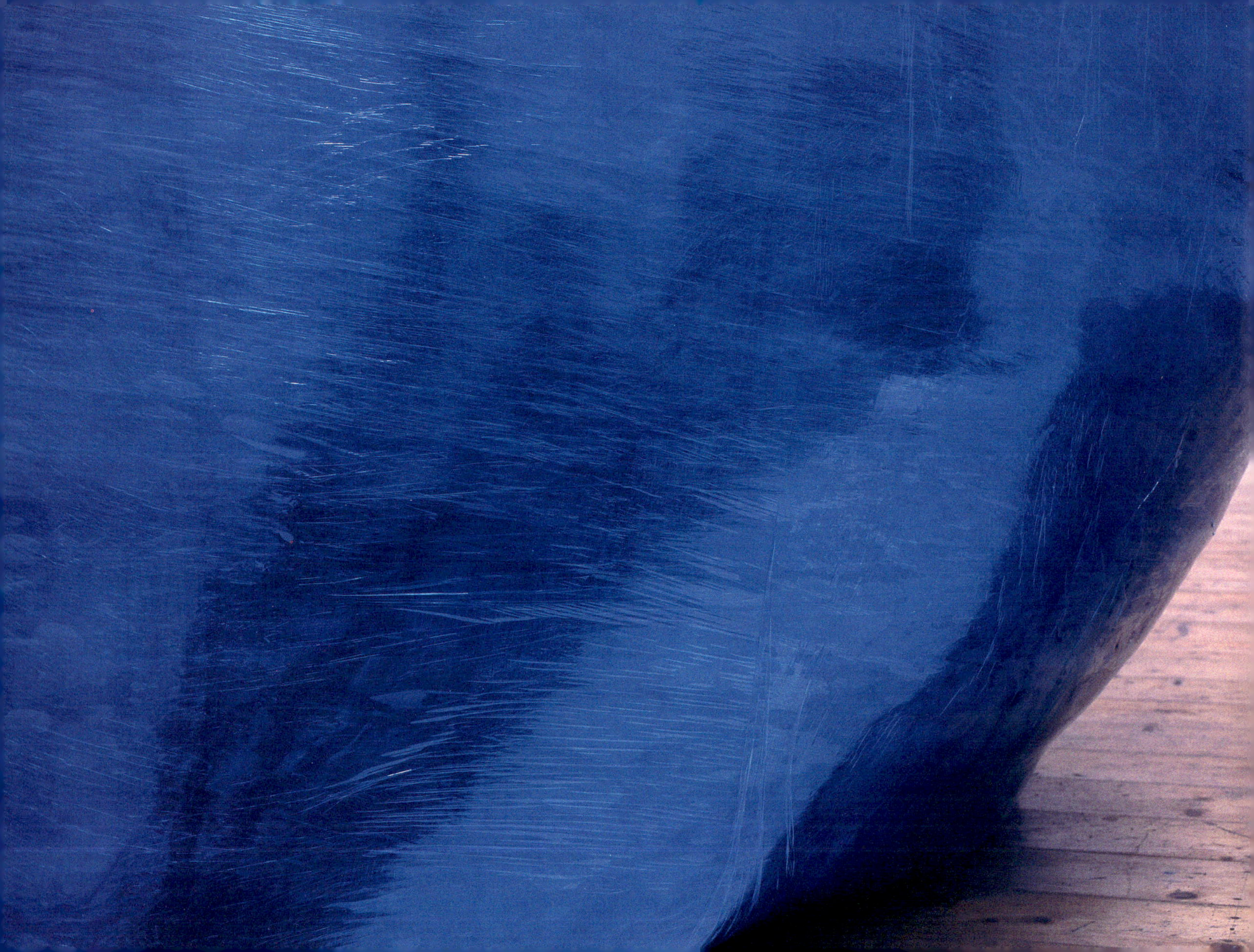

# Gereon Krebber
# Sorrysorrysosorry

herausgegeben von | edited by Stephan Mann

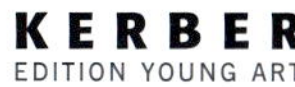

KERBER
EDITION YOUNG ART

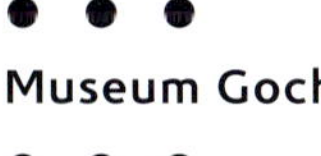

Museum Goch

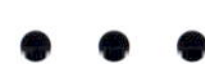

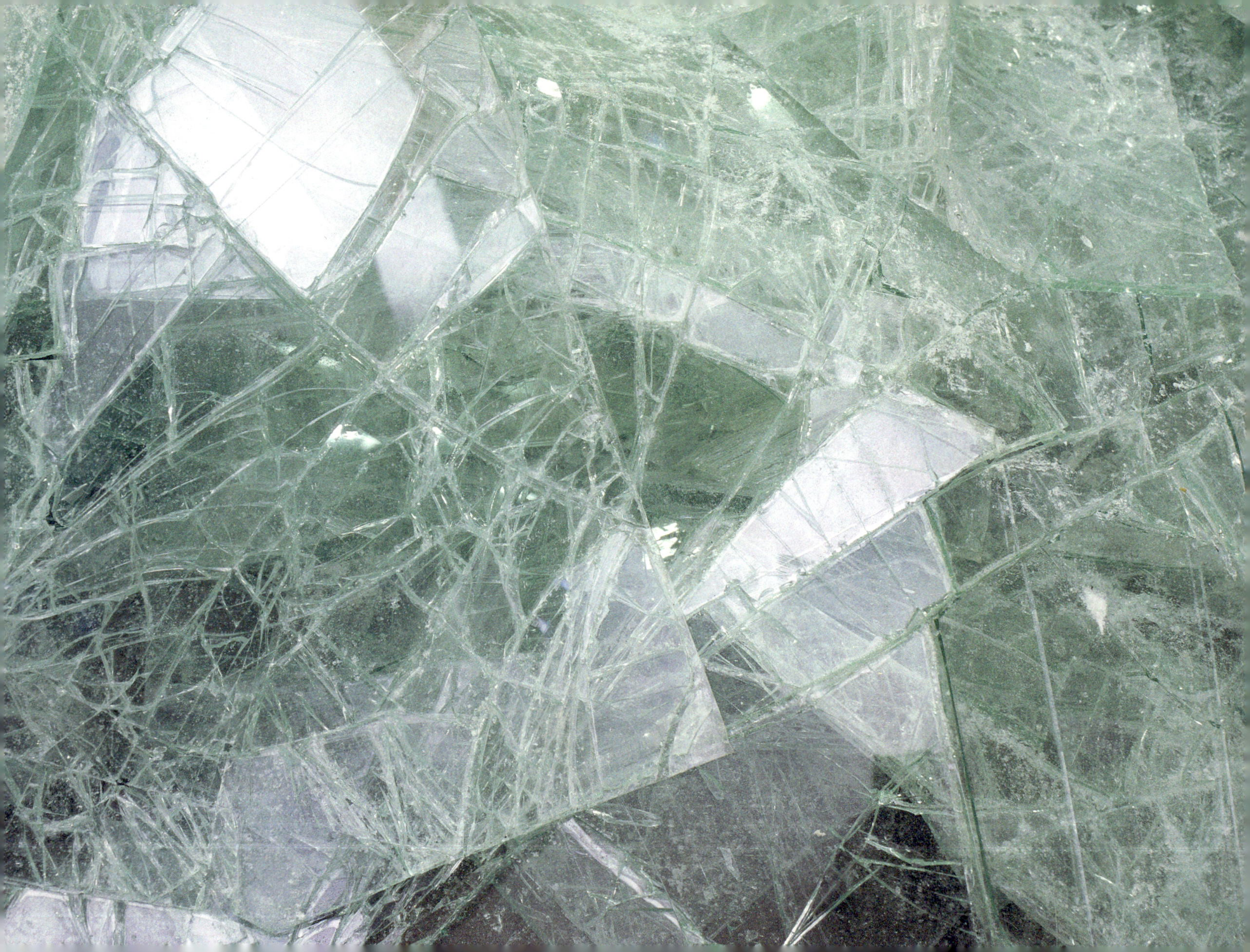

# Inhalt
# Contents

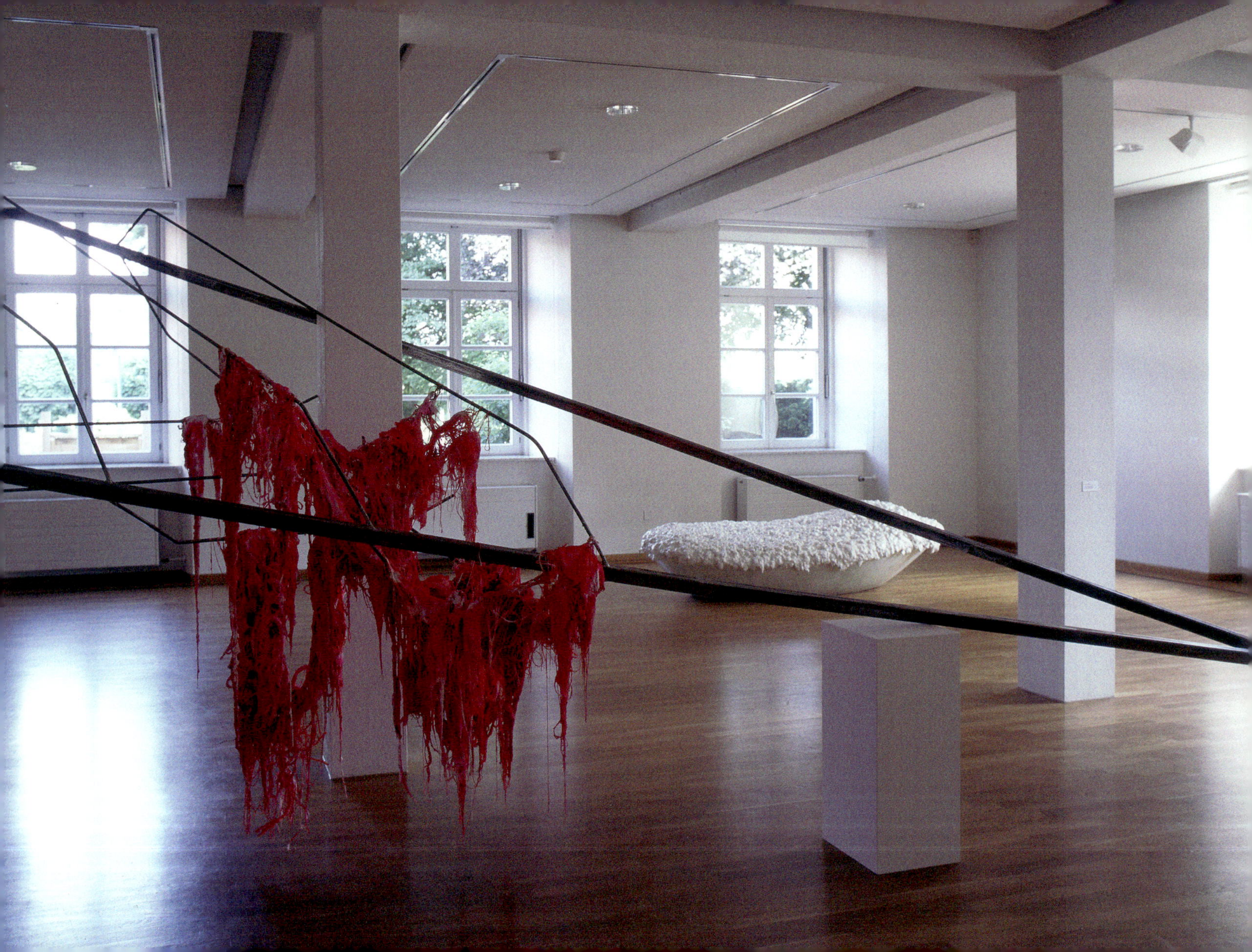

# Sorrysorrysosorry
# Gereon Krebbers Entschuldigung

Stephan Mann

Im Museum Goch korrespondieren zwei Arbeiten miteinander, die Gereon Krebber präzise für diesen Ort geschaffen hat. Im linken Ausstellungsraum schlängelt sich *Oxomoeno,* ein raupenähnliches Gebilde vom Boden über die Wand bis hin zur Decke. Mehrfach windet sich das exotische Getier und blickt von oben mit seinem leicht geneigten ‚Kopf‘ auf den Besucher herab. Das scheinbar Animalische lockt den Besucher in den Raum und zum Nähertreten. Aber es erwartet ihn keine zarte Oberfläche, vielmehr ein stacheliges, unnahbares Ding, bestückt mit unzähligen spitzen und verletzenden Stacheln.

Der Besucher weicht zurück und wird mit der Frage alleingelassen, was er hier vor sich hat. Der Wunsch nach einer haptischen Orientierung kommt hinzu und so wird sich der Mutige gewahr, dass es sich um ein Geflecht aus Hosenbügeln und Kabelbindern handelt. Fein verklebt und miteinander verdreht, schlängelt sich das Kunsttier durch den Raum.

In dem gegenüberliegenden Raum reagiert *Widget* auf diese Situation. Krebber schiebt eine spitzwinklige Dreiecksform aus Stahl dem eintretenden Besucher entgegen. Kaum betritt dieser Besucher den großen Saal mit seiner klaren Fenstergliederung und seinen beiden Mittelstützen, fühlt er sich einem Relikt aus vergangenen Tagen

gegenüber. Gestrandet im Museum, wird das schiffsähnliche Objekt zum Ausstellungsstück. Dabei scheint es zu schweben, unsichtbar mit der Wand verschraubt und auf einem Sockel platziert, der die Form der beiden Mittelstützen aufnimmt. Mit großer Leichtigkeit und Selbstverständlichkeit beherrscht das mythische Relikt den Raum. Auch hier spielt Gereon Krebber mit der Neugier seiner Besucher. Diese nähern sich einer Stahlform in die sich scheinbar zufällig so etwas wie Seetang verschlungen hat. In einer ungewöhnlichen, aggressiven roten Farbe hängt das Gebilde aus verschlungenem Allerlei herab. Auch hier erfährt der Besucher erst durch das genaue Hinsehen, was Gereon Krebber wirklich verarbeitet hat. Wie bereits für die Arbeit *Wireframe* aus dem Jahr 2007 im niederländischen Breda benutzt Krebber Zucker, Kordel, Leim und Süßigkeiten und besprüht das Gewölle mit einer leuchtenden roten Farbe. Doch anders als dort greift *Widget,* so betitelt Krebber die Gocher Installation, in den Raum und lässt den Besucher zu einem aktiven Partner der Arbeit werden.

Bereits durch ihren Umfang sprengen die Proportionen von *Widget* den Raum. Dabei ist sie so um eine der beiden Säulen konstruiert, dass dem aufmerksamen Beobachter klar wird, dass sie im Raum selbst zusammengesetzt werden musste. Aber nicht nur in ihren Maßen sprengt sie den



*Sorrysorrysosorry,*
Museum Goch, 2008:
*Widget, Bonus*

Raum. Auch in ihrer spitzwinkligen Form bringt sie eine große Dynamik in die ansonsten ruhige Architektur des Raumes.

Beide Arbeiten *Oxomoeno* und *Widget* spielen mit der Befindlichkeit des Betrachters. Er wird angesichts der Installationen in große Unsicherheit versetzt. Krebber weckt eine Fülle an Assoziationen in uns. Das sind zunächst die Unsicherheiten wegen der verwendeten Materialien. „Es sieht aber doch so aus als ob", war einer der meist gehörten Sätze in der Ausstellung. Die Besucher sind irritiert und unsicher und der Künstler lässt sie mit dieser Erfahrung allein. Auch die Objekttitel helfen da nicht weiter. Sie sind selbst rein assoziativ von Krebber erdacht und geben keinen Hinweis auf eine Deutung. „Oxomoeno: ist erstmal eine recht freie Lautfolge, mit der ich das Raupending beschreiben wollte. [...] Oxomoeno beginnt als eine onomatopoetische Zusammensetzung aus offenen ‚o' und überkreuzendem ‚x' – so wie sich die Hosenbügel kreuzen und im Querschnitt einen Schlauch ‚o' geben. Inhaltlich ist es eine Mischung zwischen Mötörhead (lustiger umlautiglastiger Rockbandname), mono (Einzeln) und Oxymoron (rhetorische Figur eines Selbstwiderspruchs wie ‚Schwarzer Schnee'). Mit Selbstwidersprüchen habe ich es ja gerne, sich schlängeln aber stachelig sein etc.", so Gereon Krebber zu dieser Arbeit.

Eine Deutung gibt es nicht im Werk des Gereon Krebber. Vielmehr wird der Besucher auf seine Empfindungen und Sinne zurückgeworfen. Er schaut, er riecht, ja er tastet die Arbeiten ab und lässt Bilder in sich entstehen, die ihn dem Geheimnis der Arbeiten näher bringen. Sicherheit, ja Deutung, hierauf wartet er vergeblich. Krebber arbeitet mit dem Erinnerungspotenzial seines Gegenübers. In welche Richtung sich der Besucher bewegt, ist ihm nicht wichtig, die Deutung bleibt allein beim Betrachter. So gesehen ist Gereon Krebber ein durch und durch sinnlicher Künstler. Seine Planungen sind sehr genau und konkret, doch die letzte Phase beim Entstehen einer Arbeit liegt ganz in seiner, dem Augenblick verhafteten Hand.

Gereon Krebbers Objekte sind Installationen und autonome Skulpturen gleichermaßen. Einerseits sind sie, wie in der Ausstellung im Museum Goch, für den konkreten Raum konzipiert und gebaut. Sie sind eingepasst in eine bestimmte architektonische Situation. Anderseits stehen die Arbeiten auch ganz für sich allein. Sie sind so eigenmächtig, dass sie sich gegen jedes Bauwerk behaupten und auch isoliert, an anderem Ort denkbar sind.

Krebber schenkt seinen Arbeiten gerne Platz. Er weiß, dass sie umlaufen werden müssen, dass der Besucher ein Teil von ihnen werden möchte und Raum braucht, um sie mit seinen Sinnen zu erfassen. So zeichnet sich auch die Gocher Installation durch eine übersichtliche Anordnung weiterer Skulpturen aus.

All diesen Arbeiten liegt das Prinzip des ‚trompe l'oeil' zugrunde, des großen Scheins oder des irritierenden Spiels mit der Wahrnehmung. Ob es die überschäumende Badewanne ist, oder der weiße Eisklotz, von Krebber verspielt *Stückchen* betitelt, stets konfrontiert er den Besucher mit einer Fülle bekannter Bilder und Assoziationen mit denen er aber schließlich, das Objekt genau betrachtend

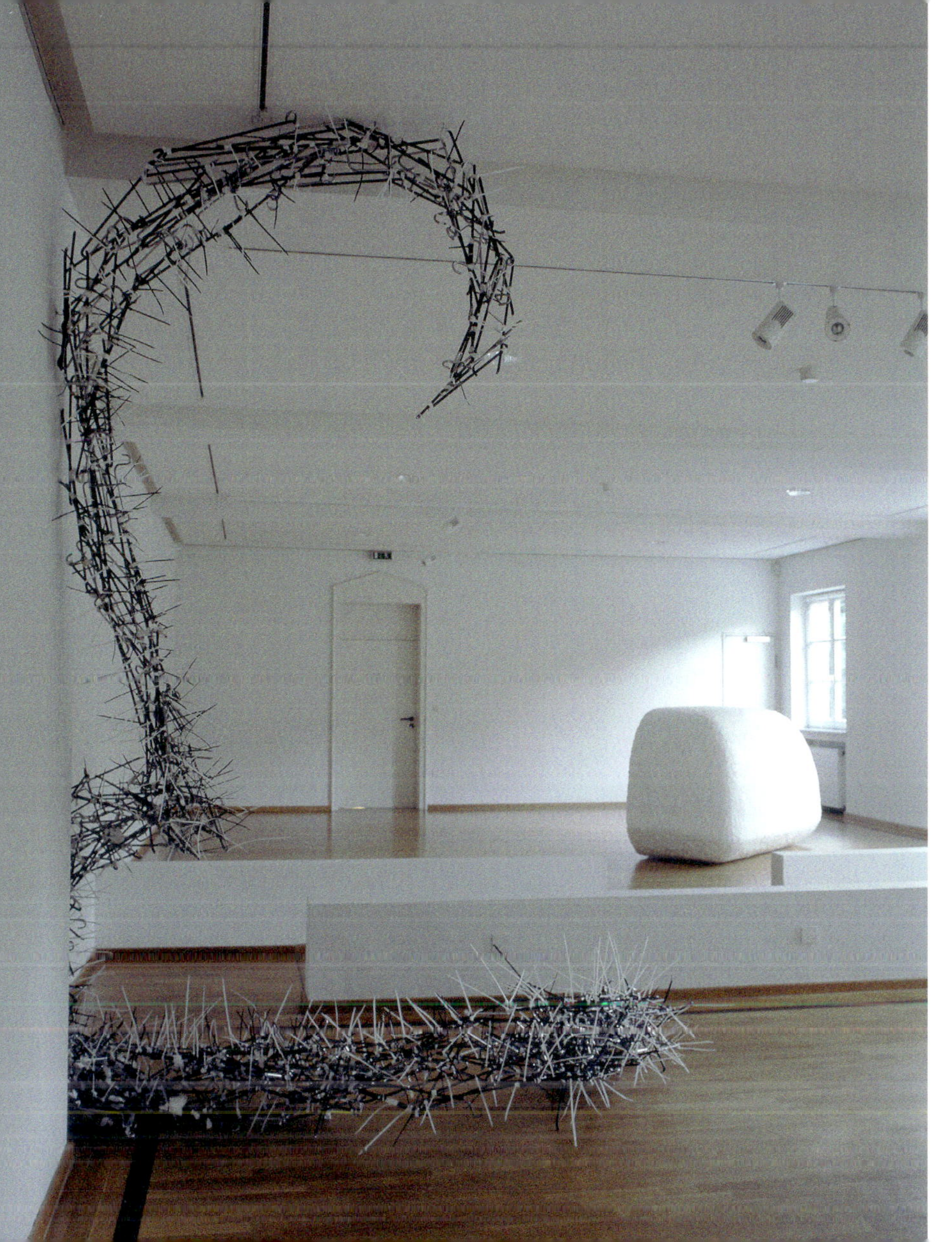

fragend alleingelassen wird. Es sieht so aus als ob und ist es doch nicht, oder doch? Für das Spielerische, die Ironie mit der Gereon Krebber den Besucher hinters Licht führt, entschuldigt sich der Künstler in unserer Ausstellung und gibt ihr den Titel *Sorrysorrysosorry.* Was will man mehr?

Auch für den *Sockel,* jenes klare und funktionale Element eines jeden Museums, das nur dienend das kostbare Objekt zur Wirkung bringt, es wird für Gereon Krebber zum unsicheren Faktor eines jeden Museumstechnikers. Die Ecke angekratzt, die Standfläche schief und auch das Material hält nicht das, was es dem Anschein nach verspricht: Gips und Farbe. Aus dem so scheinbar stand-haf-ten Sockel wird selbst ein Objekt von größter Fragilität. Hierfür entschuldigt sich der Künstler: „Sorrysorrysosorry".

Bei aller Ernsthaftigkeit, lassen sich diese Arbeiten mit viel Humor lesen. Sie spielen mit Bekanntem und überführen dieses in eine neue Kunstwirklichkeit. Der Schein wird zelebriert in Krebbers Installationen. Und wie so oft entpuppt er sich als nichts anderes als ein Spiel. Krebber schreckt hierfür vor nichts zurück. Jedes Material kommt ihm gerade recht. Auch die beliebten süßen Zuckerketten verarbeitet er gern.

Gereon Krebber verführt uns immer wieder neu. Er entlarvt die Oberfläche und damit den schönen Schein unserer Gegenwart.

*Sorrysorrysosorry,*
Museum Goch, 2008:
*Oxomoeno, Stückchen*

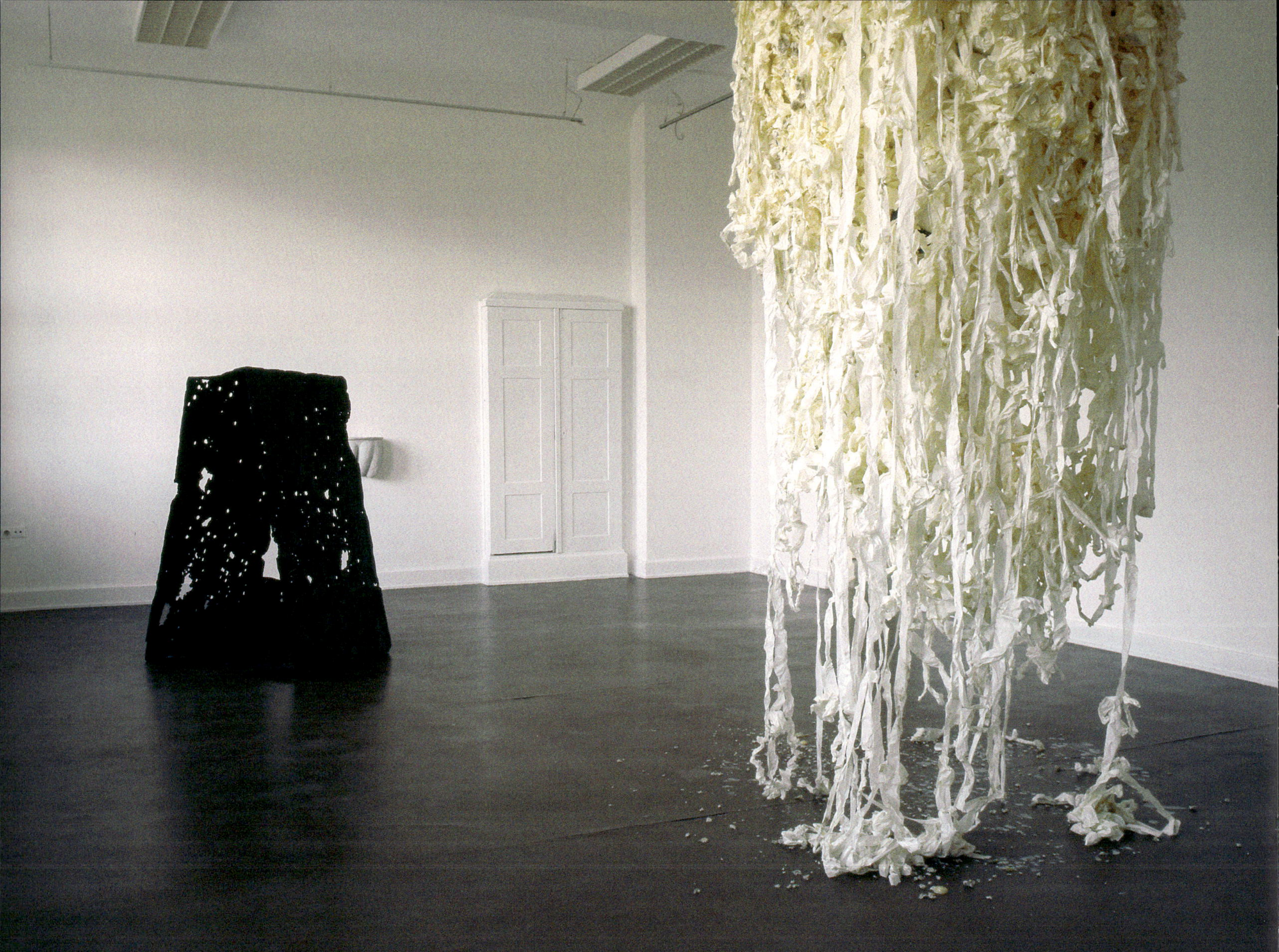

# Take a walk on the wild side
# Gereon Krebber in Essen

Uwe Schramm

Auch für den geübten Kunstbeobachter zählt die Begegnung mit Gereon Krebbers plastischer Ding- und Vorstellungswelt zu den ebenso nachhaltigen wie irritierenden Erlebnissen. In seinen Ausstellungen trifft man auf blau eingefärbte Spaghettis, die zum Trocknen über ein frei stehendes Metallgestänge aufgehängt sind; ein wabbeliger, leuchtend orangefarbener Gelantinekeil schmiegt sich wie ein überdimensionales Haribo-Konfekt an eine Treppenstufe oder Weihwasserbecken ähnliche Hohlformen sind mit Coca Cola gefüllt. Rollen aus Gips und Styropor lassen Assoziationen an tiefgekühltes Tiramisu aufkeimen, fremdartige, kokonhafte Gebilde wuchern aus gelben Kabelröhren und die Böden der Ausstellungsräume bedecken Pfützen aus glibberig-schaumiger Substanz, die in ihrer grünlich schimmernden Transparenz ungesunde Erinnerungen an menschliche Auswürfe wecken.

Lustvoll überschreitet Krebber die materialbezogenen Dogmen klassischer Bildhauerei. Zur Visualisierung seiner künstlerischen Ideen greift er vorzugsweise auf unkonventionelle materielle Lösungen zurück, die das Kunstverständnis manch eines Betrachters auf eine harte Probe stellen. Dabei erscheint Krebbers Findungsreichtum bei der Auswahl seiner Werkstoffe schier unerschöpflich. Das plastische Ausdrucksvermögen des Künstlers gewinnt seine Gestalt durch die Verwendung von Abfallsäcken, Klebeband, Zahncreme, Klebepunkten, Zucker, Silikon, Gelatine, Hosenbügeln, Beton, Glyzerin, Kabelbindern, Folien, Luftballons und weiteren organischen und künstlich erzeugten Stoffen, Werkstoffe – die in ihrer gesamten Bandbreite die Verfügbarkeit profaner, täglich benutzbarer Materialien eindrucksvoll abbilden.

Krebbers Rückgriff auf kunstferne Materialien gehorcht jedoch keinem bloßen Selbstzweck. Der Künstler will die pure Rationalität als maßgebliche Kategorie der Weltwahrnehmung vergessen machen, um den Betrachter mit sinnlichen Erfahrungsweisen zu konfrontieren, die ihn auf die Komplexität seiner menschlichen Existenz zurückzuführen.

Mit der Verwendung bestimmter Materialien und ihrer gegebenen Assoziationsdichte läßt Krebber Erinnerungen an Gebilde unserer täglichen Erscheinungswelt aufkeimen, die verstören, irritieren und die eigene Weltsicht infrage stellen. Krebber spielt mit Assoziationsgewächsen, die bewusst den „guten Geschmack" empfindlich stören. Sie berühren den Betrachter wie Dinge oder Wesen aus einer anderen Welt und wirken umso intensiver, je mehr sie der eigenen Wirklichkeitserfahrung nahekommen oder aus ihr die eigene Gestalt beziehen.

Jene Irritation und Störungen, die im Umgang mit Krebbers Werken entstehen, haben ihren Ursprung darin, dass der Künstler in der Präsenz

*Droopy*, Kunsthaus Essen, 2008: *Slice of a barricada, Triple bun, Droopy*

seiner Plastiken gezielt diejenigen Ebenen des menschlichen Körpers anspricht, die zu dessen lebenserhaltendem Funktionskreislauf gehören, im gesellschaftlichen Leben jedoch üblicherweise zu den unausgesprochenen Tabus zählen. So reinszeniert er in seinen Plastiken beispielsweise lustvoll den Ausscheidungsprozess oder dessen Resultate und setzt visuelle sowie olfaktorische Reize ein, die unmittelbar sozial antrainierte Reflexe von Ekel oder Anstand auslösen. Gleichzeitig jedoch verführt die schillernde Materialität seiner Installationen die Besucher zu einer solchen Nähe der Betrachtung, dass der emotionale Widerstreit zwischen Faszination und Ekel unausweichlich erscheint.

Krebbers Plastiken suchen oder finden auf subversiven Wegen die Vergleichbarkeit und analogen Verschränkungen zum menschlichen Körper, sowohl in physikalischer als auch in biochemischer Hinsicht. Tabubrüche, Provokationen und Infragestellungen bestimmen dabei das intendierte Maß an Widersprüchen und gefühlsbesetzten Reaktionen des Rezipienten, die sich mit der Ausdruckspräsenz von Krebbers Plastiken stets verbinden.

### When life begins

Nachdem sich Gereon Krebber entschlossen hatte, ein Ausstellungsprojekt im Kunsthaus Essen zu realisieren und eine Besichtigung der zur Verfügung stehenden Ausstellungsräume Klarheit über den Ort des zukünftigen Geschehens brachte, formulierte der Künstler innerhalb kürzester Zeit die Umrisse seiner Ausstellungsidee. Mit beeindruckender Souveränität und Genauigkeit erfasste

Krebber die besondere Spannung des Raumes, dessen architektonischen Besonderheiten und die eigenwillige, allenfalls unterschwellig wahrzunehmende Atmosphäre des Ortes.

Krebber ging durch sämtliche Räume, vermaß mit seinem eigenen Körper und ausgebreiteten Armen Wände, Türöffnungen und Fensternischen und entschied, dass eigens für den größten, mit Pfeilern und einer durchgehenden Fensterreihe bestückten Raum etwas Großes, die Raumdimensionen Sprengendes geschaffen werden sollte. Die kantigen Pfeiler sollten über die gesamte Ausdehnung des Raumes hinweg von einer weichen, rundlich-länglichen Form, ähnlich der einer Schlange oder eines Wurmes sanft umspielt werden, der den zukünftigen Ausstellungsbesucher durch seine eleganten Biegungen und Windungen dazu nötigt, mit Vorsicht über auf dem Boden liegende Auswüchse und Stümpfe hinwegzusteigen.

Zusätzlich zu diesem körperlich-sinnlichen Erlebnis sollte sich ein visuelles Überraschungsmoment einstellen – durch die Konfrontation mit den von Krebber vorgesehenen Materialien. Um dieses Ziel zu erreichen, griff Krebber bei der Realisierung seiner spektakulären Raumintervention nicht auf den von Bildhauern üblicherweise bevorzugten Materialfundus zurück, sondern ließ Werkstoffe zum Einsatz gelangen, die sonst eher in Lebensmittelmärkten das handelsübliche Erscheinungsbild bestimmen. Eine simple Holzkonstruktion wurde solange Schicht für Schicht zunächst mit Silberfolie und dann mit leuchtend grüner Klarsichtfolie umwickelt, bis eine fremdartige, organisch anmutende Form entstanden war, deren

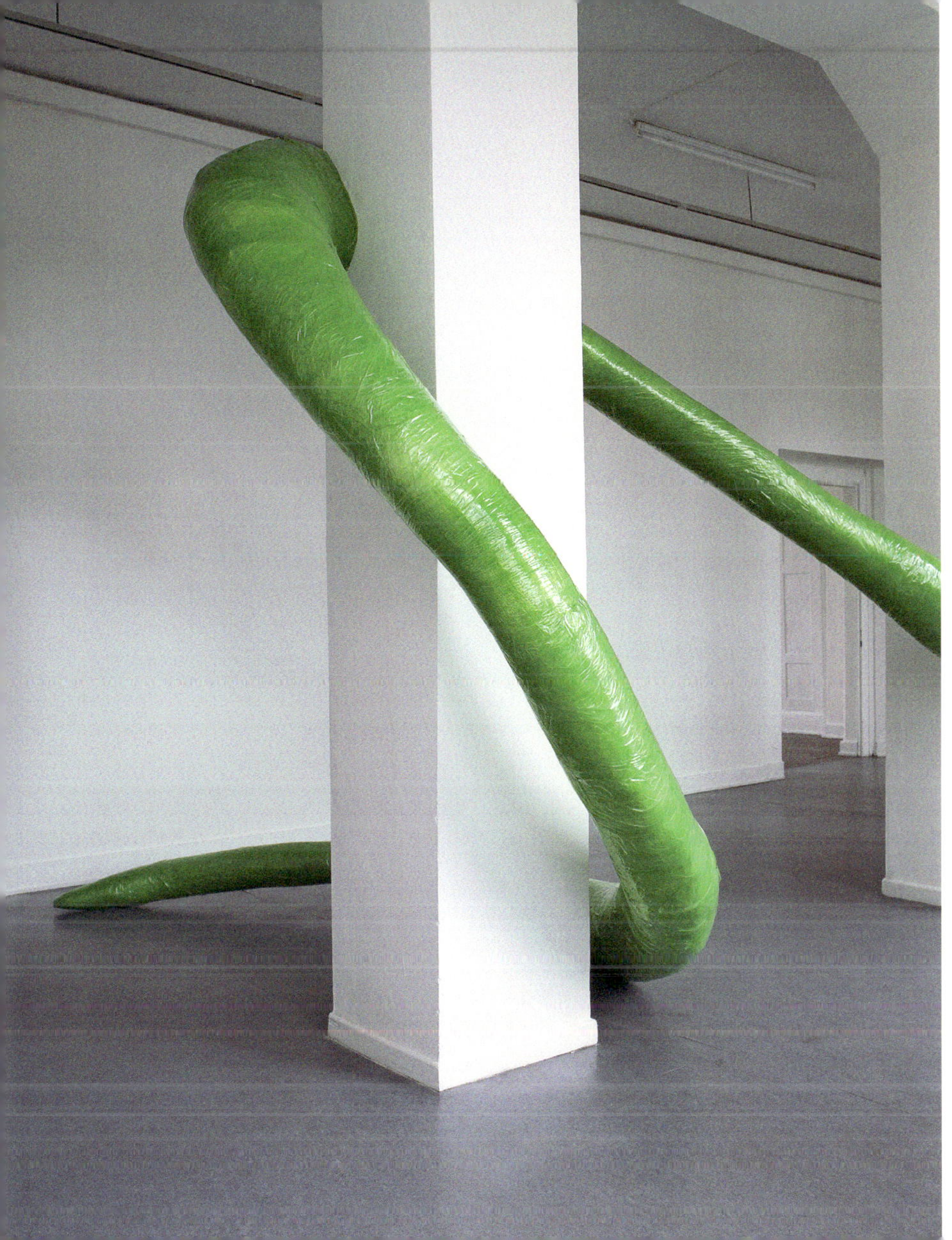

kantige Trägerkonstruktion für den Betrachter vollkommen unsichtbar war. Raum, Architektur und plastische Gestalt bildeten plötzlich eine untrennbare Einheit, deren besondere visuelle Präsenz den gesamten Raum in Schwingungen versetzte und ein Gefühl des Fließens vermittelte, das die gewohnten Konstanten der Wahrnehmung außer Kraft setzte.

Krebber unterwandert unsere vorgefasste Sicht der Welt und der Dinge sanft, aber sehr bestimmt und höchst wirksam. Dies betrifft insbesondere die Architektur, die durch Krebbers künstlerische Eingriffe buchstäblich ein neues Gesicht erhält und damit zu einer überraschenden Form der sinnlichen Erscheinung findet.

Als optisches Gegenstück zu *Vymbo*, wie Krebber seine dinggewordene Linie im Raum genannt hat, sollte *Droopy* den Ausstellungsbesucher nicht nur mit einer außergewöhnlichen materiellen Form umfangen, sondern ihn darüber hinaus auch mit einem unverwechselbaren Geruch begrüßen. Aus der Auffassung heraus, dass sich die Präsenz seiner Plastiken nicht allein auf deren physische und visuelle Fassbarkeit beschränkt, sondern sich diese ganz selbstverständlich auch auf weitere sinnliche Erlebniswelten ausdehnt, schuf Krebber ein fremdartig wirkendes Objekt, das, von der Decke hängend, den gesamten Raum sowohl durch seine körperhafte Gestalt als auch durch den von ihr ausgehenden Geruch beherrschte. Den Kern von *Droopy* bildete eine Anzahl aufgeblasener Luftballons, die durch unzählige Meter Klebeband zu einem zusammenhängenden knotenartigen Gebilde verbunden wurden. Die Oberfläche der Ballone

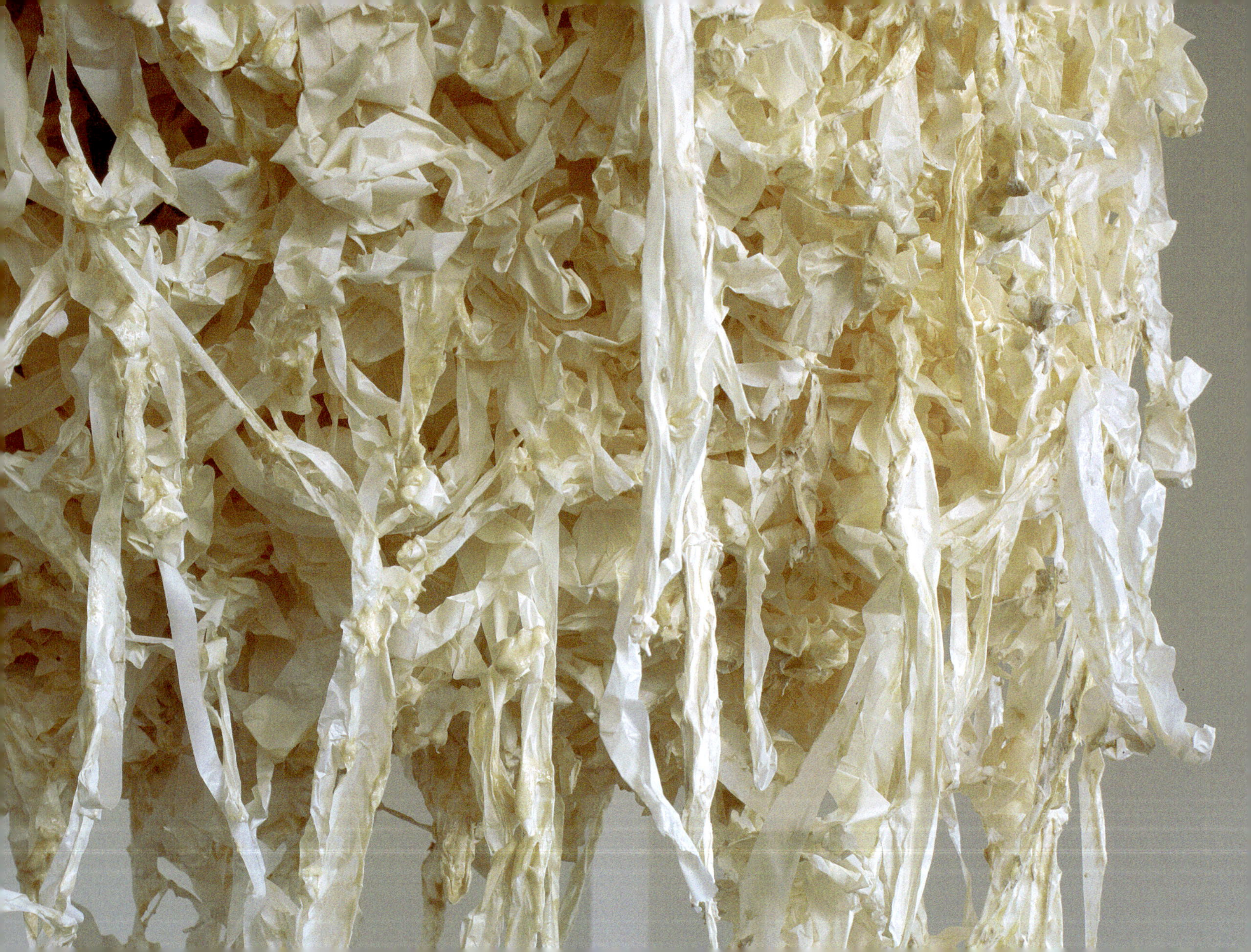

war vollständig mit Klebebandwürsten bedeckt, die zum Teil bis auf den Boden herunterhingen. Die so entstandene blasenhaft aufgeworfene Form bestrich Krebber akribisch mit einem Gemisch aus geblich-weißer Mayonnaise und Kleister, das an manchen Stellen aufreizend langsam wieder zu Boden tropfte. Das Ganze erinnerte an eine Qualle, deren Tentakeln in den Raum hineinragten, oder an einen Kokon, der neues unbekanntes Leben auszubrüten schien.

Die Reaktionen des Ausstellungspublikums fielen durchaus ambivalent aus. Sie schwankten zwischen Faszination und Ekel, Neugierde und Abstoßung, zwischen dem unwiderstehlichen Drang, das ‚Nest‘ berühren zu wollen, und dem Respekt vor dem offensichtlichen Eigenleben des Materials, das eine weitere Annäherung geradezu verbot.

*Droopy* visualisiert eindrucksvoll die Faszination des Künstlers für einen Umgang mit Materialien, dessen Wirkung und Reaktion er selbst nicht bis ins Letzte zu kontrollieren vermag. Die Arbeit an der plastischen Gestalt wird so zu einem Experiment mit zuweilen ungewissem Ausgang. Sie veranschaulicht Krebbers Lust, sich innerhalb seiner künstlerischen Arbeit dem Risiko des Unbekannten, Unkontrollierbaren kontrolliert hinzugeben, um daraus für sich selbst und den Betrachter neue, aufregende Erfahrungswelten entstehen zu lassen. Eingeschlossen in sein künstlerisches Konzept ist eine selbsttätig verlaufende Materialperformance, die eine Metamorphose seiner Objekte zur Folge hat.

So veränderte auch *Droopy* im Laufe der Ausstellungszeit die einstmalige Gestalt. Die Luftballons verloren an Spannkraft und ließen immer mehr Klebebandkringel zu Boden fallen. Die Farbe veränderte sich langsam und zunehmend bis ins Gelbliche. Wie ein organisches Lebewesen schien Krebbers Skulptur zu leben, sich zu bewegen und zu verändern. Das Geräusch herabfallenden Materials durchdrang dann und wann die Ausstellungsräume. Unter dem Objekt bildete sich eine zarte Lache aus gelblich flüssigem Schleim, der allmählich unangenehm zu riechen begann.

### Killing me softly

Es sind gerade diese dominanten materiellen Eigenschaften seiner plastischen Gebilde, die die übergreifende Absicht des Künstlers sichtbar machen, klassische Bildhauerthemen zu einer neuen Lösung zu führen. Krebbers unkonventionelle künstlerische Vorgehensweise zielt darauf, traditionelle plastische Gestaltungsaufgaben, die sich an Begriffen wie Leichtigkeit und Schwere, Masse und Leere, Transparenz und Fülle, Balance, Stabilität und Linearität orientieren, zu konterkarieren und damit der Kunst entscheidende Wege für ein erweitertes Ausdruckspotenzial zu ebnen. Die Lust an der Provokation begleitet ihn dabei. Bewusst erzeugt Krebber ein Gefühl der Unruhe und Bedrängnis, gewollt beschreitet er den schmalen Grat zwischen Anziehung und Abstoßung, zwischen Faszination und Ablehnung – Ärgernisse inklusive.

„I had the idea“, sagte Gereon Krebber einmal in einem Interview, „of declaring war on the viewer. Literally saying ‚Hey. I want to kill you‘“.

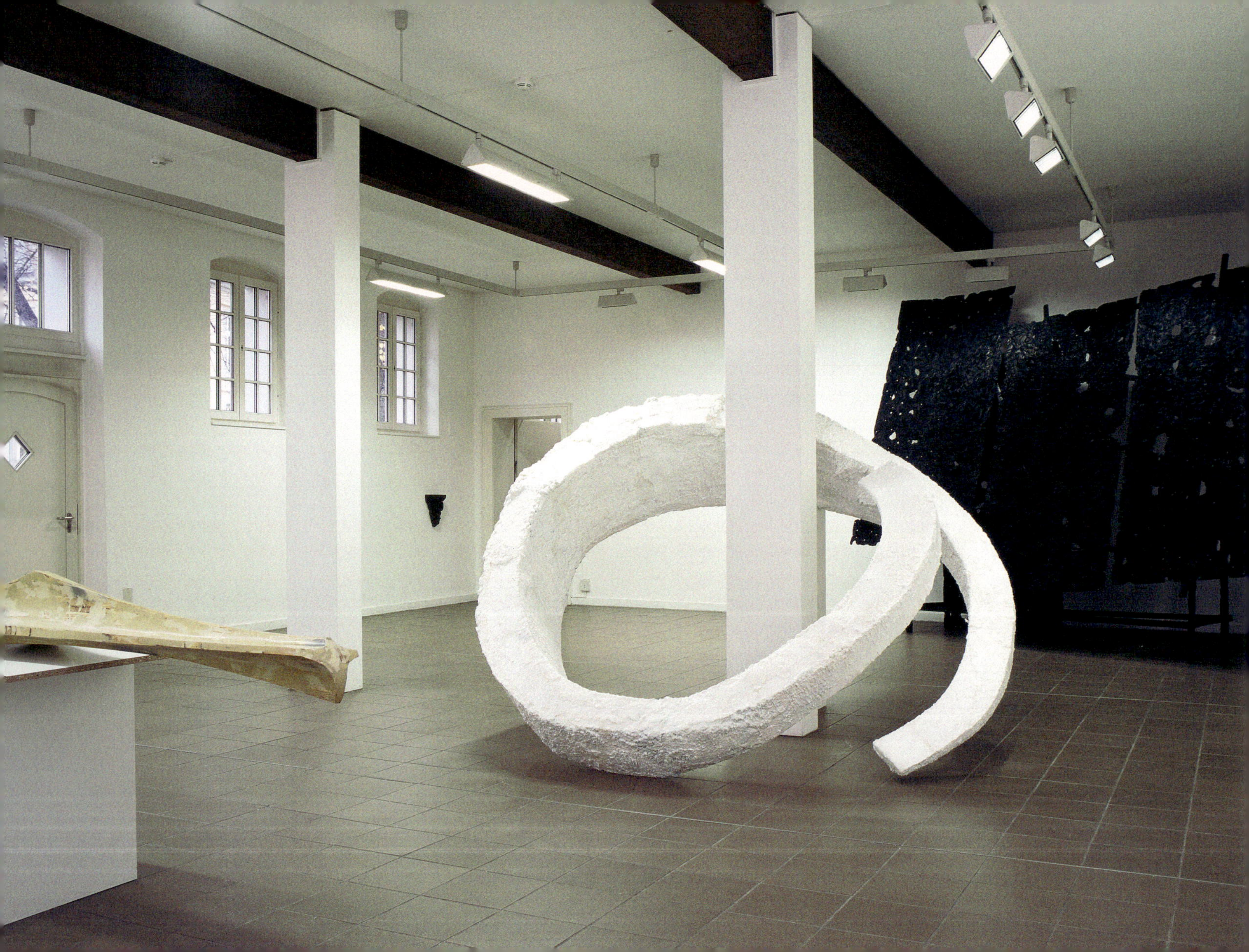

# Schon, noch, nicht mehr
# Zu den Arbeiten von Gereon Krebber

Susanne Wedewer

„A work of art is above all an adventure of the mind."

Eugene Ionesco

*Superliminal,* der Titel der Ausstellung im Kunstverein Leverkusen, ist – um es vorweg zu nehmen – ein Kunstwort, eine Wortschöpfung Krebbers. ‚Super' im Sinne von über, überragend, von großartig, aber auch übertrieben schwingt hier mit und ebenso der Klang von Limit, von limitiert als begrenzt und damit exklusiv, begehrt. Krebber liebt dieses gedankliche Spiel mit den Möglichkeiten, wie sie sich aus dem Unbestimmten, nicht klar Definierten ergeben – auch bei seinen Skulpturen.

Denn selbst wenn wir deren Materialität zu bestimmen, ihre Form mit Verweis auf bekannt erscheinende Gebrauchsgegenständen zu umschreiben vermögen, so schleicht sich während dieses Prozesses der eigentlich klärenden Wahrnehmung doch auch immer wieder Zweifel an der Richtigkeit des soeben Festgestellten ein. Zu irritierend ist häufig der Gegensatz zwischen dem Material, das wir in seiner Funktionalität zu kennen glauben, und der aus ihm entstandenen plastischen Formung: künstlich/organisch; hart/weich; fest/flussig. So lässt Krebber beispielsweise Glas die Treppe ‚hinunterfließen' – in ganzen Stücken erstarrt, markiert es diese Spur, aufgebrochen, gebrochen ohne zerbrochen zu sein. Fisschollen ähnlich,

doch ohne die Dramatik gefährlich spitzer Bruchstellen. Das berühmte Gemälde *Das Eismeer* (1823/24) von Caspar David Friedrich kommt vor Augen, ein Bild, das lange Zeit unter dem Titel *Die gescheiterte Hoffnung* firmierte und höchst unterschiedliche Lesarten evozierte. Diese reichen von den Schrecken der Polarwelt über das Göttliche der Natur versus die Vergänglichkeit des Menschen bis hin zu politischen Deutungen. Für uns Betrachter des 21. Jahrhunderts ist es allerdings primär dieses von Friedrich so nachhaltig geprägte Bild vom Eis, das durch die Installation von Gereon Krebber wachgerufen wird, ohne inhaltliche Festlegungen. Und auch dem Bildhauer geht es zunächst einmal vor allem um das Material, darum, dessen Möglichkeiten auszuloten wie hier erstmals die des Verbundglases.

Der 1973 geborene Gereon Krebber arbeitet oftmals mit Gegenständen des täglichen Lebens, deren jeweilige Materialität, räumliche Qualität oder Oberflächenbeschaffenheit er für seine plastischen Arbeiten nutzt. Und mit alltäglichen Werkstoffen – Holz, Beton, Styropor, Acrylharz oder Glas – die er verbrennt, verkohlt, verspachtelt, verputzt, schmilzt auf der Suche nach jener Form, wie sie für einen Moment – wie erstarrt – entsteht aus dem stets labilen Gleichgewichts von schon, noch, nicht mehr.

Die Skulptur als festgehaltener Moment eines Prozesses, einer Veränderung, ist keineswegs ein neuer Gedanke, galt doch, den geeigneten Moment zu finden, spätestens seit Lessing als deren vornehmste Aufgabe. Gereon Krebber weiß um die Geschichte seines Mediums, weiß um die Arbeiten von Imi Knoebel, auch um die Vorgänger der Minimal Art. Doch deren, wie er sagt, „orthodoxe Haltung" in Bezug auf die Ortsspezifik der Arbeiten interessiert ihn nicht, für ihn ist Raum, ist Architektur und ihre Struktur ein Material von vielen. Was ihn interessiert, ist vielmehr jener Schwebezustand einer Arbeit, wie er sich aus dem Spiel, dem Experiment mit dem Material entwickelt – wie weit kann ich gehen, etwa, wenn ich Schichtholzplatten zunächst mit verschiedenen Werkzeugen und anschließlich mit dem Flammenwerfer malträtiere? Wann versagt mir das Material seine Dienste?

So stehen manche der Skulpturen von Krebber auf der Kippe zum völligen Zerfall – auch dies im Unterschied zu der im Zusammenhang mit seinem Werk viel zitierten Minimal Art. Daraus ergibt sich konsequenterweise, dass immer auch einige Arbeiten nach dem Ende einer Ausstellung ‚entsorgt' werden, sei es, weil sie in sich zusammenfallen, sei es, weil sie, vor Ort entstanden, von diesem nicht als unzerstörtes Ganzes mehr zu entfernen sind, sei es, weil sie an anderen Orten andere Formungen beanspruchen.

Doch Spuren des Zerfalls wie Spuren des Entstehungsprozesses sind bei Gereon Krebber werkkonstituierend! Seine plastischen Arbeiten künden, wie Julia Höner bereits in ihrem Text zu der Arbeit *Slink* festgestellt hat, „von Vergänglichkeit und Verbrauch und führen ihre eigene Konsumierbarkeit durch das Betriebssystem Kunst ad absurdum."[1] Denn Gereon Krebber beugt sich nicht dem Dogma der Unveränderlichkeit, der Einmaligkeit eines Kunstwerks. Vielmehr benutzt er einzelne seiner Arbeiten wie Buchstaben, die es immer wieder neu zusammenzusetzen gilt – der Raum dient ihm dabei als Grammatik, die die Diktion vorgibt.

Installationen entstehen, manchmal recht leicht wirkende Inszenierungen entweder von einem einzelnen, raumgreifenden Hauptakteur oder, wie in Leverkusen, einem ganzen Ensemble. Autonom, jedes für sich und doch Teil des Zusammenspiels untereinander, mit dem Raum, dem Ort – „Wirken nicht manche Materialien so, als sei bei Bayer etwas schiefgelaufen?" (Krebber)[2] – und dem Betrachter. Und dieses Zusammenspiel funktioniert, auch wenn, wie Carl Andre es 1980 formulierte, „Kunst [...] keine Form der Kommunikation [ist]. Kunst kann, wie Elektrizität, Hilfsmittel zur Kommunikation sein, aber ihr Wesen ist genauso wenig Kommunikation wie das der Elektrizität. Kunst ist eine der Arten, das zu ertragen, womit wir uns nie abfinden werden, dem Tod zum Beispiel."[3] Gereon Krebber gelingt dies auf einer Ebene, die sich beinahe mit der berühmten Formulierung von der „Leichtigkeit des Seins" umschreiben ließe, meldeten sich da nicht Zweifel, Zweifel an unserer Wahrnehmung, an dem vermeintlichen So-Sein des von uns Wahrgenommenen. Und so lassen auch wir uns, angesteckt von der in jeder Arbeit deutlich spürbaren Neugierde Krebbers, immer wieder ein auf das gedankliche und das bereits Form gewordene Spiel mit dem Möglichen.

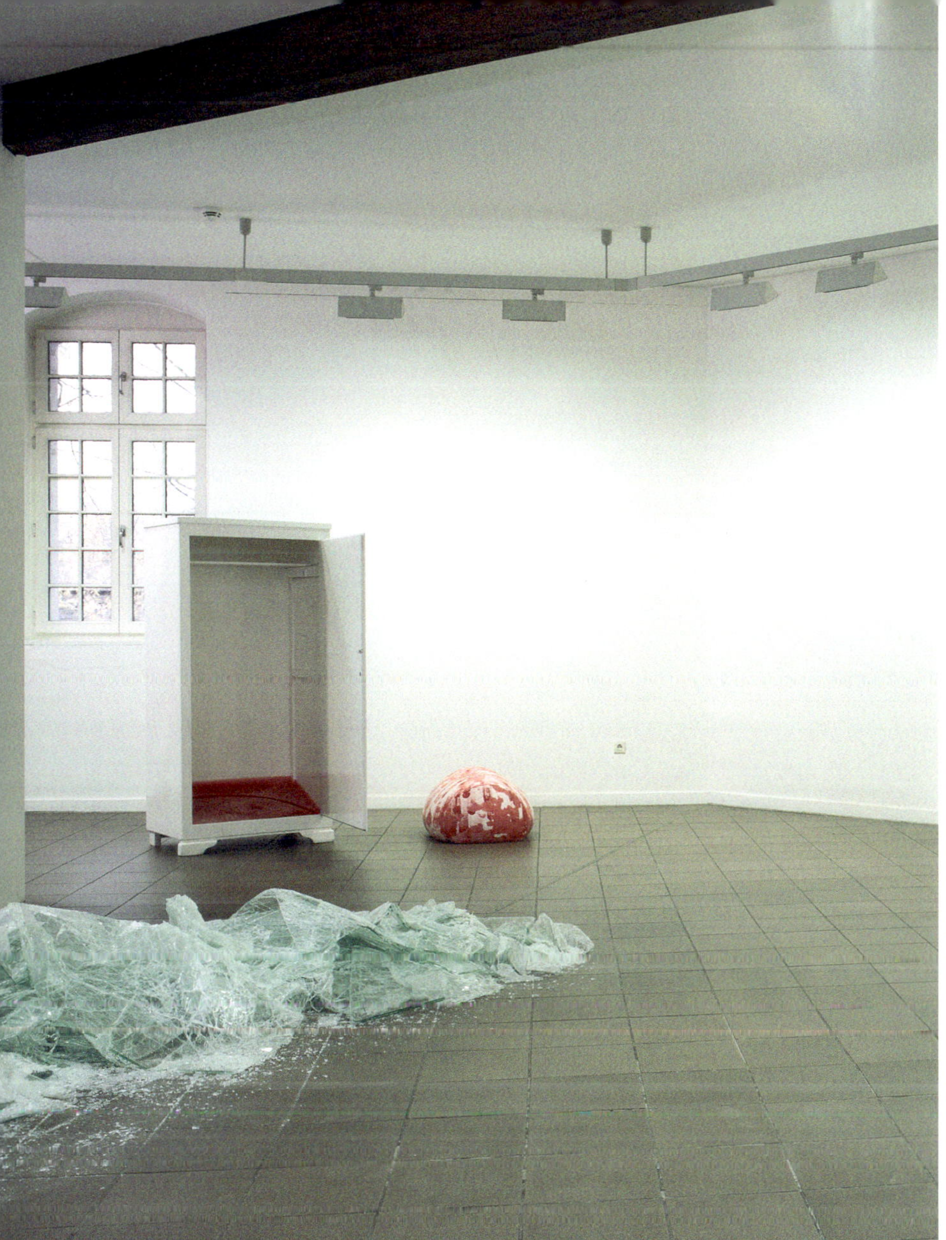

*Superliminal*, Kunstverein Leverkusen Schloß Morsbroich, 2008: *Zunge (Tongue), Gulpy, Drop*

1 Julia Höner, „Komm, wir machen mal 'ne Hänge-probe", in: Gereon Krebber, *Slink*, hrsg. von Jochen Heufelder, Fuhrwerkswaage Kunstraum, Köln 2007.
2 Gespräch mit dem Künstler, während des Aufbaus von *Superliminal*, Kunstverein Leverkusen 2008.
3 Paul Sutinen: „Carl Andre – The Turner of Mat-ter (1980)", in: Ausstellungs-katalog *Carl Andre Sculptor 1996*, Krefeld, Wolfsburg 1996, S. 52, in der Überset-zung von Brigitte Kalthoff.

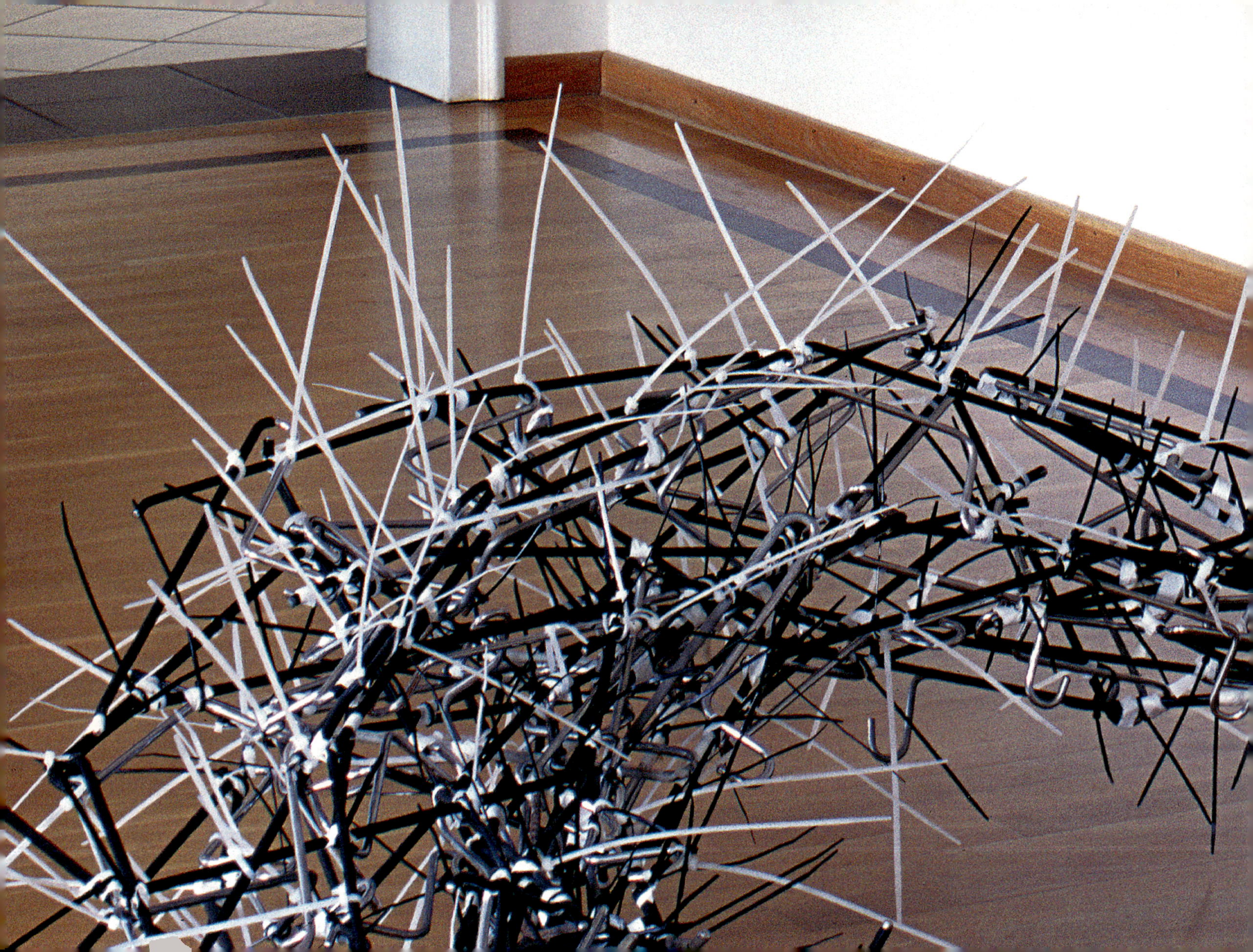

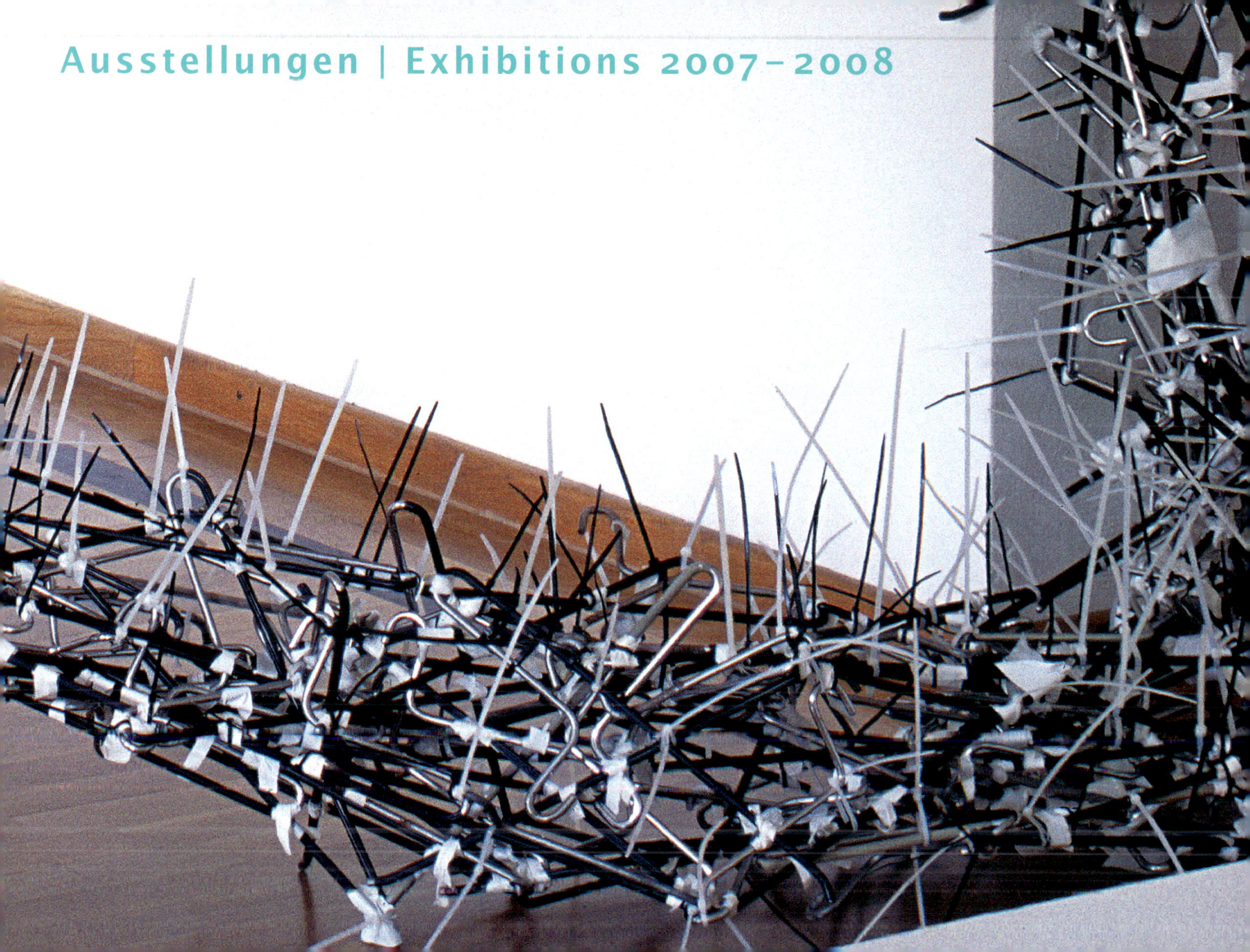

# Triband
# Kunstklub Berlin

2.3.–11.3.2007

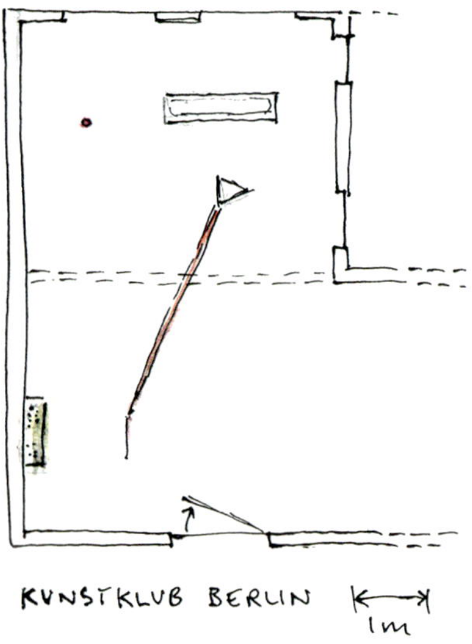



*Tränke,* 2007
Betonspachtel, Gips, Holz,
abgeschnittene Bar
Concrete filler, plaster,
timber, cut off bar
L: 1,3 m

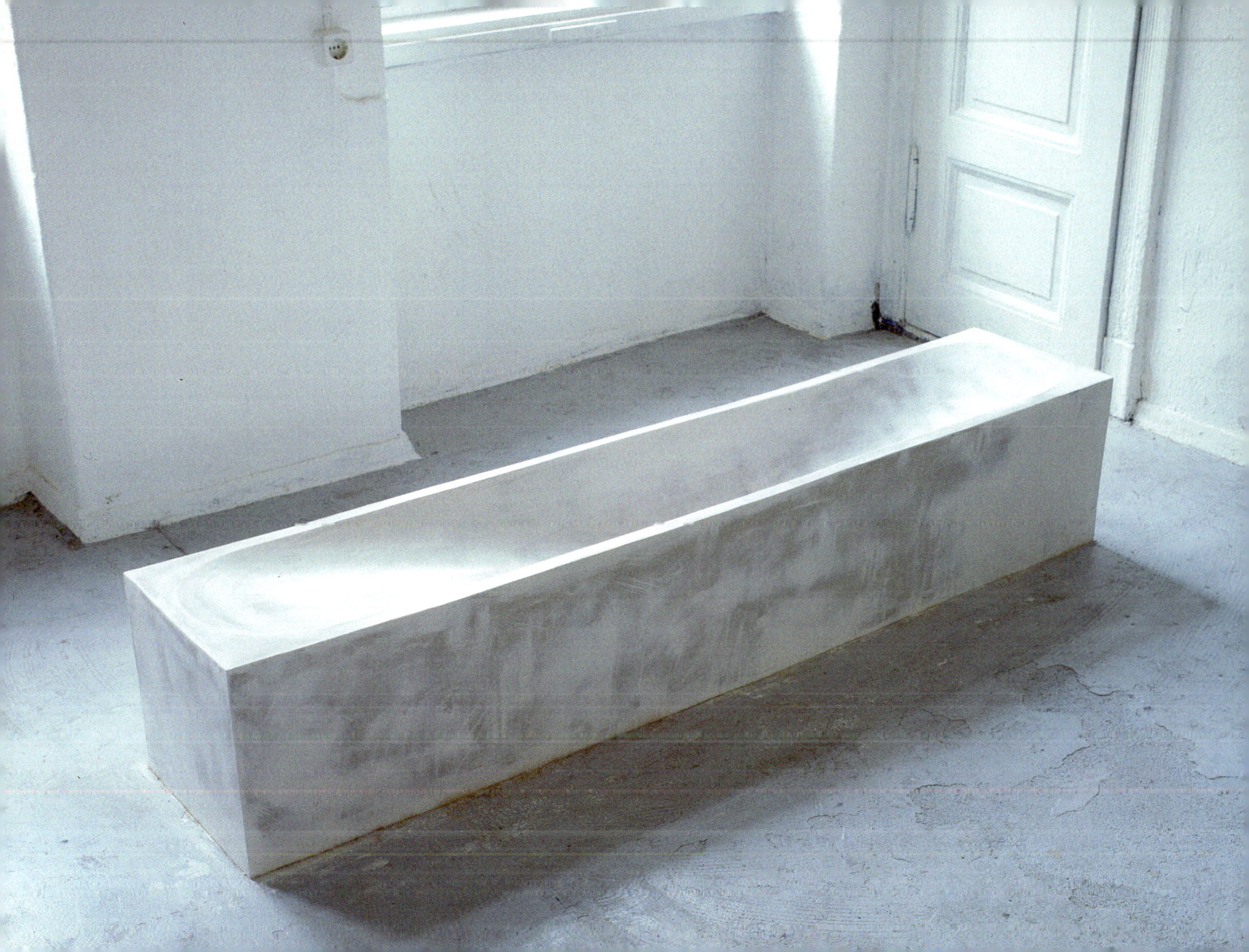

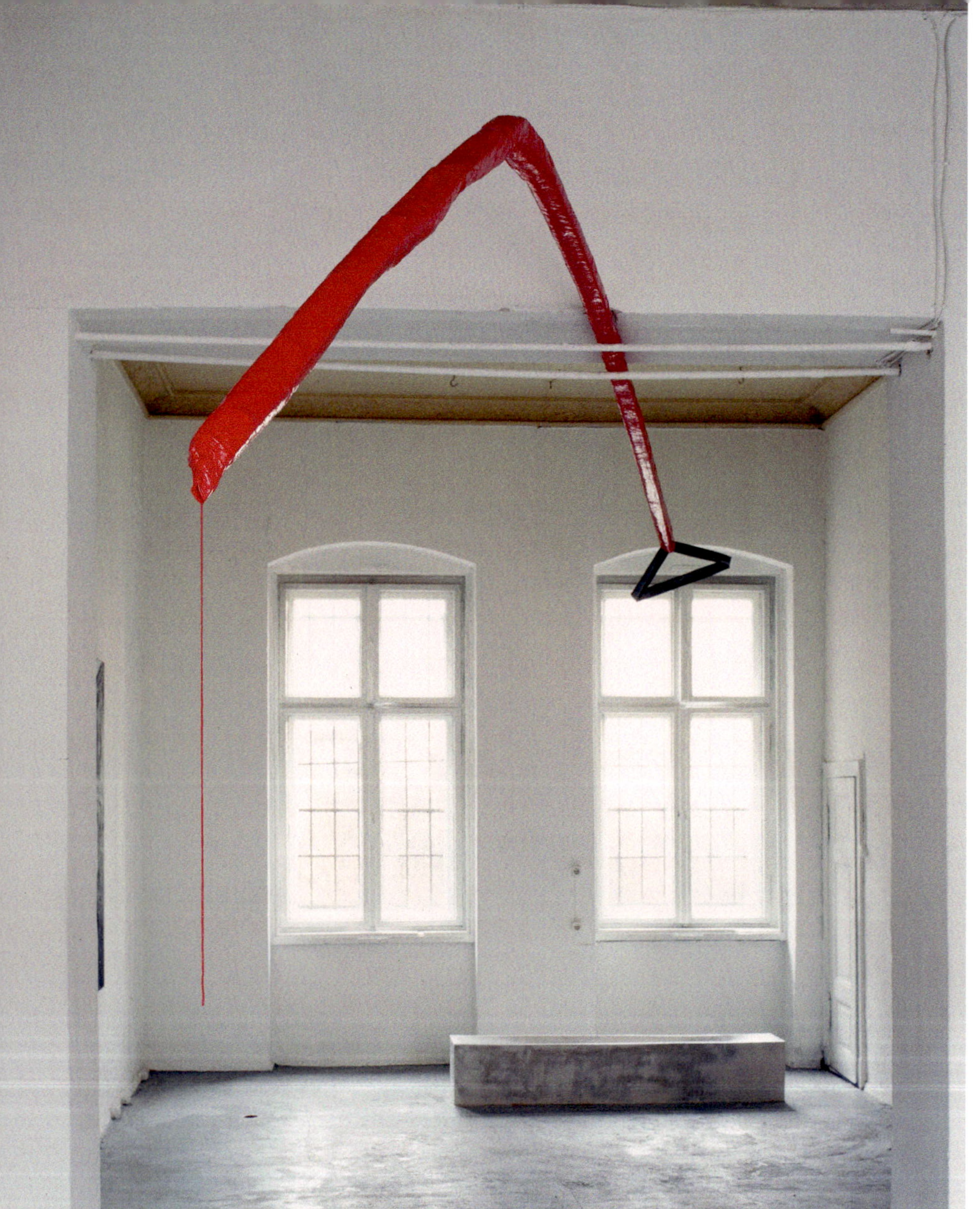


*Reach,* 2007
Süßigkeit, Folie, Holz, Blech
Candy, foil, timber, tin
L: 3,8 m

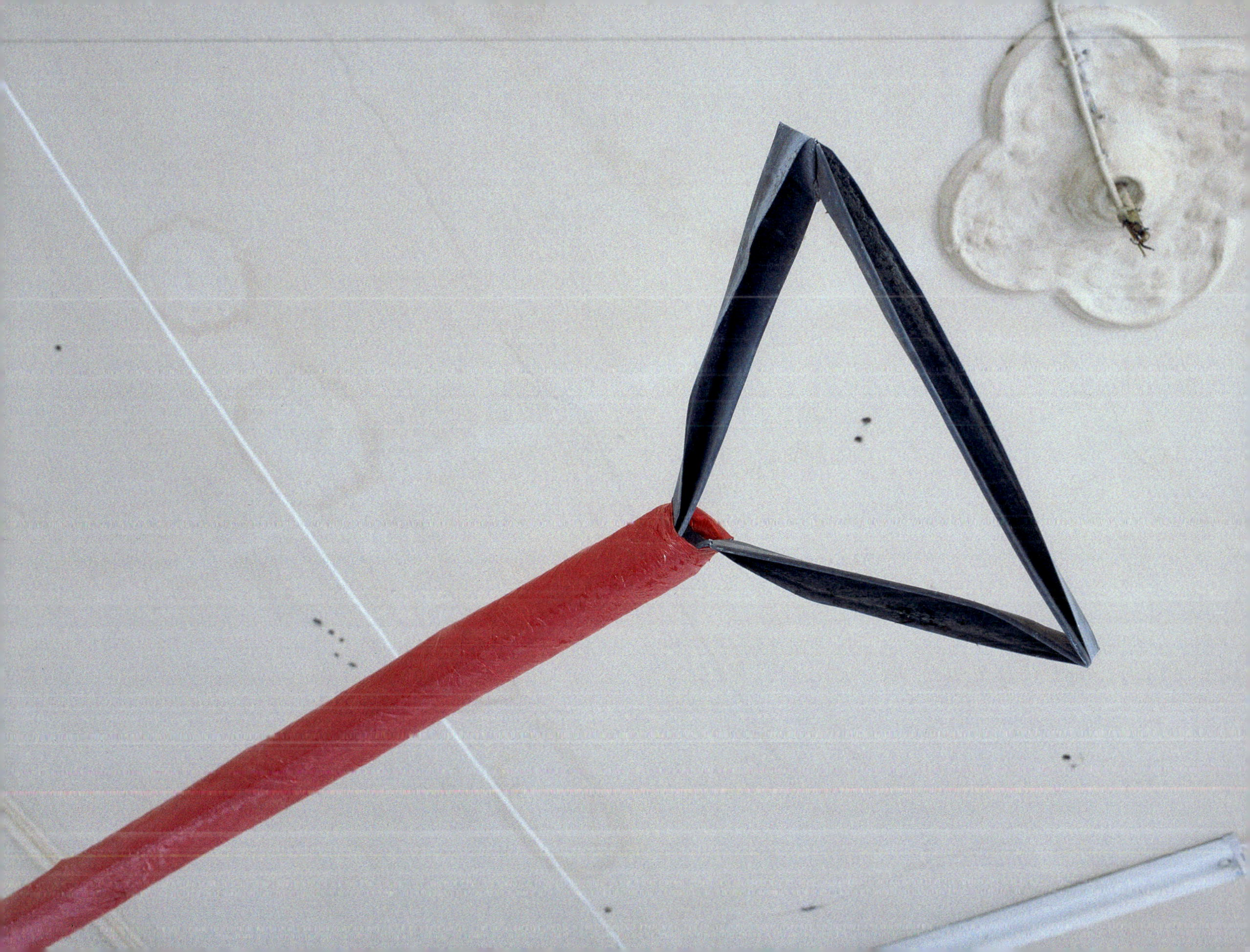

# Leichter getan als gesagt
# Galerie Jarmuschek & Partner, Berlin

28. 4. – 2. 6. 2007

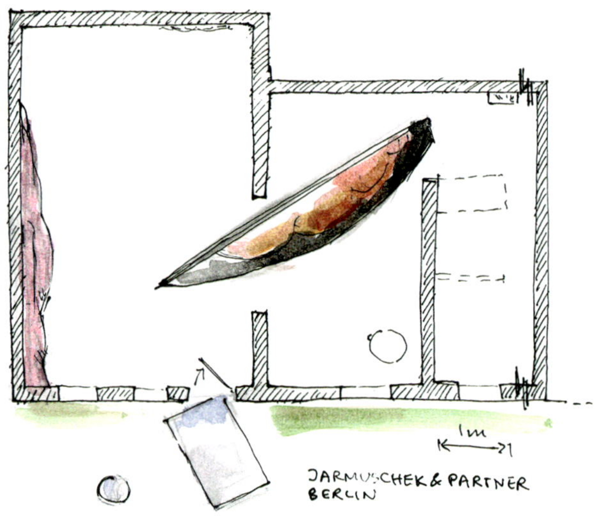


*Poller, Slab*, 2007
Beton, Pigment
Concrete, pigment
Poller H: 0,7 m
Slab H: 1,6 m

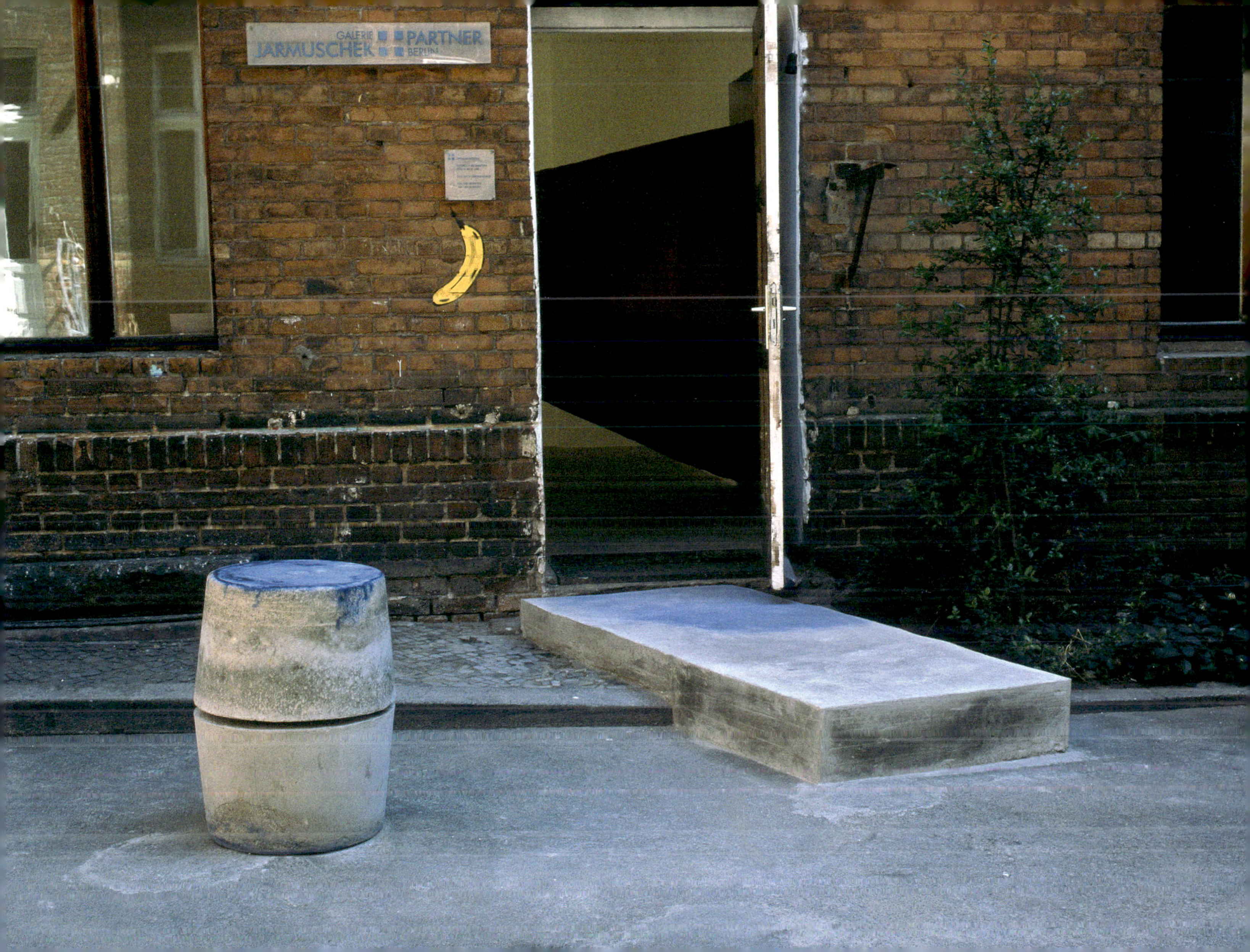

GALERIE
JARMUSCHEK ■ ■ PARTNER
BERLIN

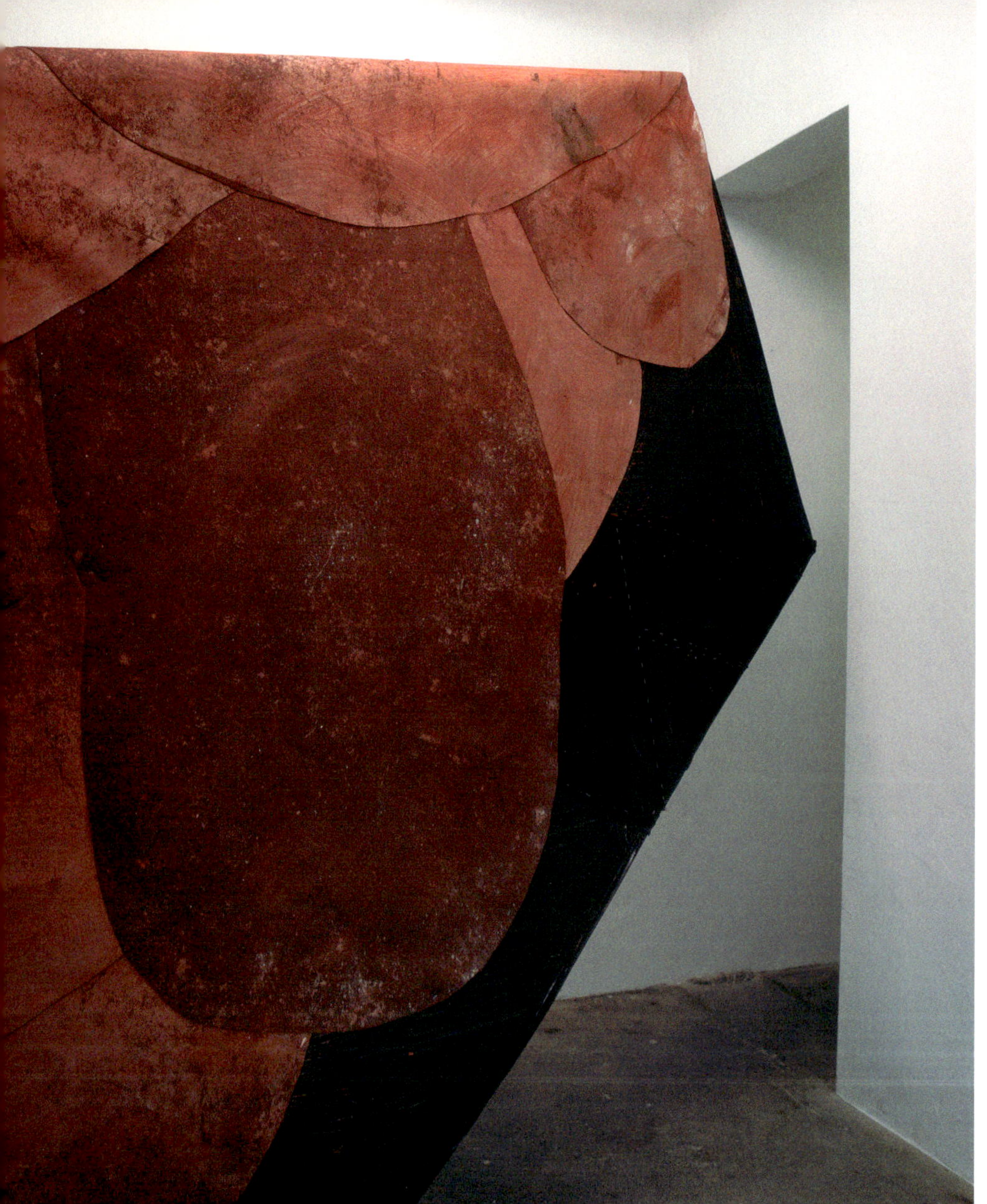

*Slice*, 2007
Teppich, Farbe, Nylon,
Folie, Holz
Carpet, paint, nylon, foil,
timber
L: 4,8 m

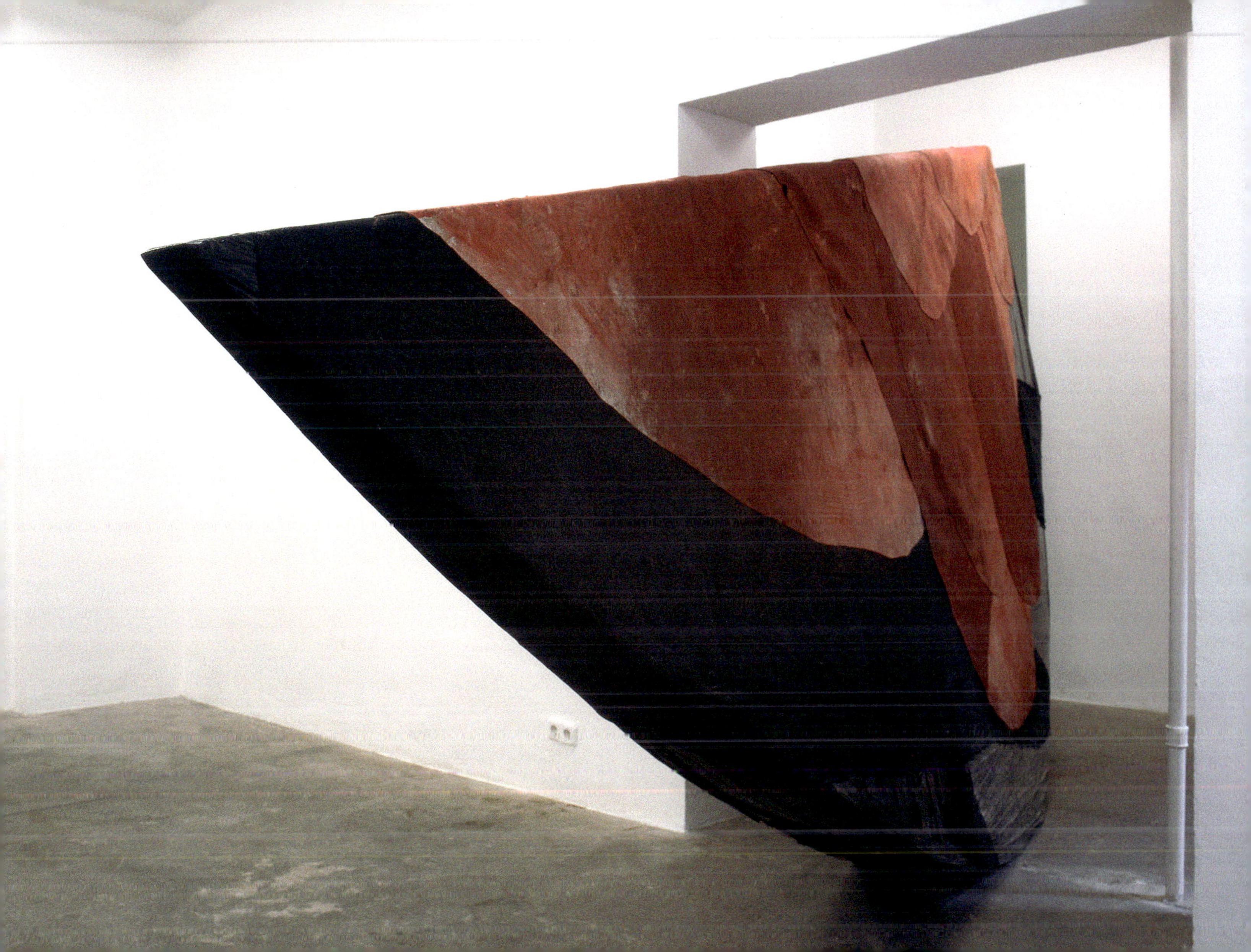

# Gereon Krebber
# Grundy Art Gallery, Blackpool

5.5.–16.6.2007

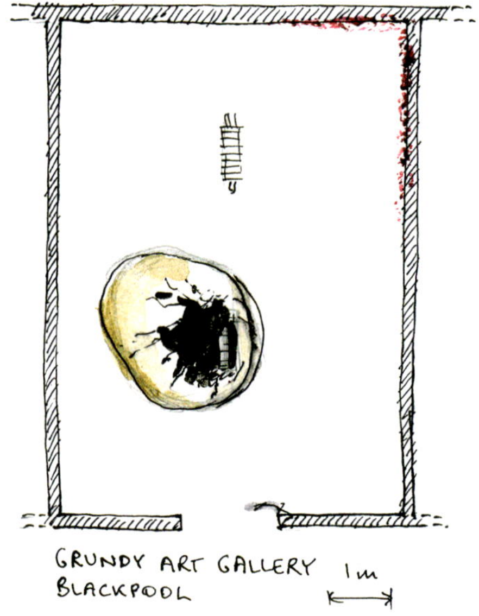





*Blackpool blobster,* 2007
Lack, Farbe, Putzgips,
Styropor, Heizkörper
Varnish, paint, bonding coat,
polystyrene, heating unit
L: 4 m

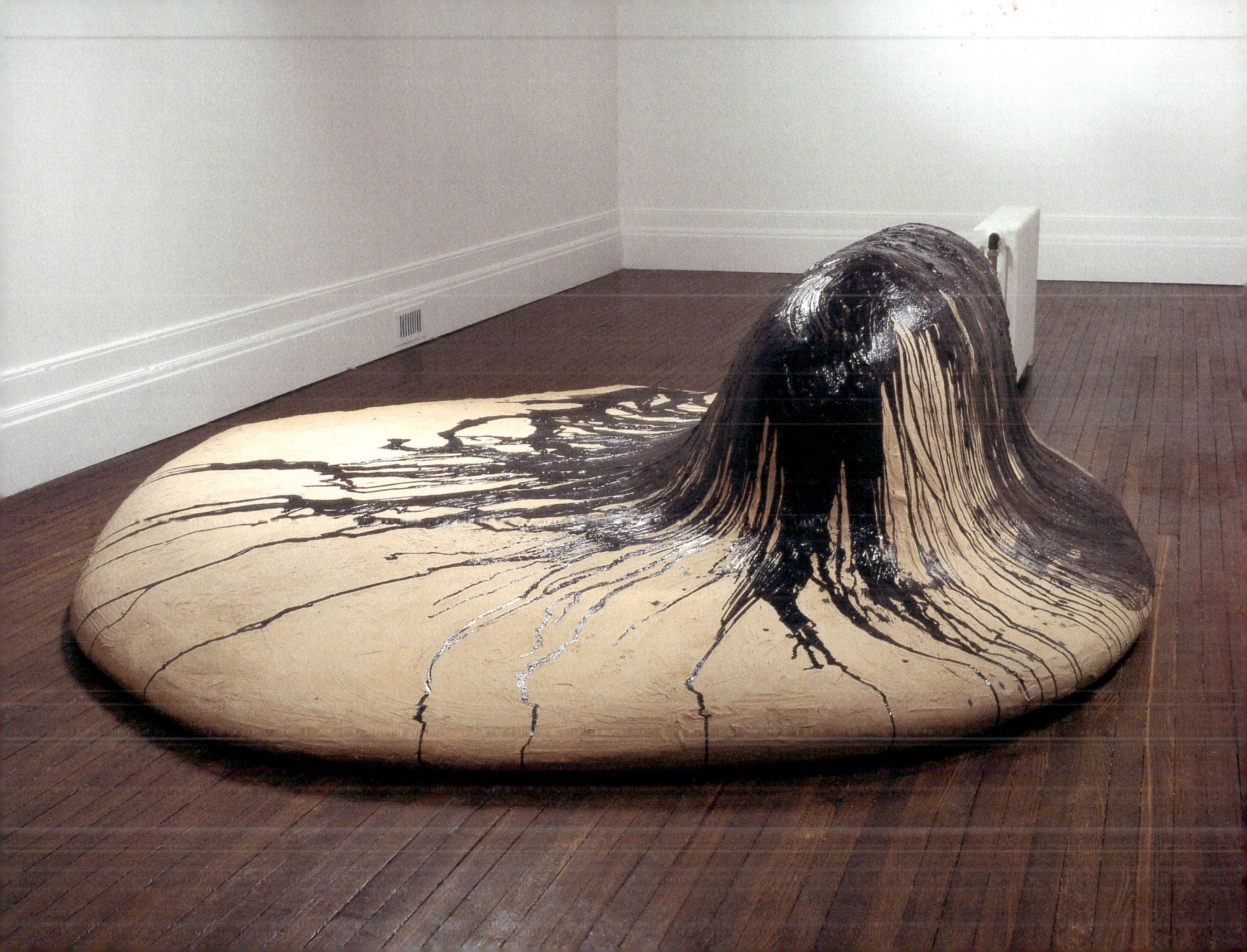

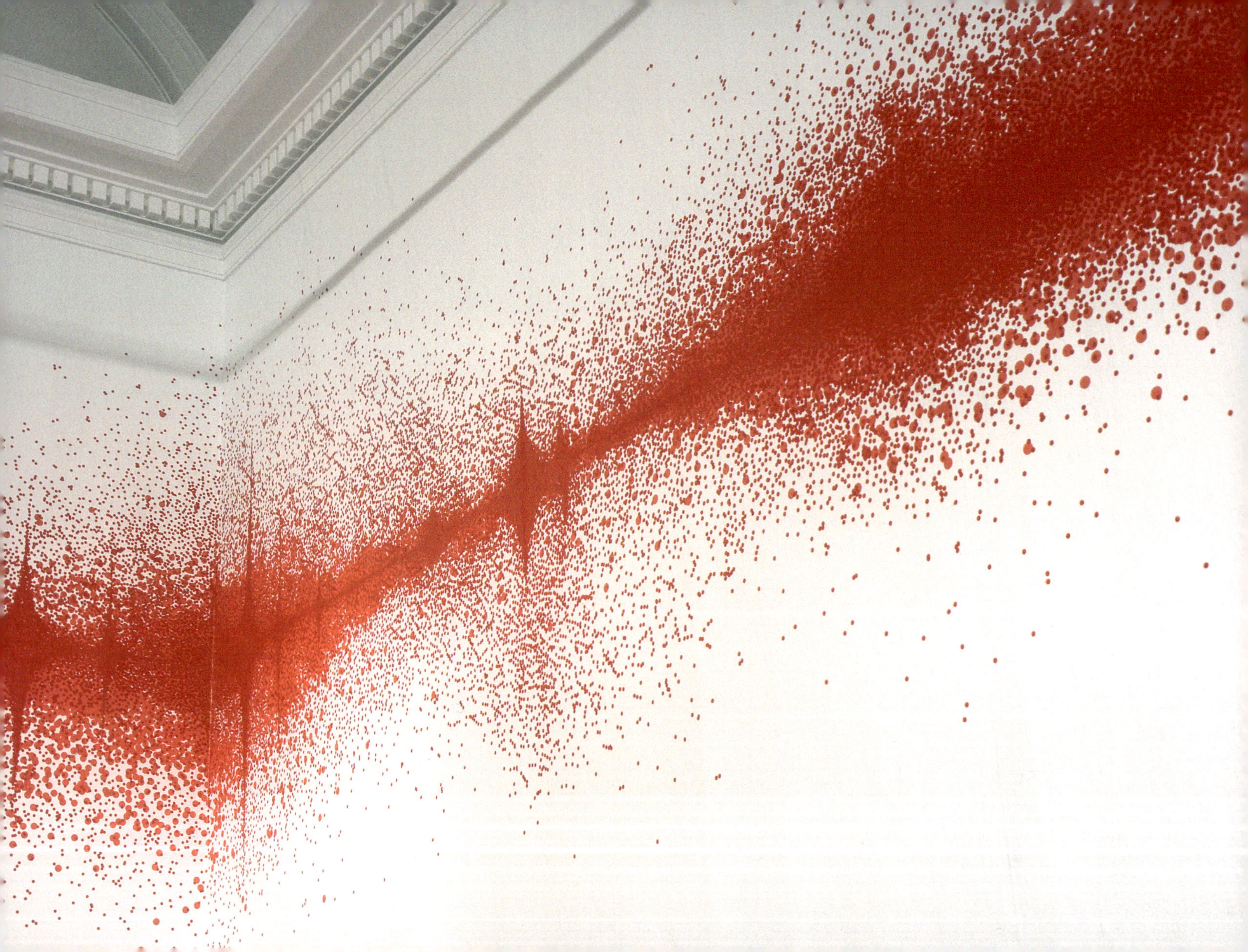

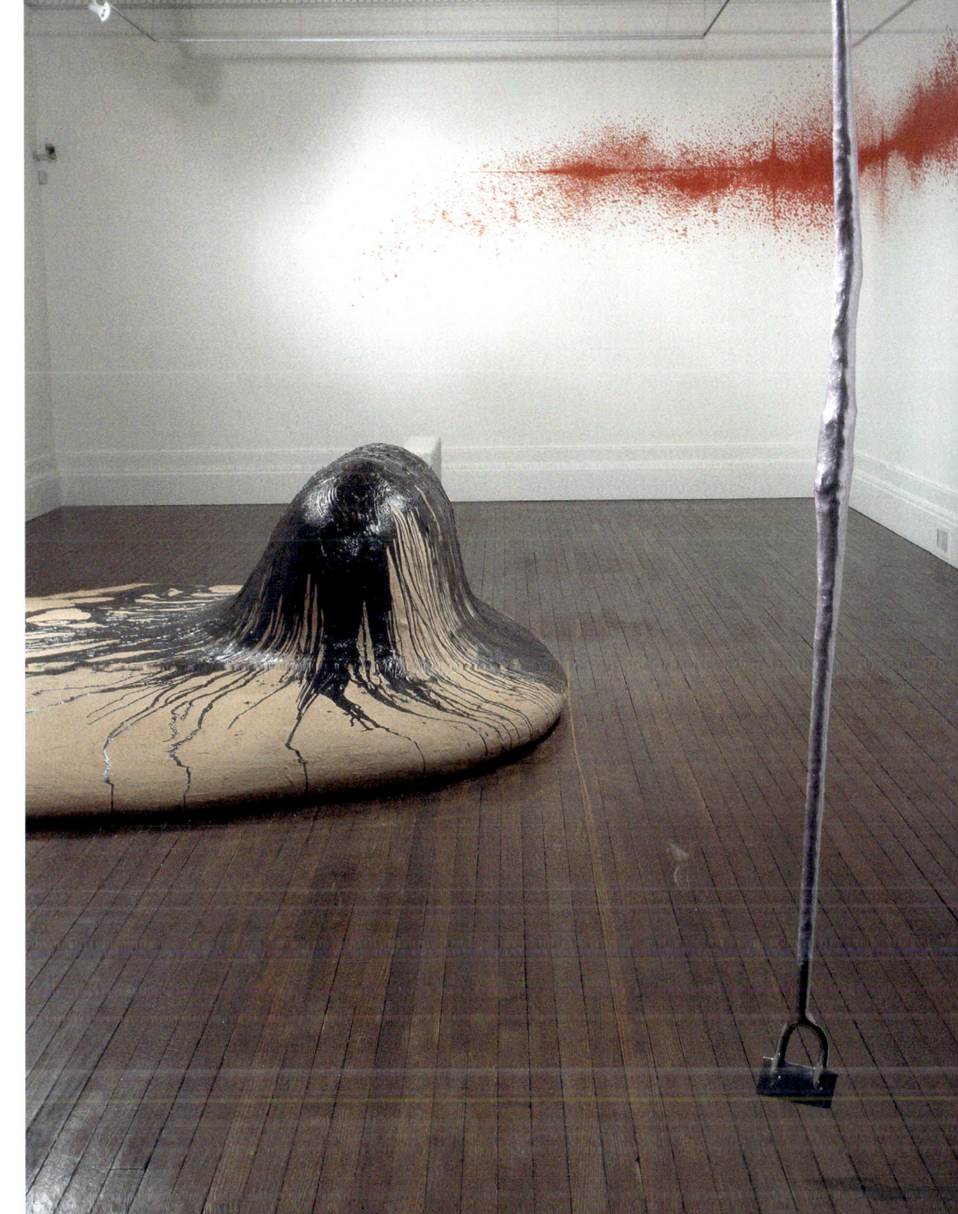

*Blink,* 2007
Klebepunkte rot
Marking dots, red
L: 8 m

*Hoe (Hacke),* 2007
Folie, Gartengeräte, Haken
Folie, gardening tools, hooks
H: 2,8 m

# Slurp
# Stiftung DKM, Duisburg

13.7.–28.10.2007

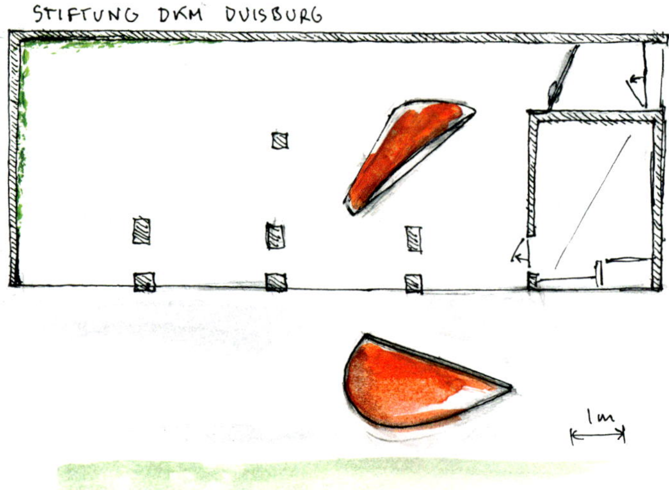





Außenansicht Galerie DKM
Outside view Galerie DKM
*Grüne Kreise, Slurp*

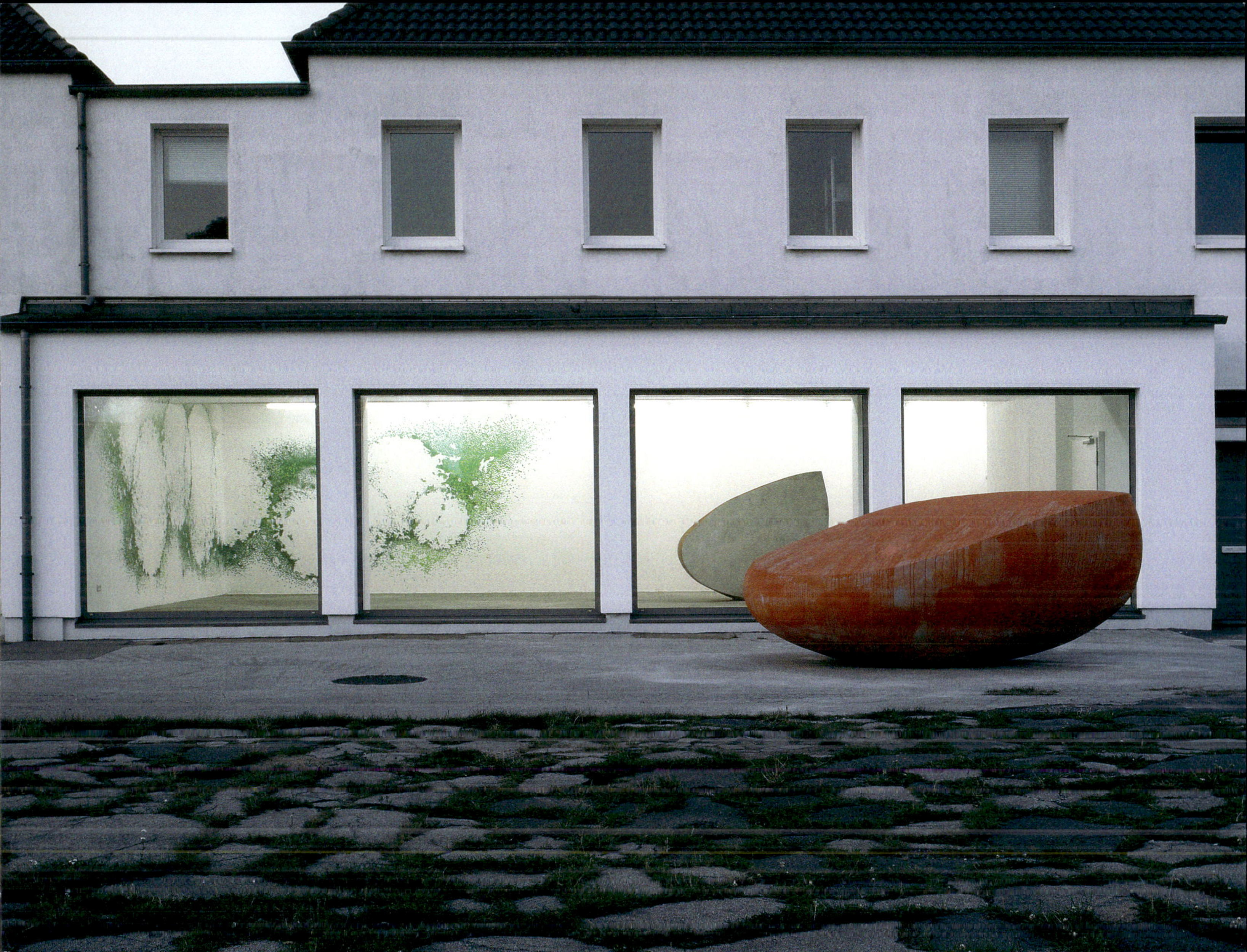

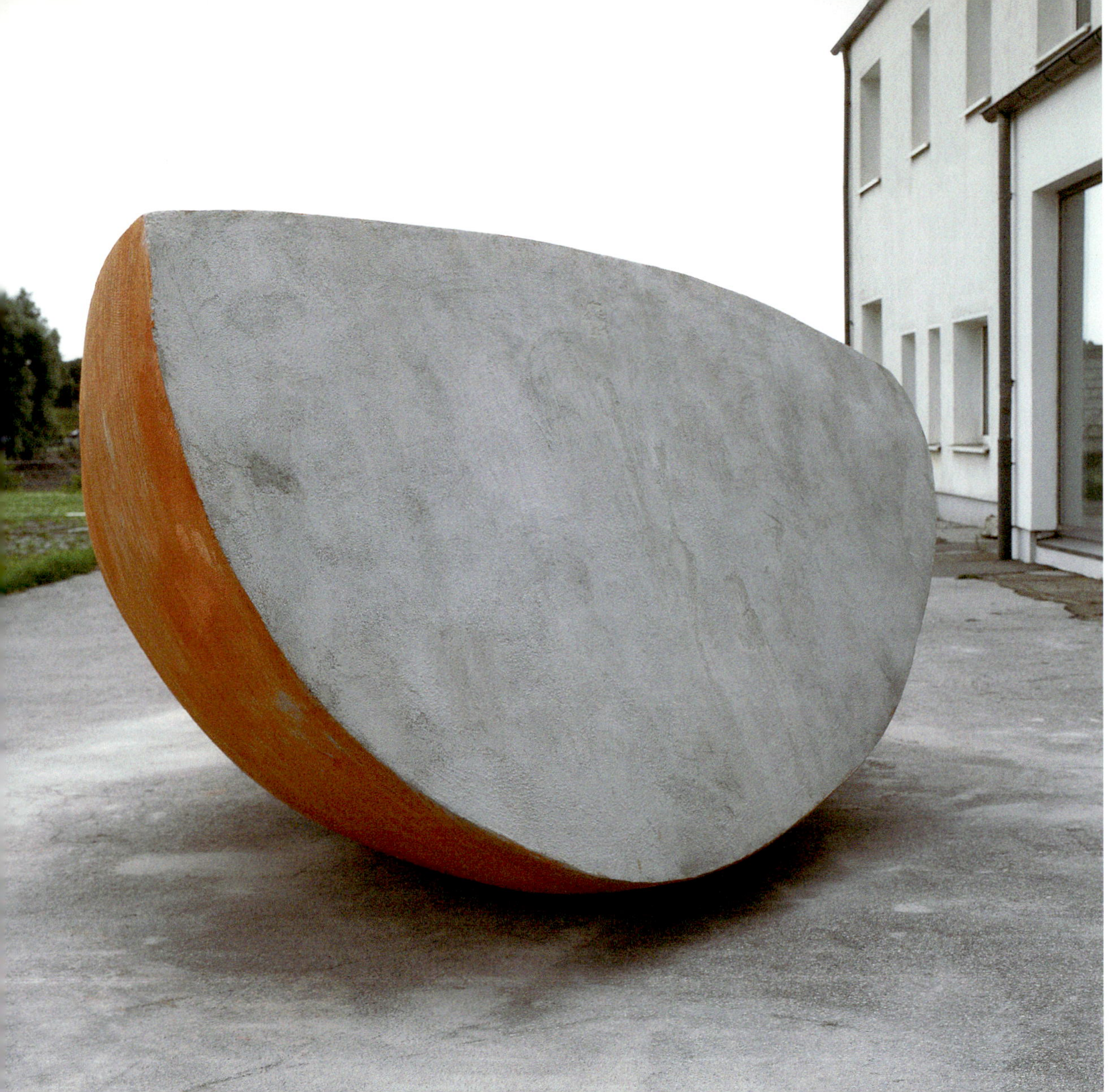


*Slurp*, 2007
Zweiteilig | two parts
Leichtputz, Styropor, Farbe
Lightweight wall plastering,
polystyrene, paint
B: 4,5 m pro Stück |
each part

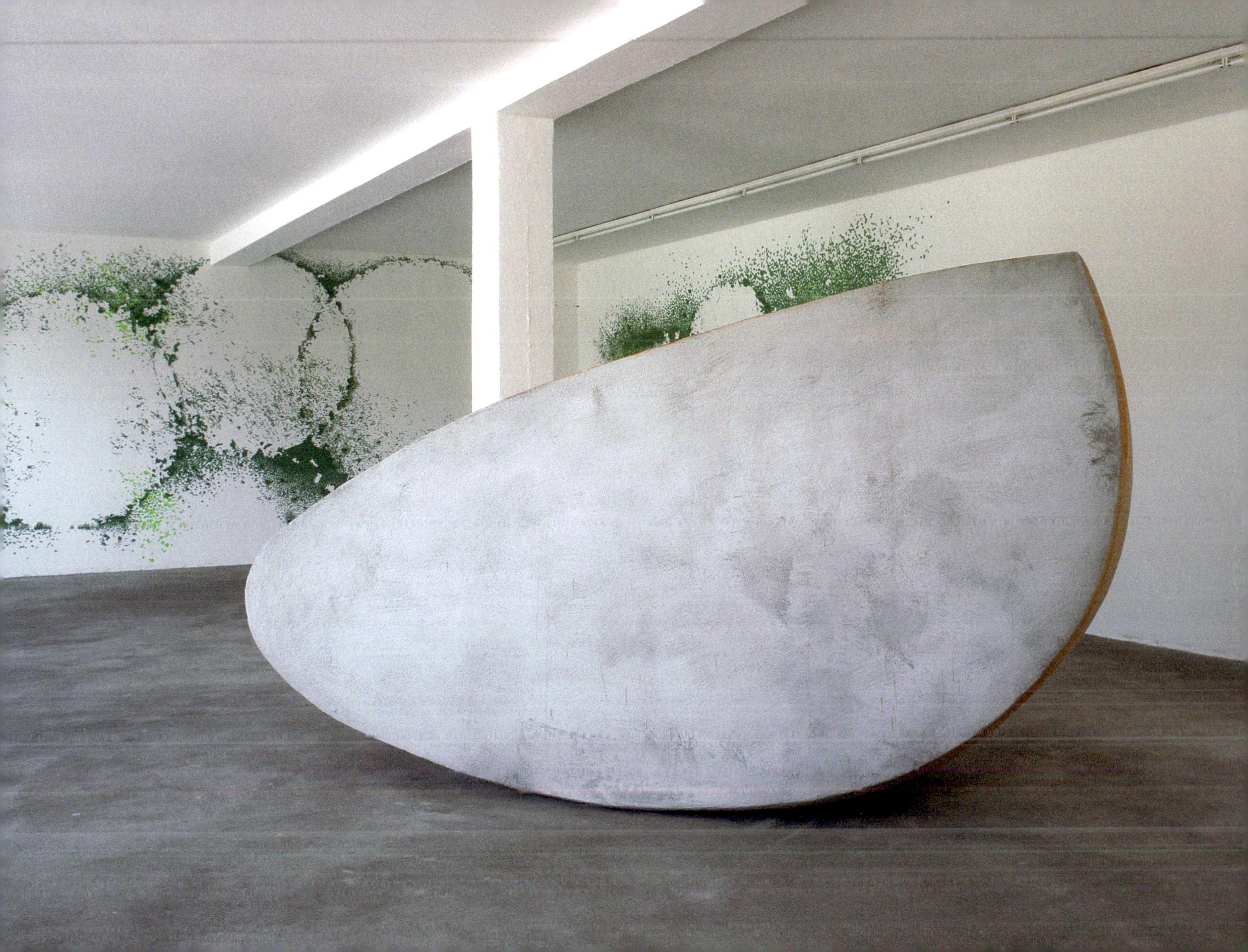

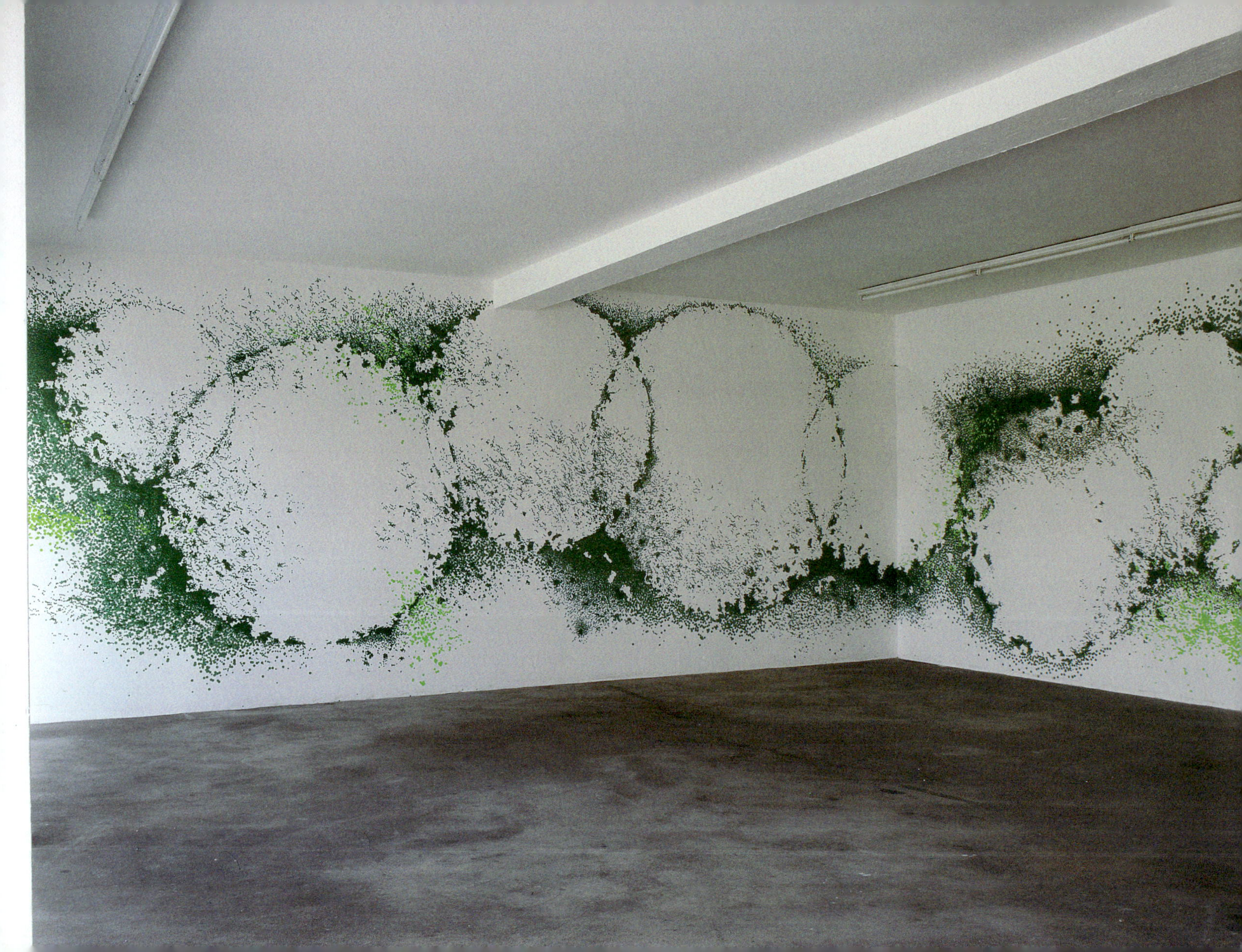

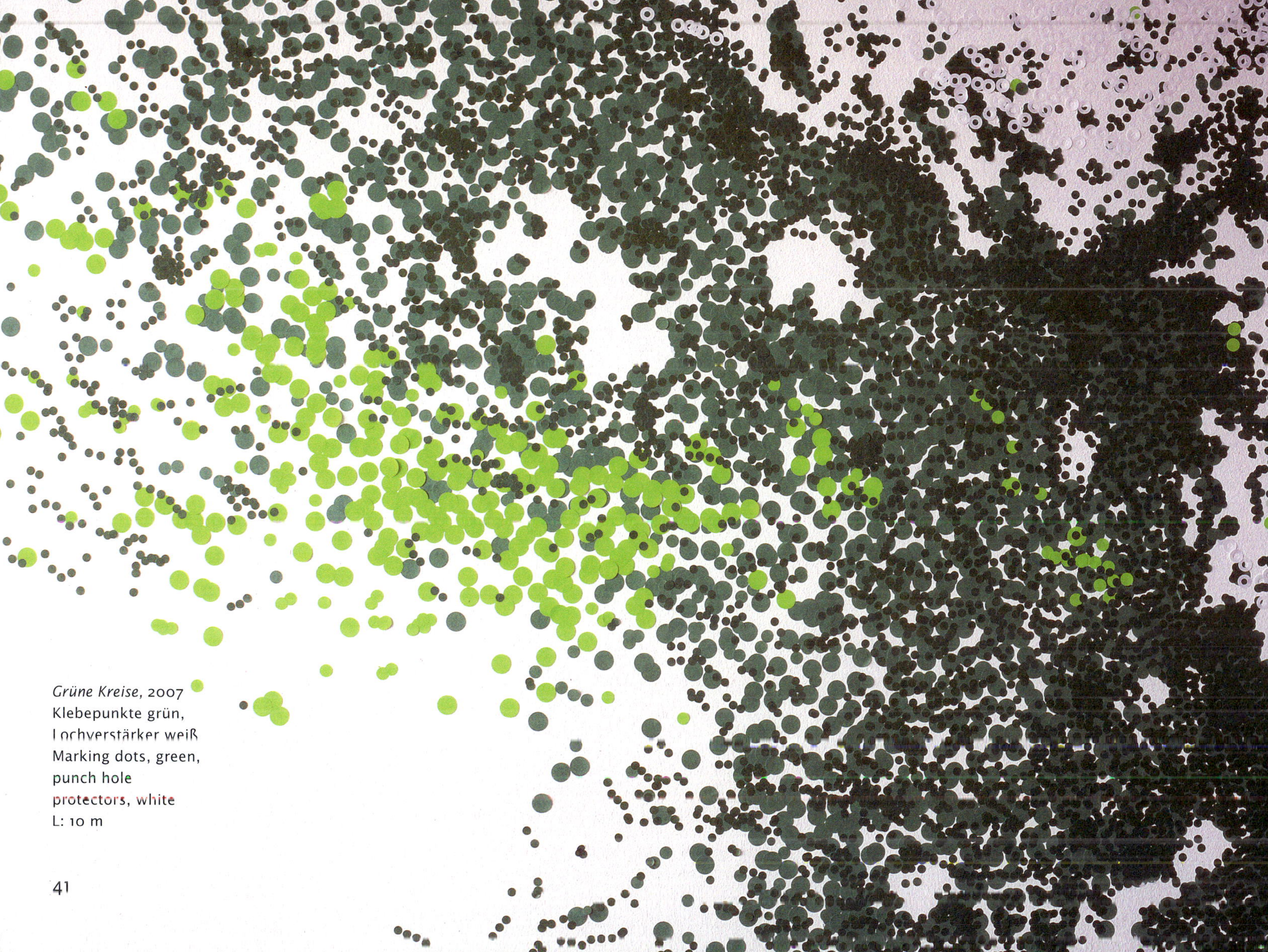

*Grüne Kreise*, 2007
Klebepunkte grün,
Lochverstärker weiß
Marking dots, green,
punch hole
protectors, white
L: 10 m

41

# Eye love candy
## KOP Stichting, NL-Breda

1. 9. – 14. 10. 2007

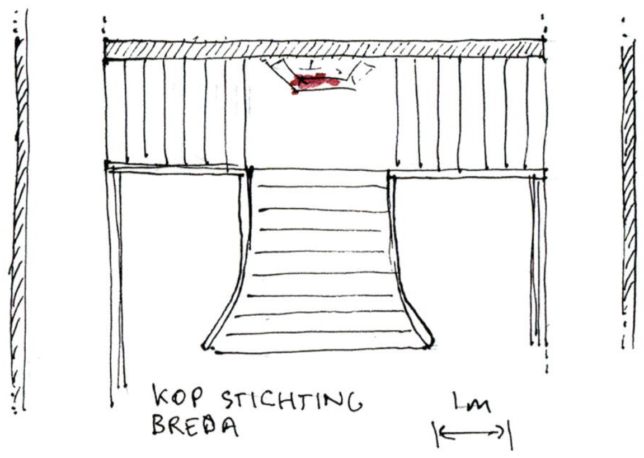

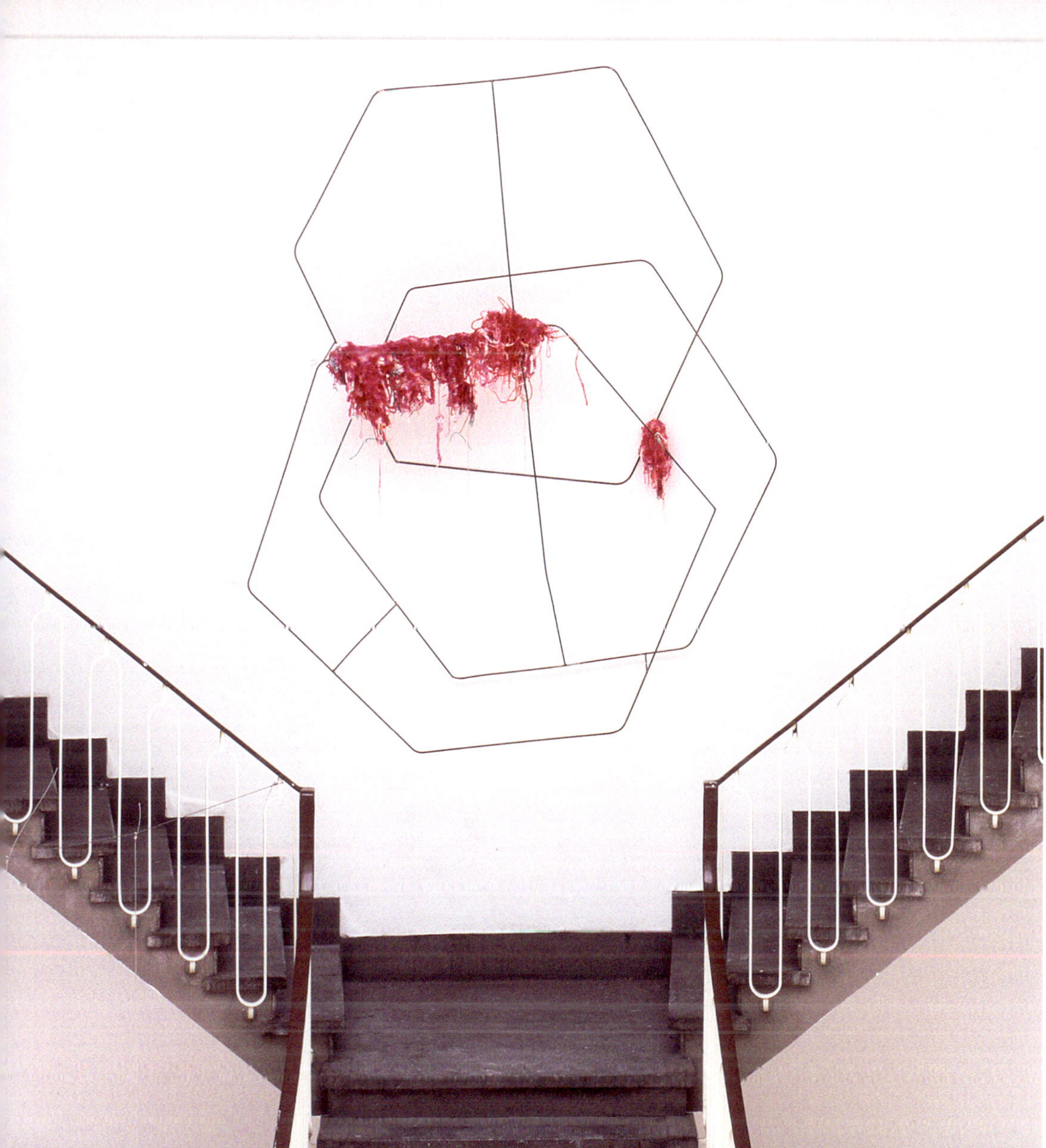

*Wireframe,* 2007
Stahl, Kordel, Zucker, Leim,
Süßigkeiten, Sprühfarbe
Steel, cord, sugar, glue,
candy, spray paint
H: 2,4 m

# Slink
## Fuhrwerkswaage Kunstraum, Köln

9.9.–23.9.2007

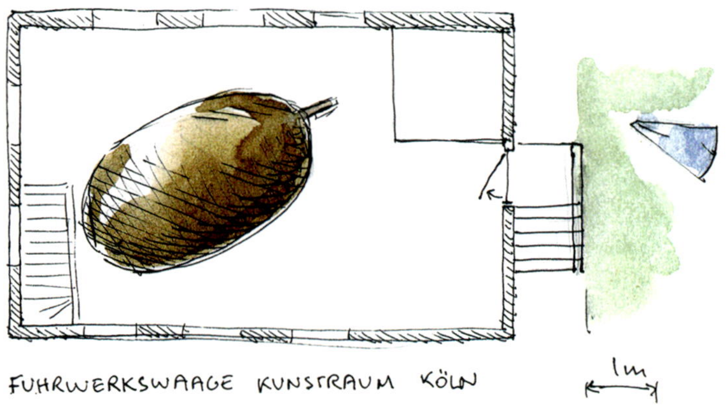




*Slink*, 2007
Klebeband, Holz,
Aufhängung
Tape, timber,
hanging device
L: 7,6 m


44

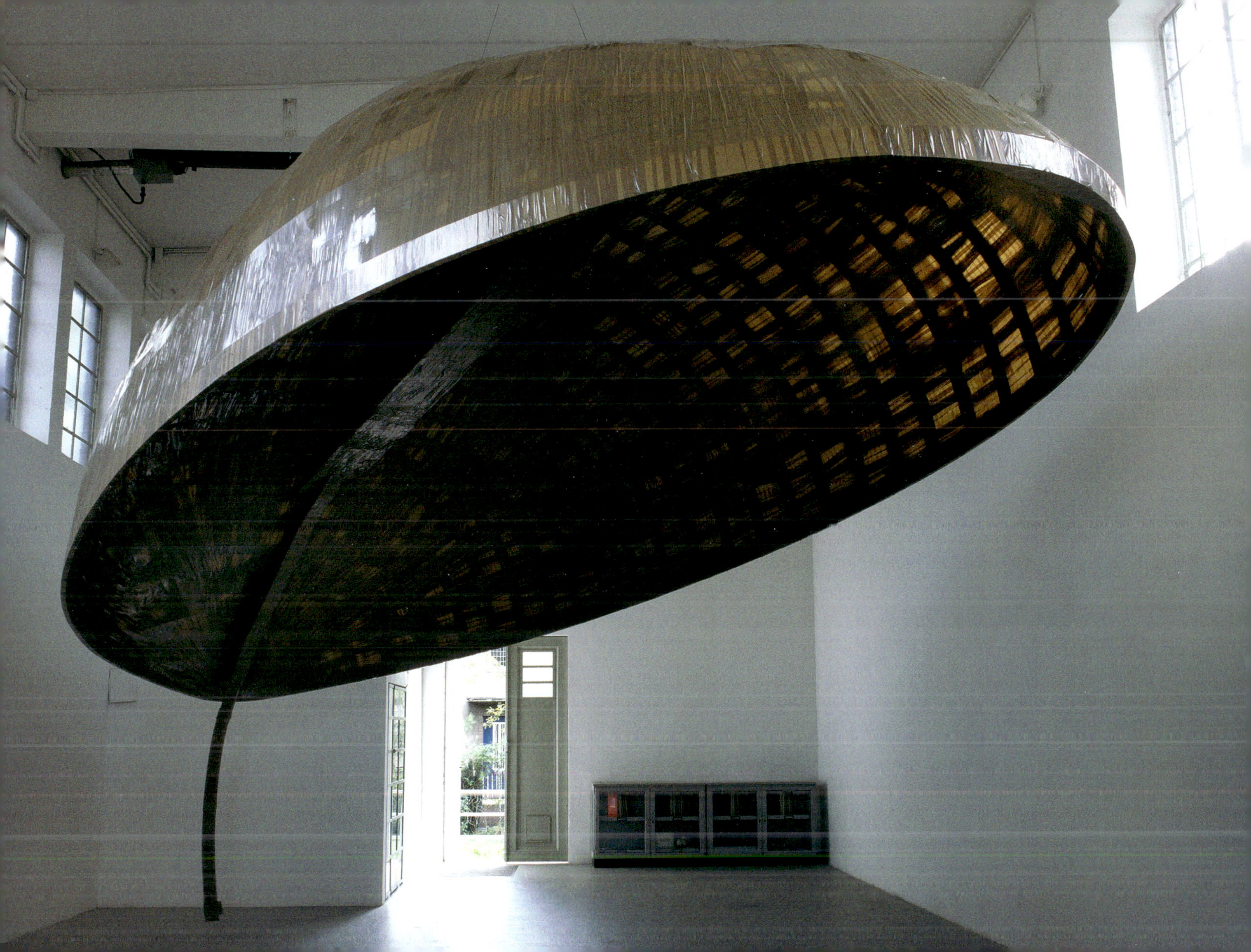

# Dreizueins
## Kunsthalle Recklinghausen

7.10.–18.11.2007

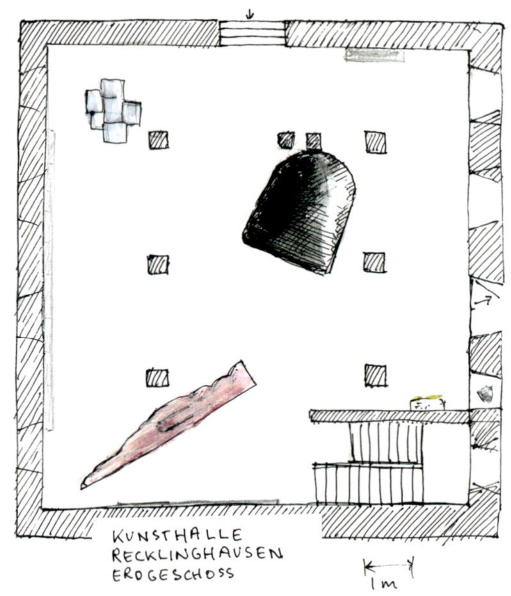





*Puppe, Stacky, Pad*

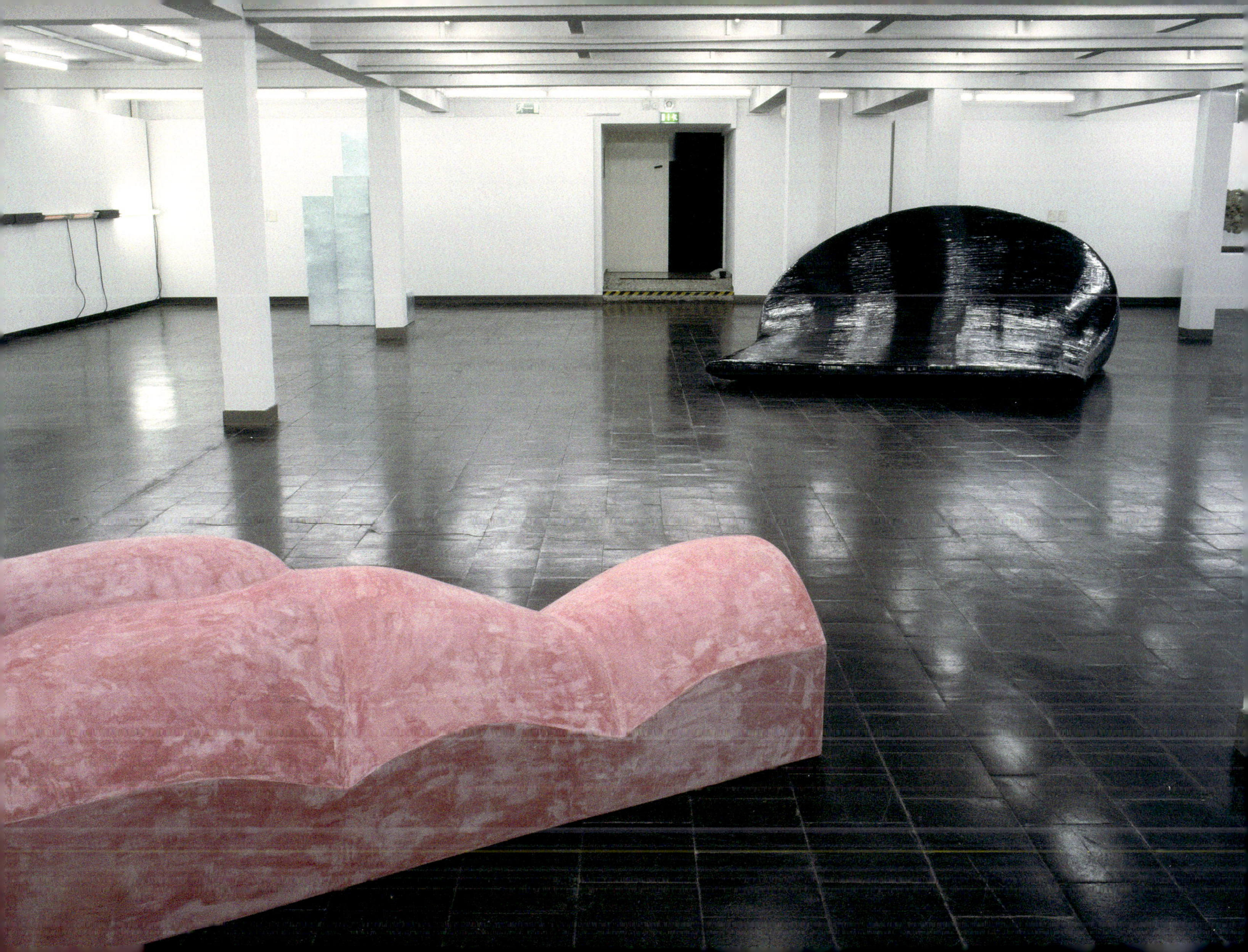

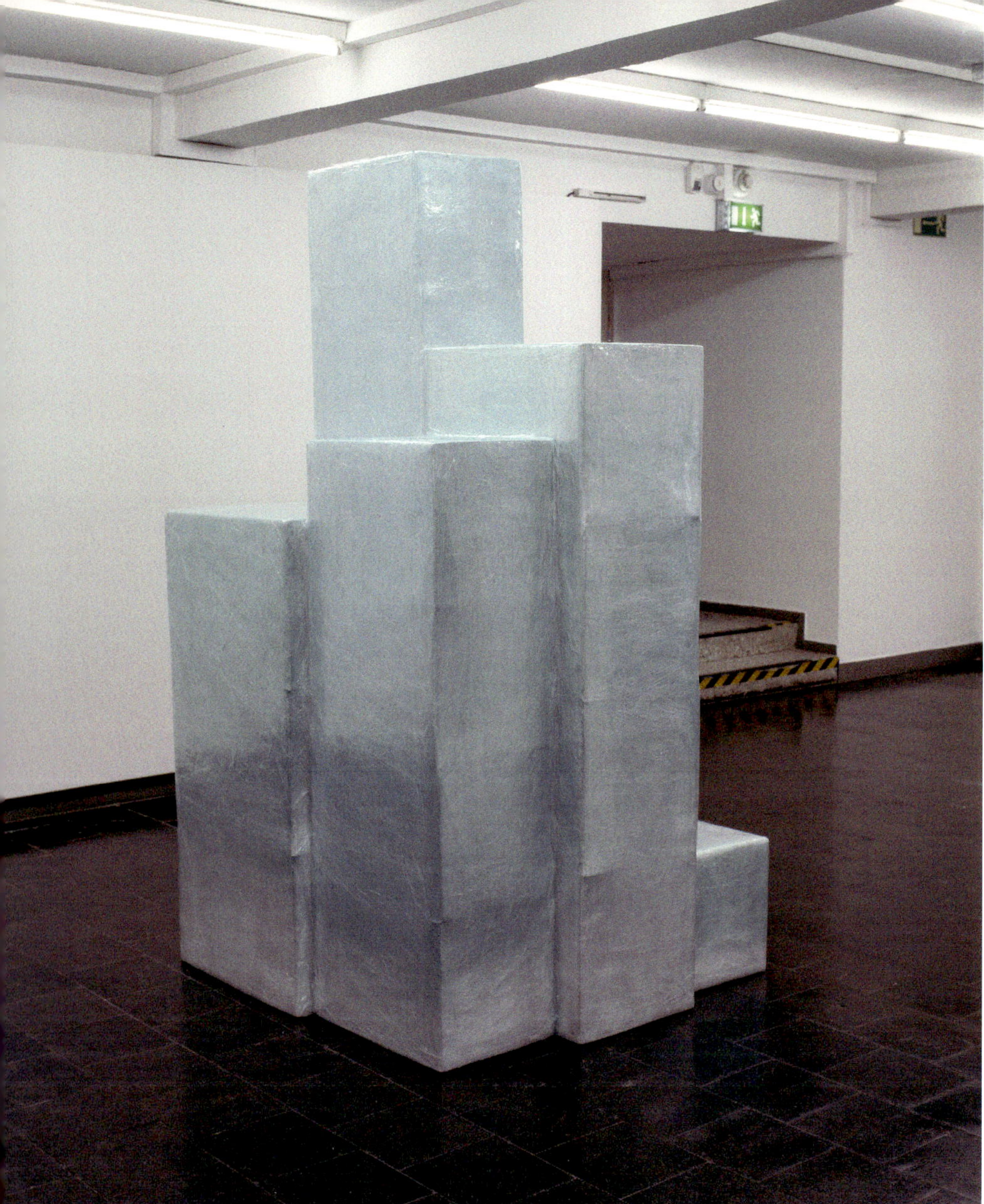

*Stacky,* 2007
Folie, Umzugkartons
Foil, cardboard boxes
H: 2,1 m

*Puppe,* 2007
Farbe, Spachtel, Styropor
Paint, filler, polystyrene
L: 5,5 m

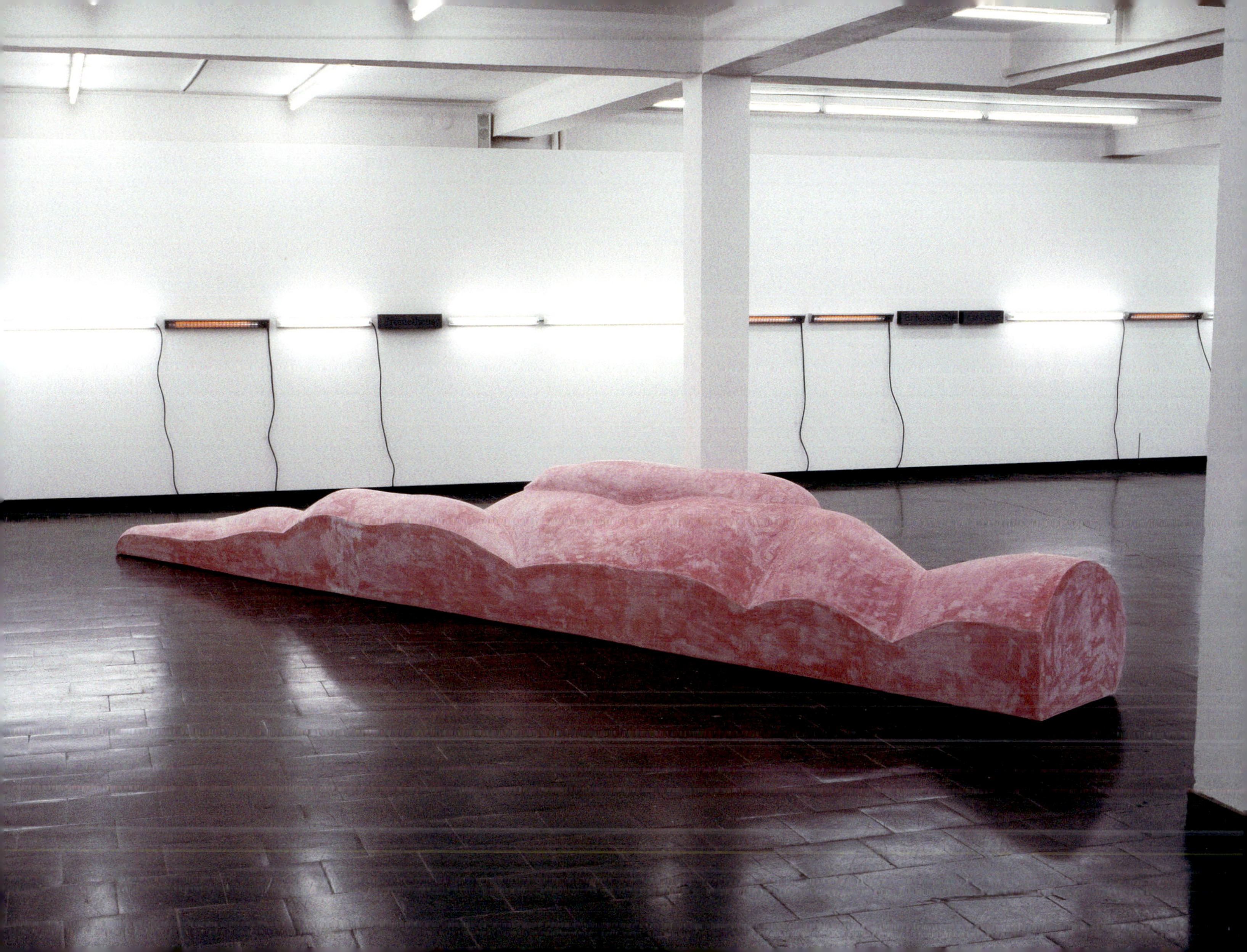

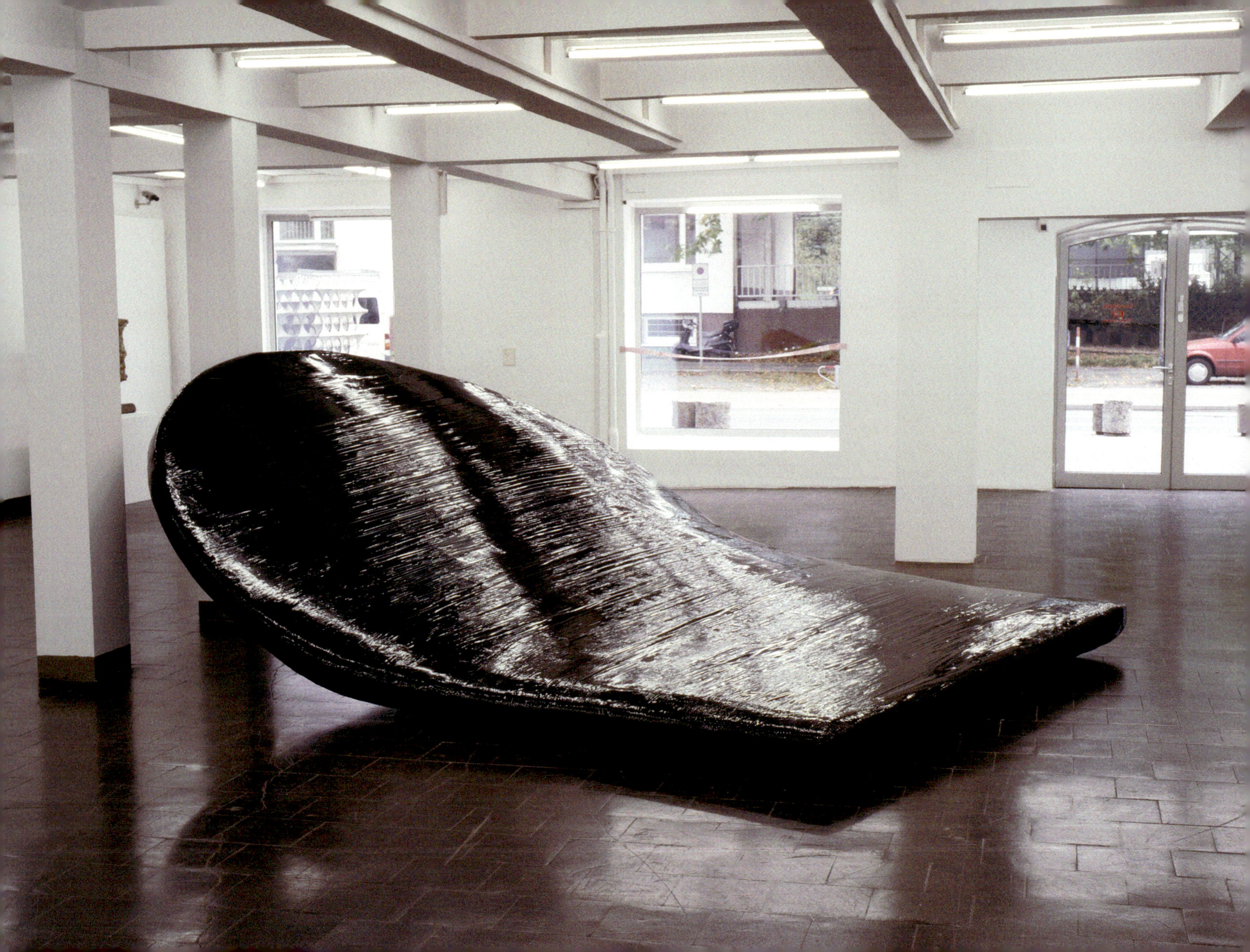

*Pad,* 2007
Folie, Füllmaterial,
Holz, Trennwand
Foil, debris, timber,
partition wall
B: 2,3 m

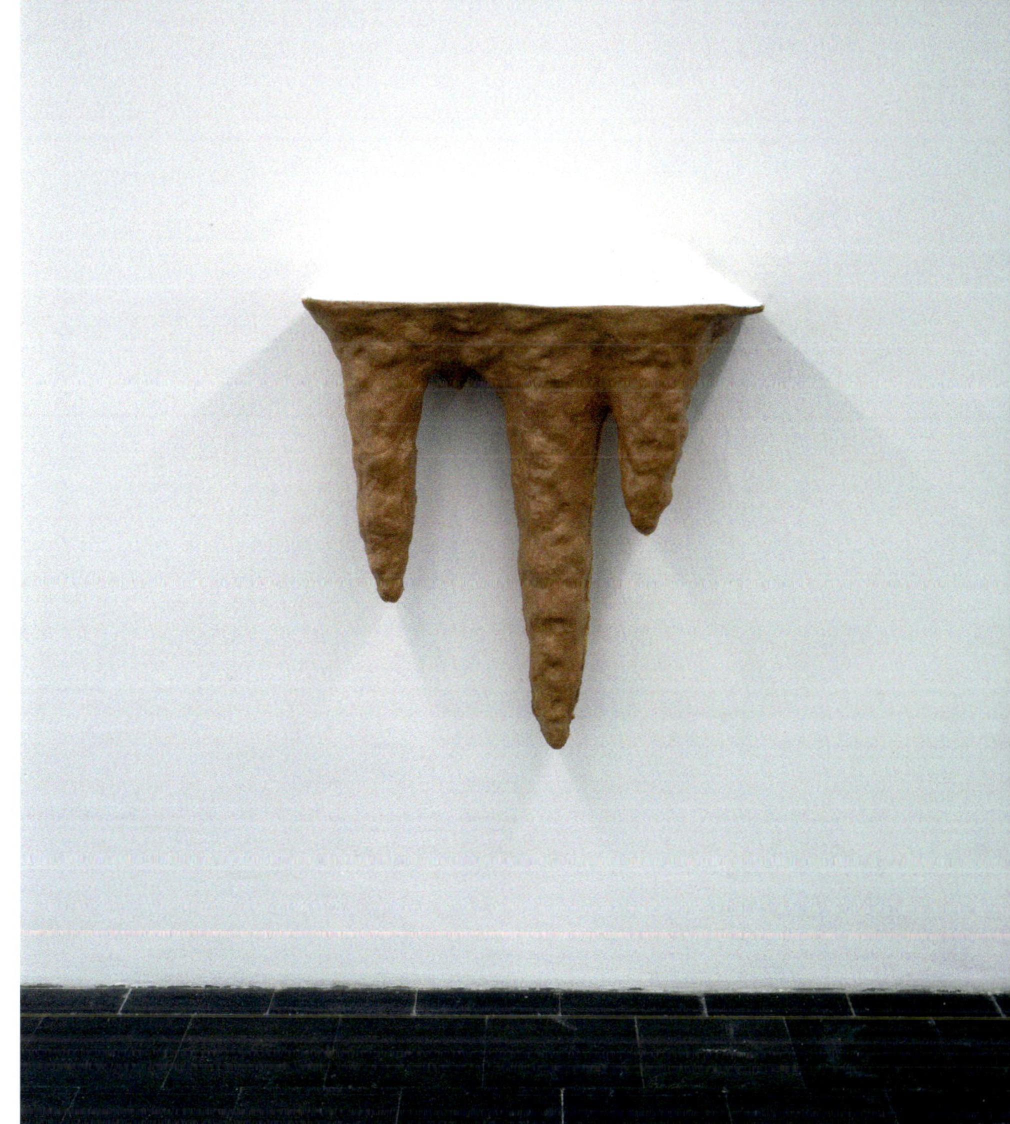

# Kunstpreis junger westen 2007
# Kunsthalle Recklinghausen

2.12.2007–3.2.2008

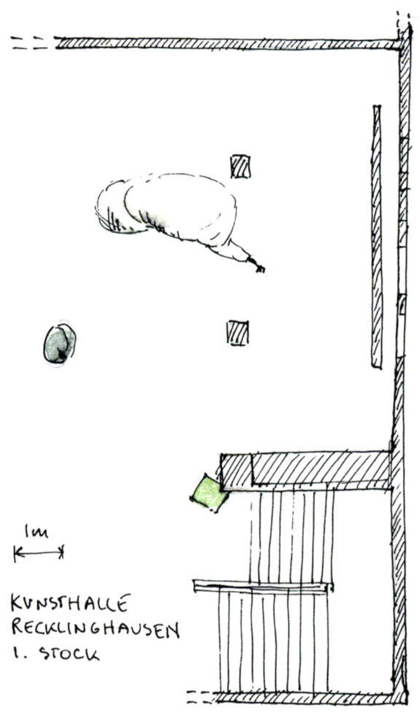



*Wibble wobble*, 2007
Gelatine, Glyzerin,
Pigment
Gelatine, glycerine,
pigment
L: 0,5 m

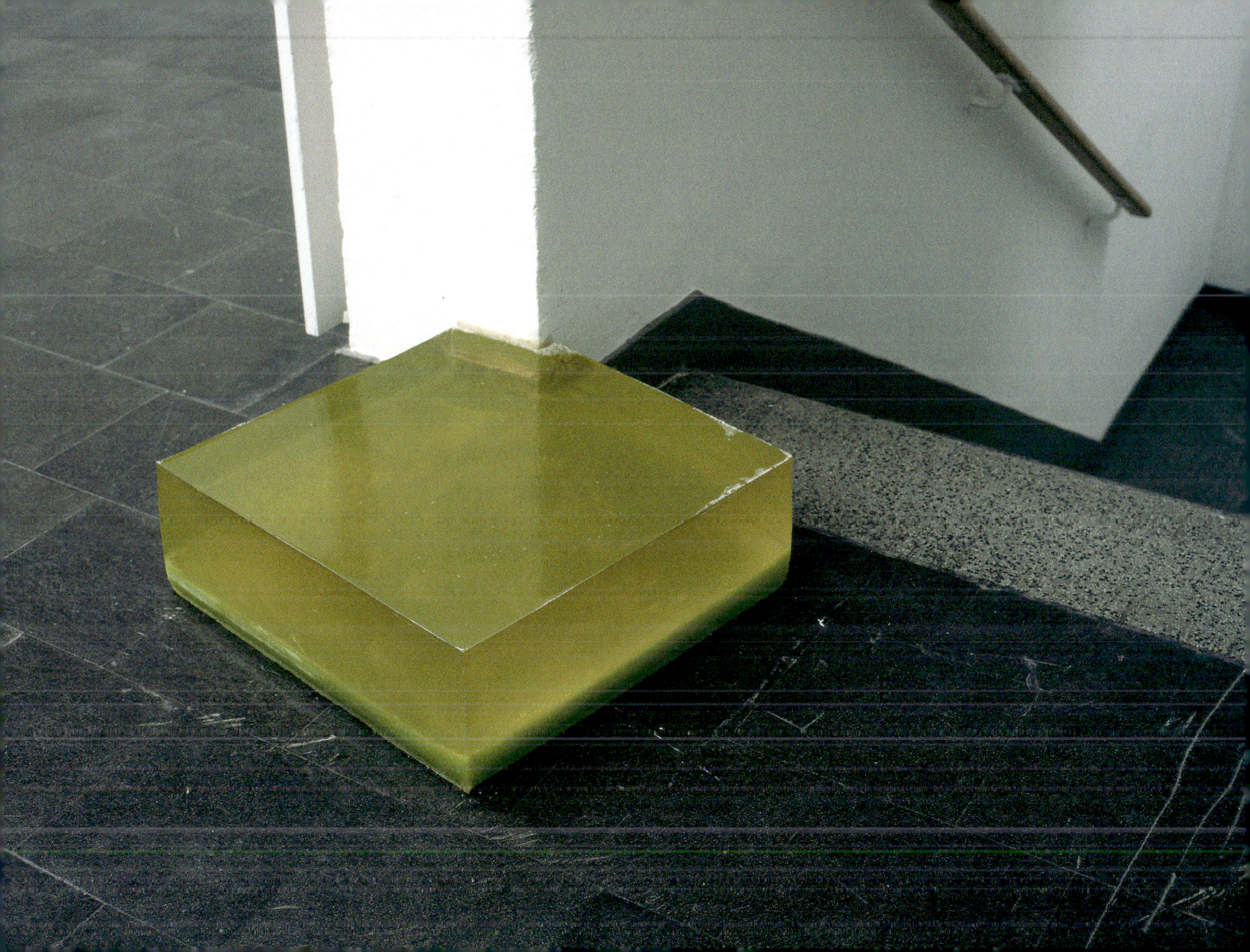

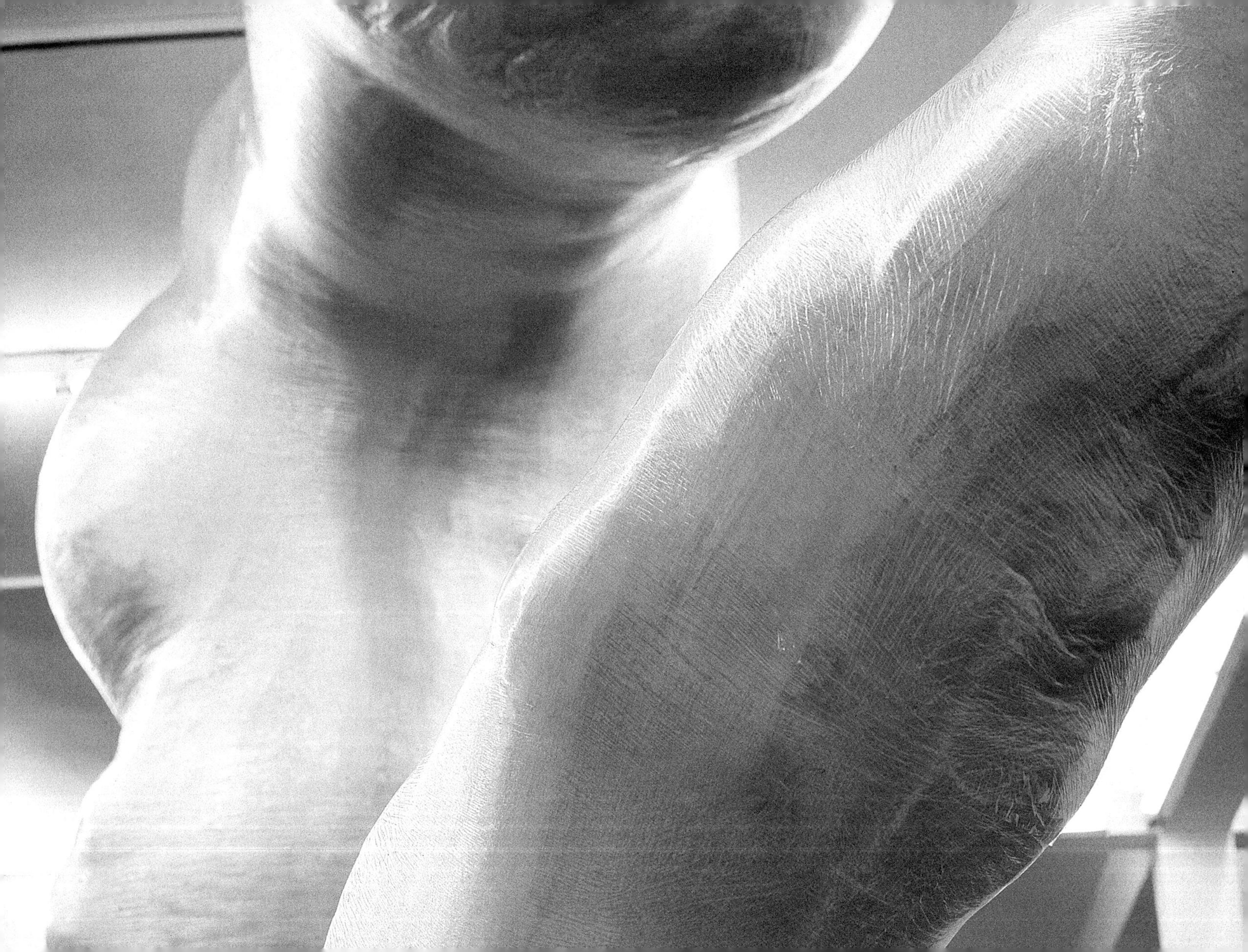

*Thug,* 2007
Folie, Klebeband,
Ballons, Holz,
Brechstange
Foil, tape, balloons,
timber, crow bar
H: 3,6 m

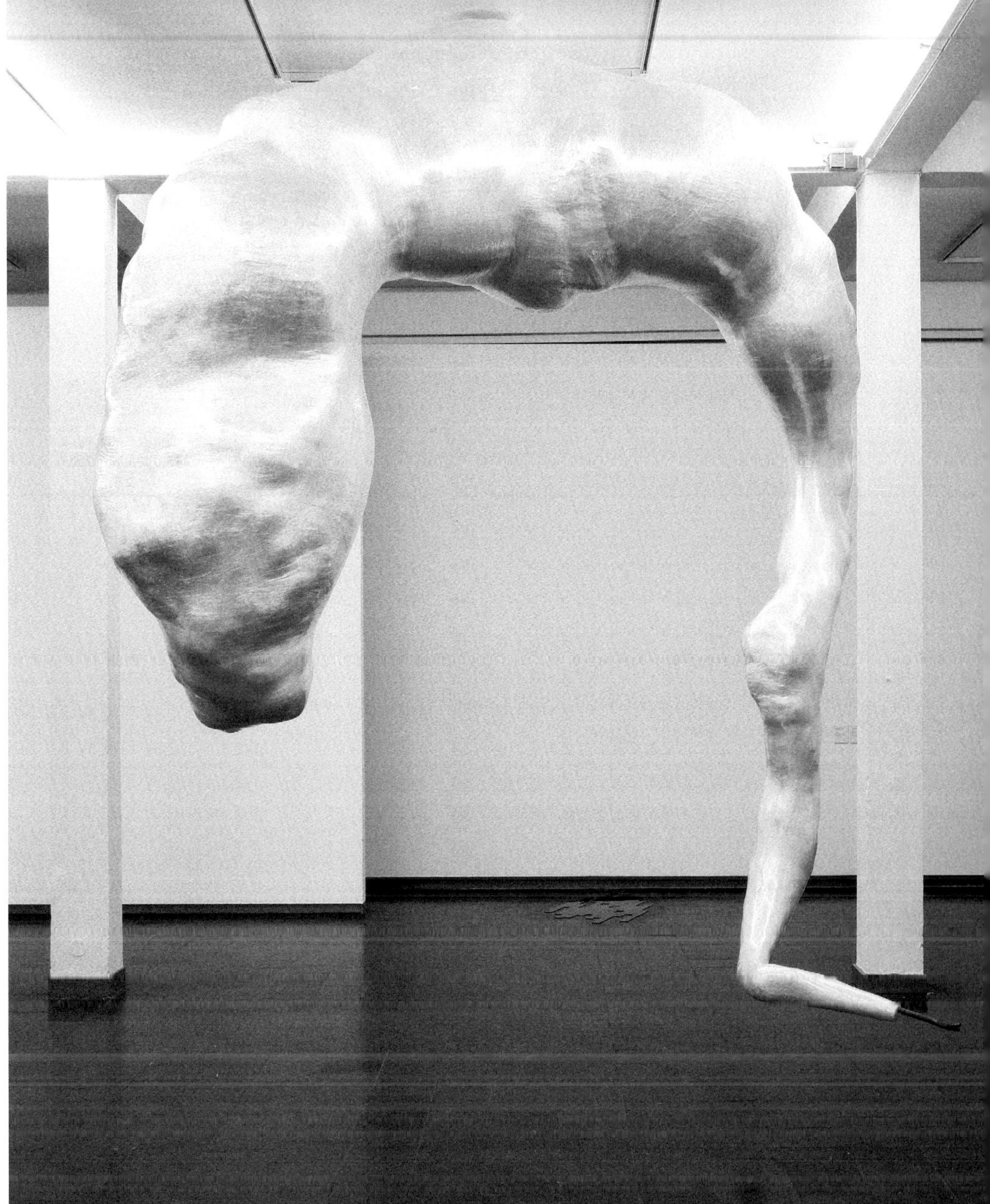

# Better is something you build
# Kevin Kavanagh Gallery, Dublin

7.2.–1.3.2008

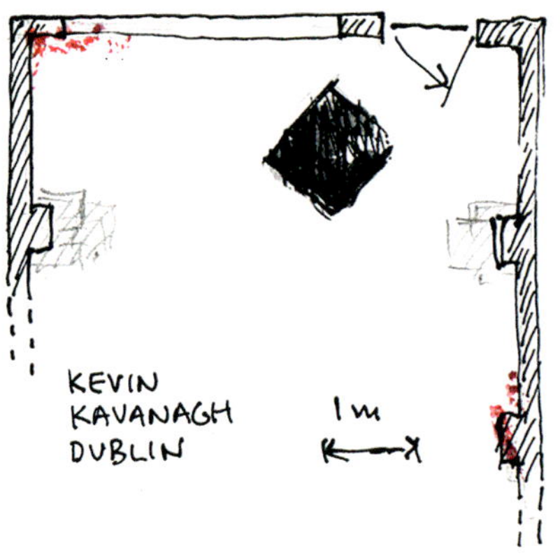



*Two stripes (Zwei Streifen)*, 2008
Klebepunkte, rot
Marking dots, red
L: 1,4 m

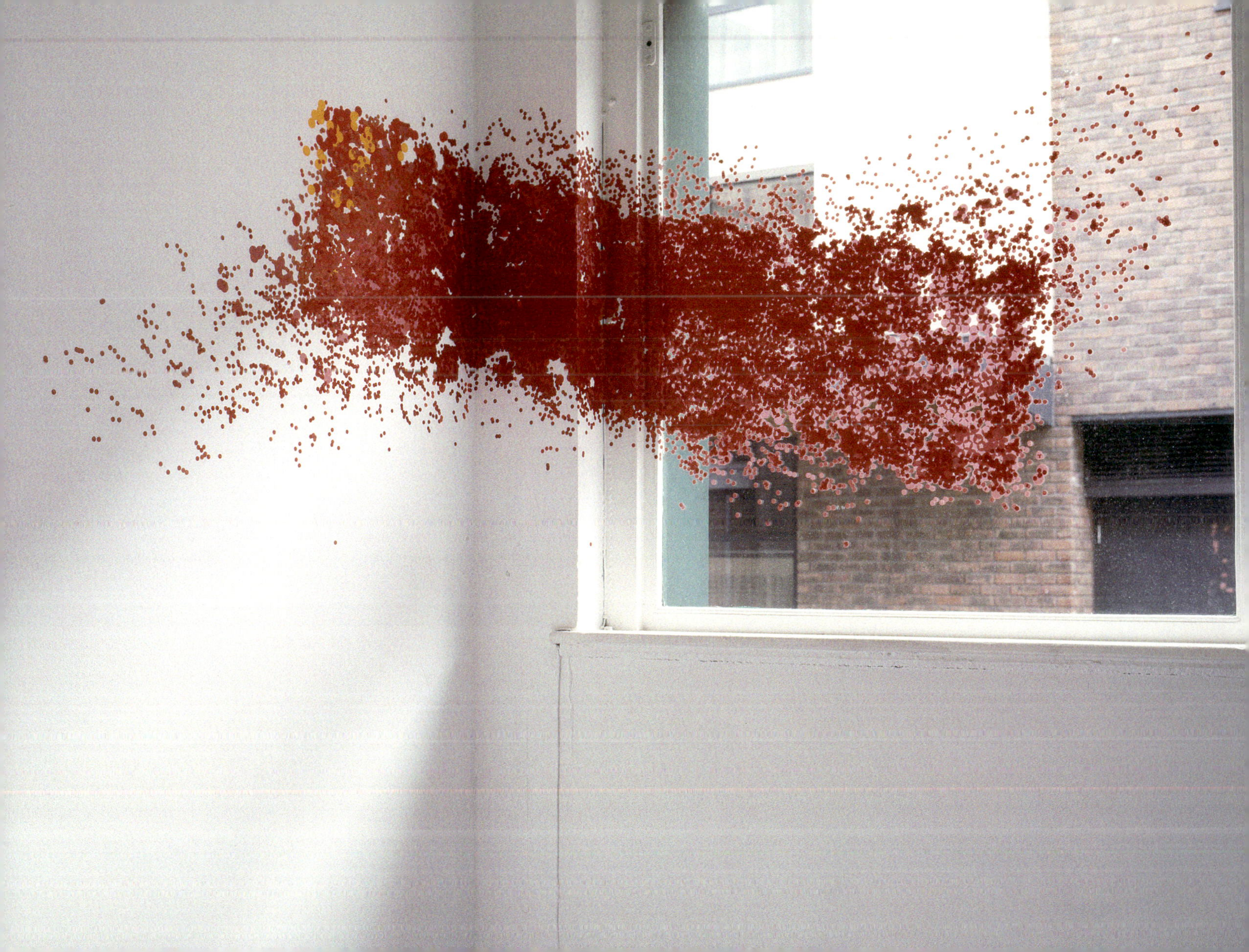

# Frischzelle_08
# Kunstmuseum Stuttgart

8.3.–11.5.2008

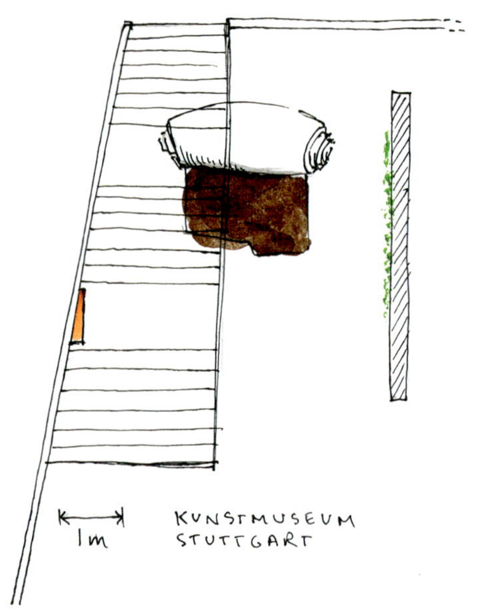




*Ausgleichstück (Orange bar),* 2008
Gelatine, Glyzerin, Pigment
Gelatine, glycerine, pigment
L: 1,4 m

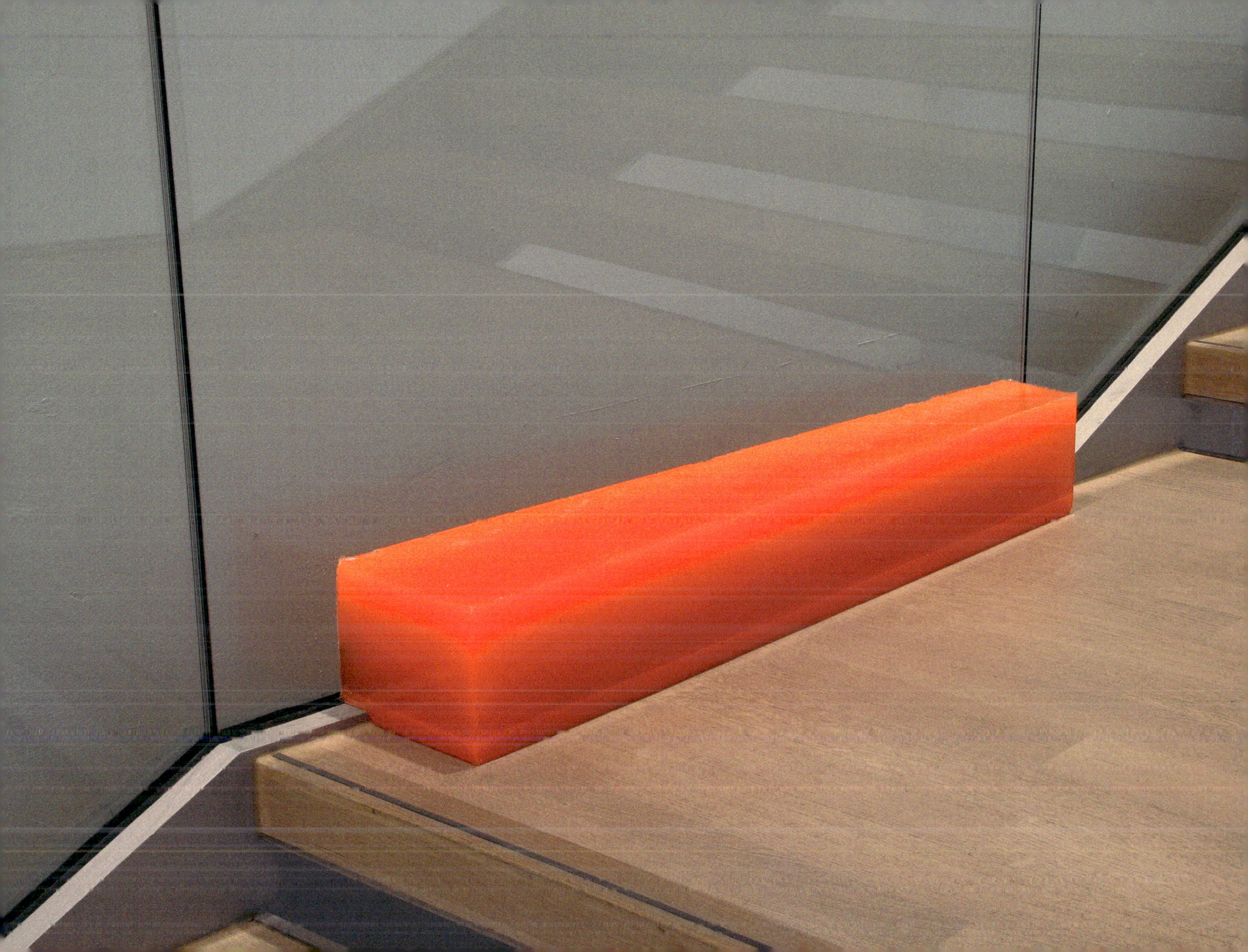

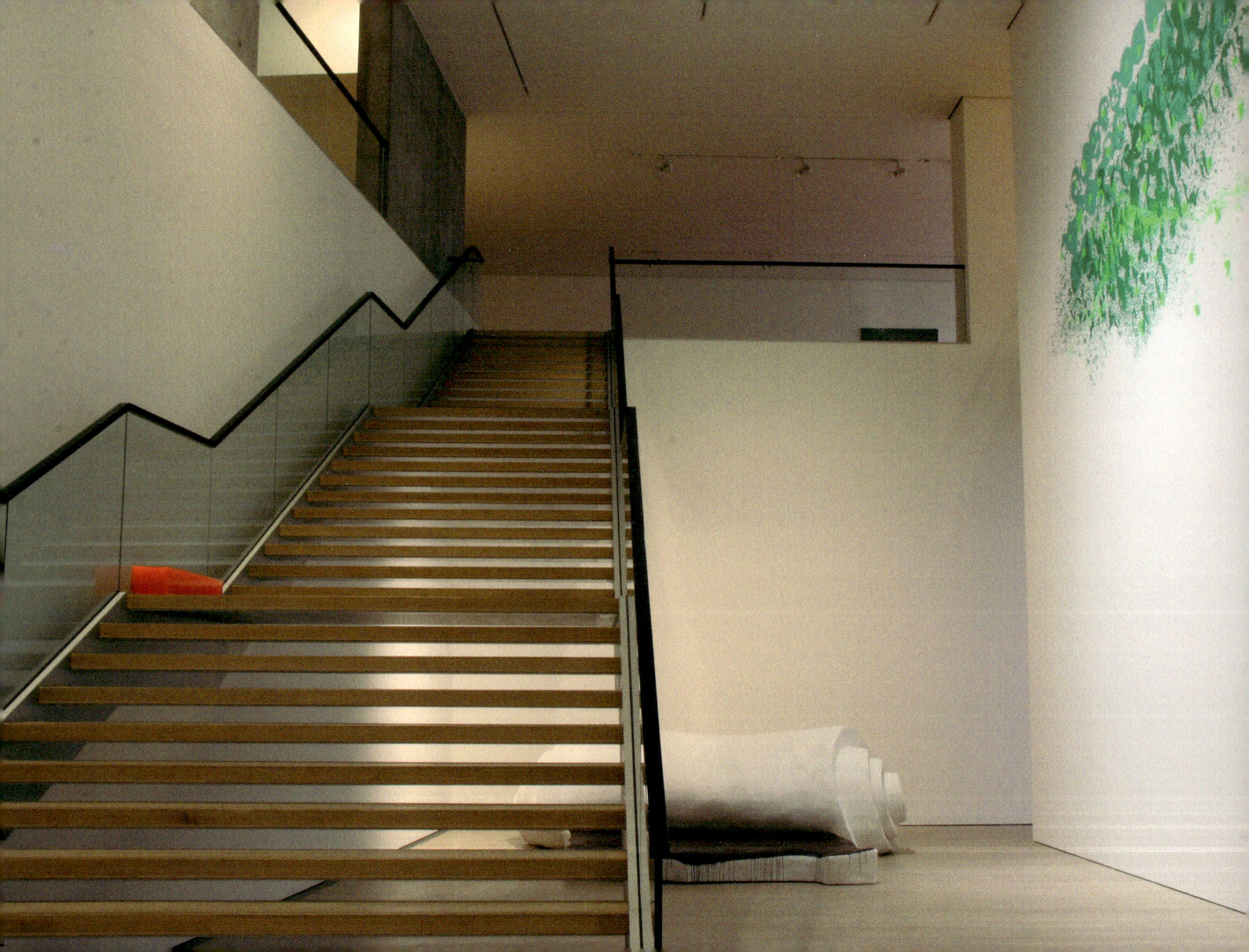

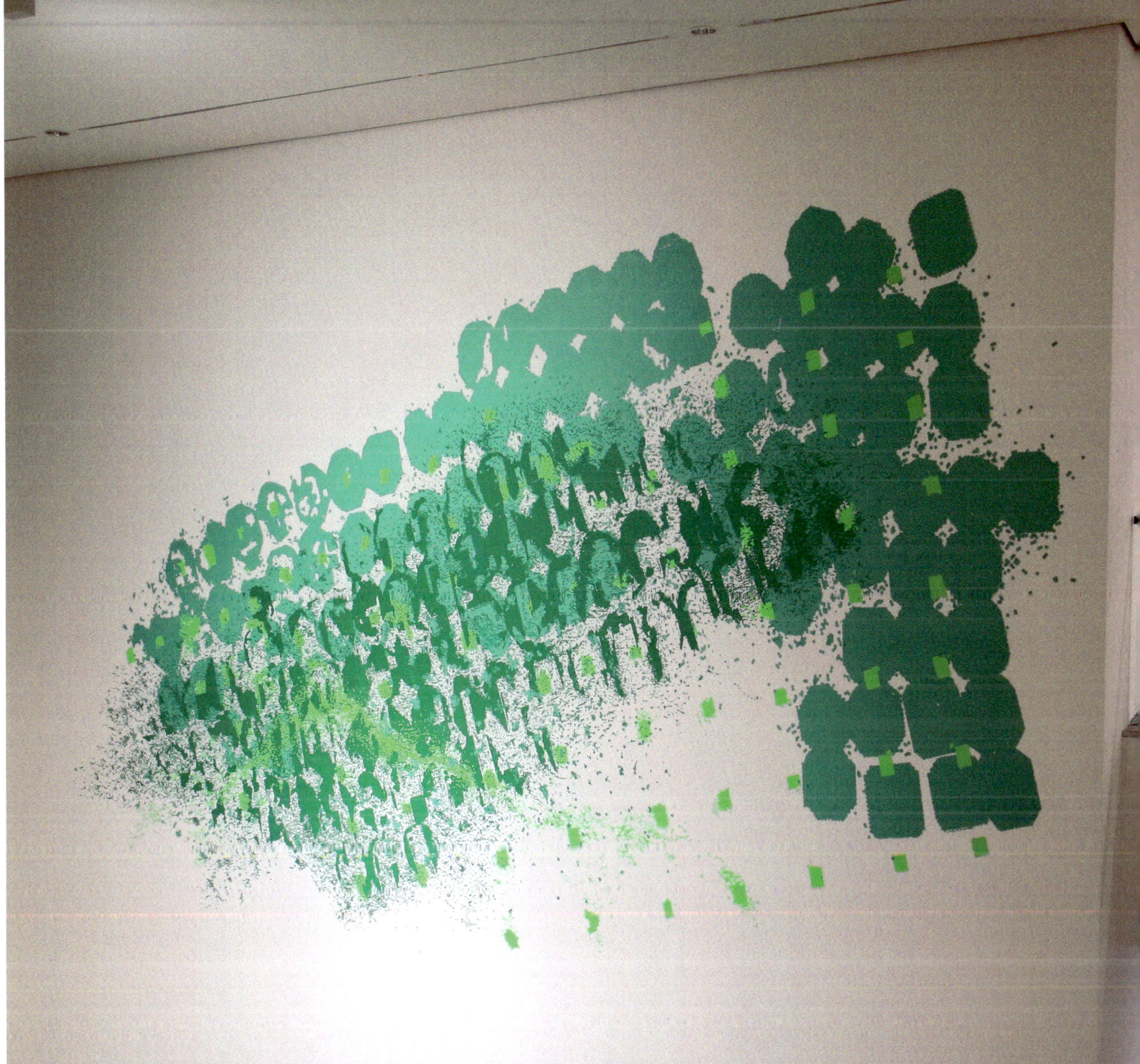

Mesophyll, 2008
Klebepunkte grün
Marking dots, green
L: 7 m

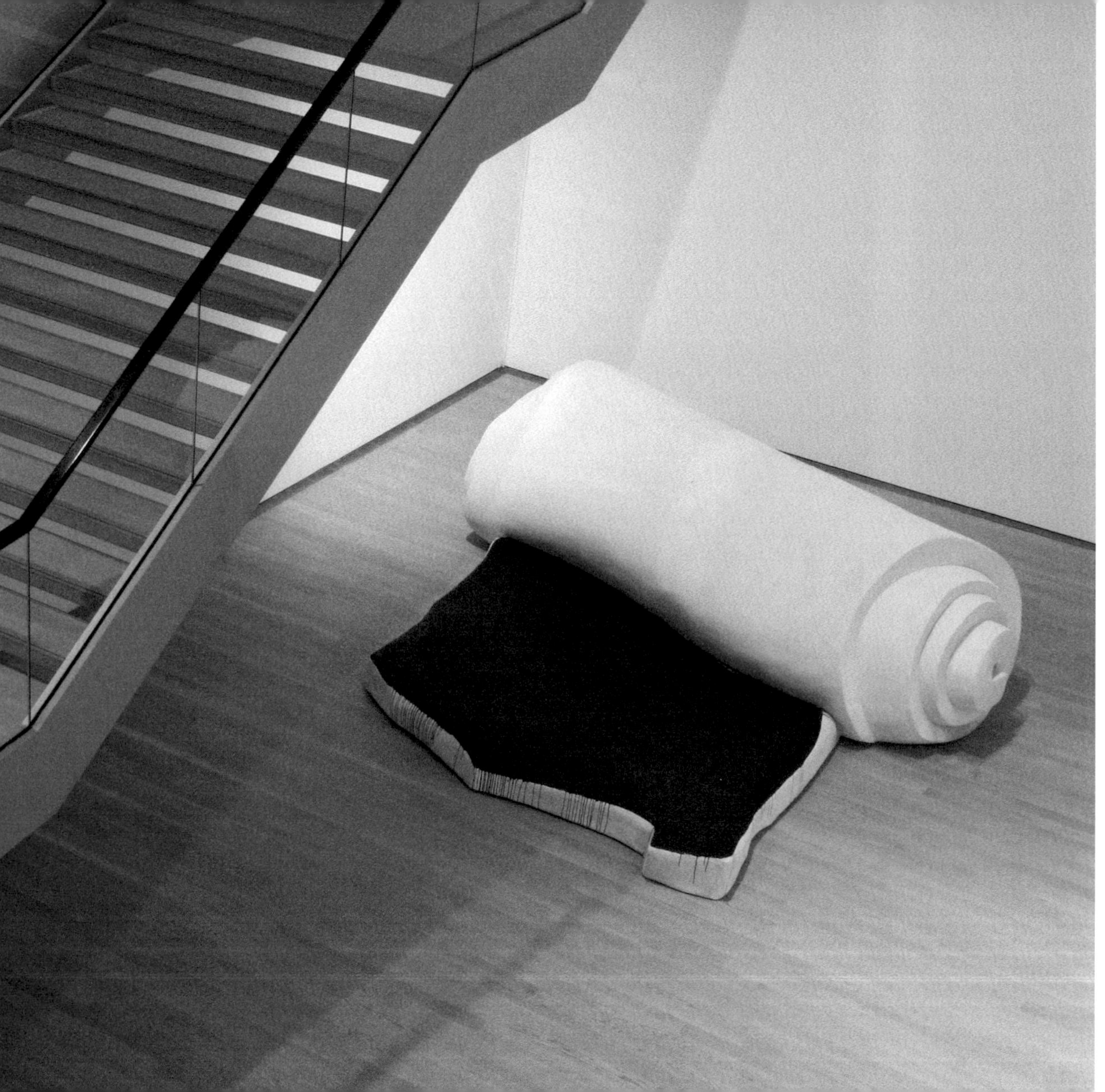

*Rolle (Roll)*, 2008
Putz, Dispersion, Styropor
Wall plastering, paint,
polystyrene
B: 3,6 m
Sammlung | Collection
Ciesielski, Vallendar

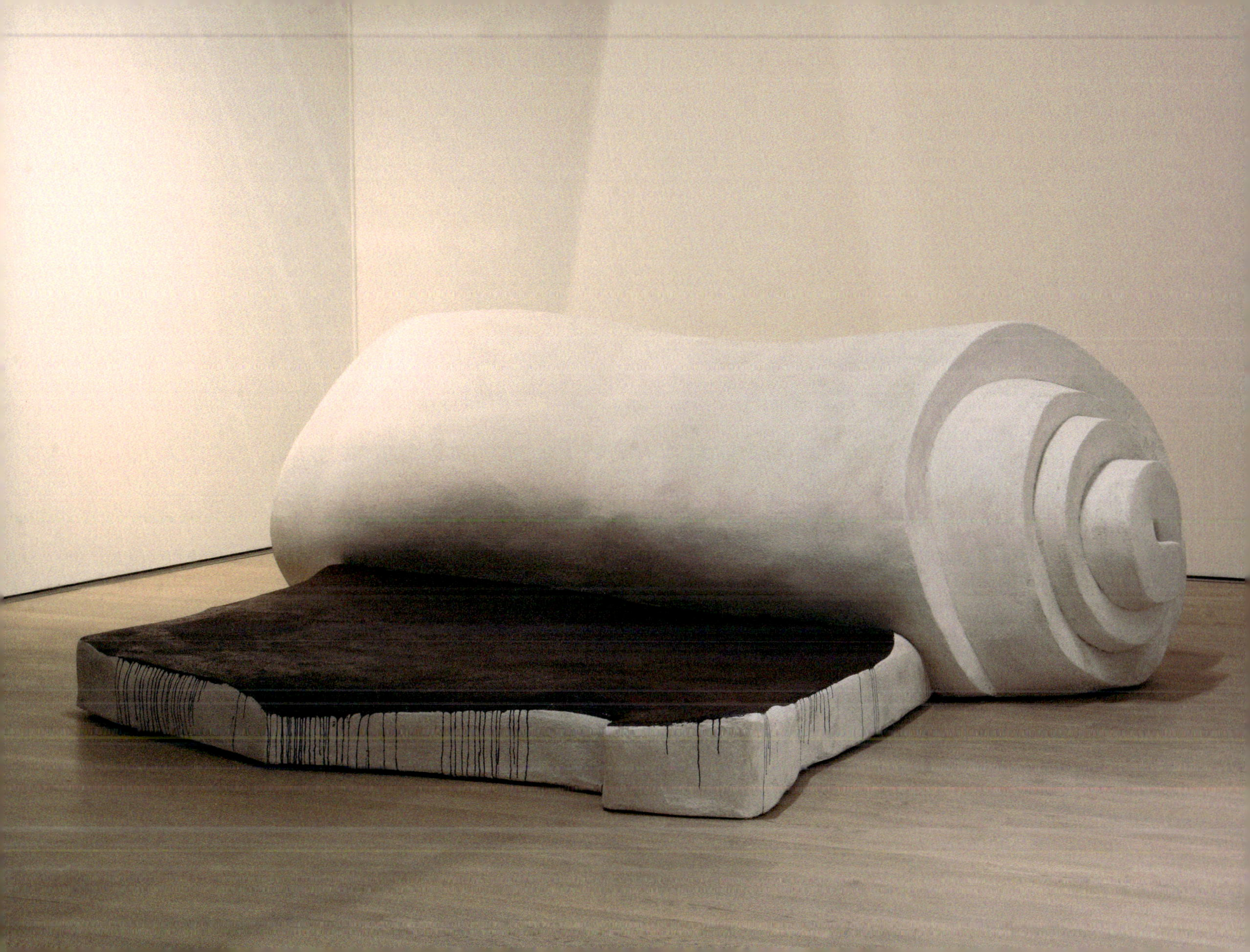

# Droopy
# Kunsthaus Essen

28.3.–27.4.2008

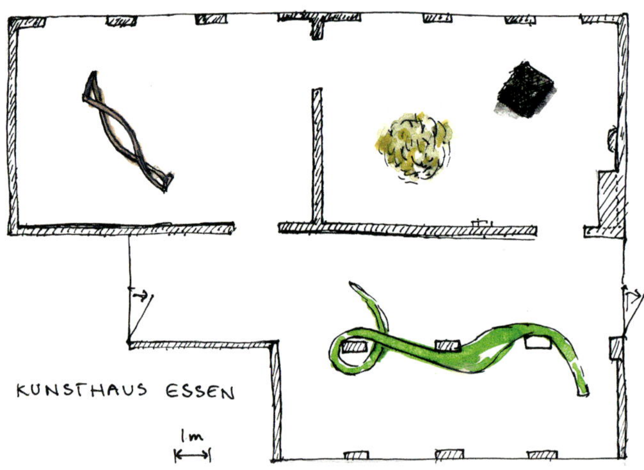



*Vymbo*, 2008
Folie, Packmaterial,
Klebeband, Holz
Foil, packaging materials,
tape, timber
L: 9 m

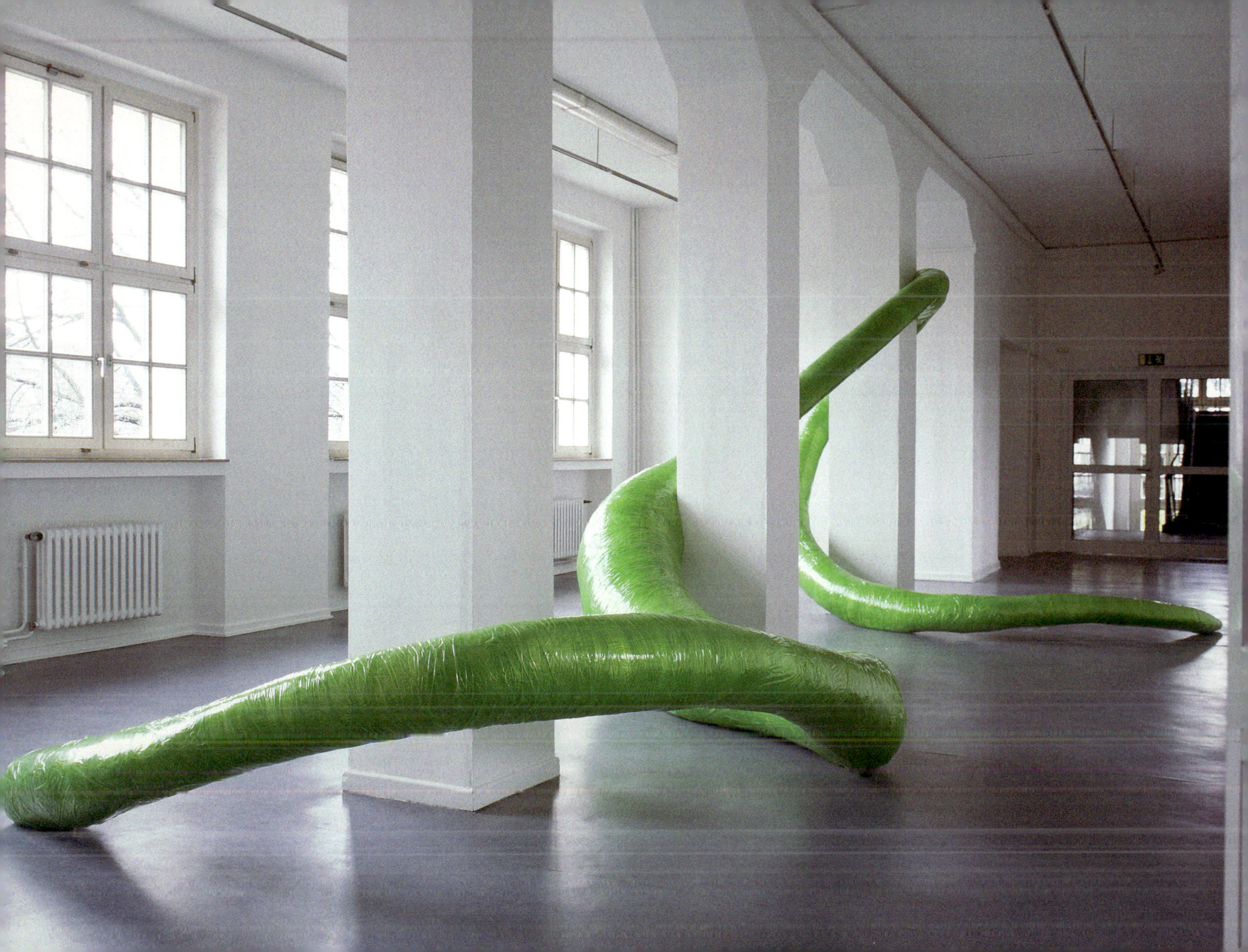

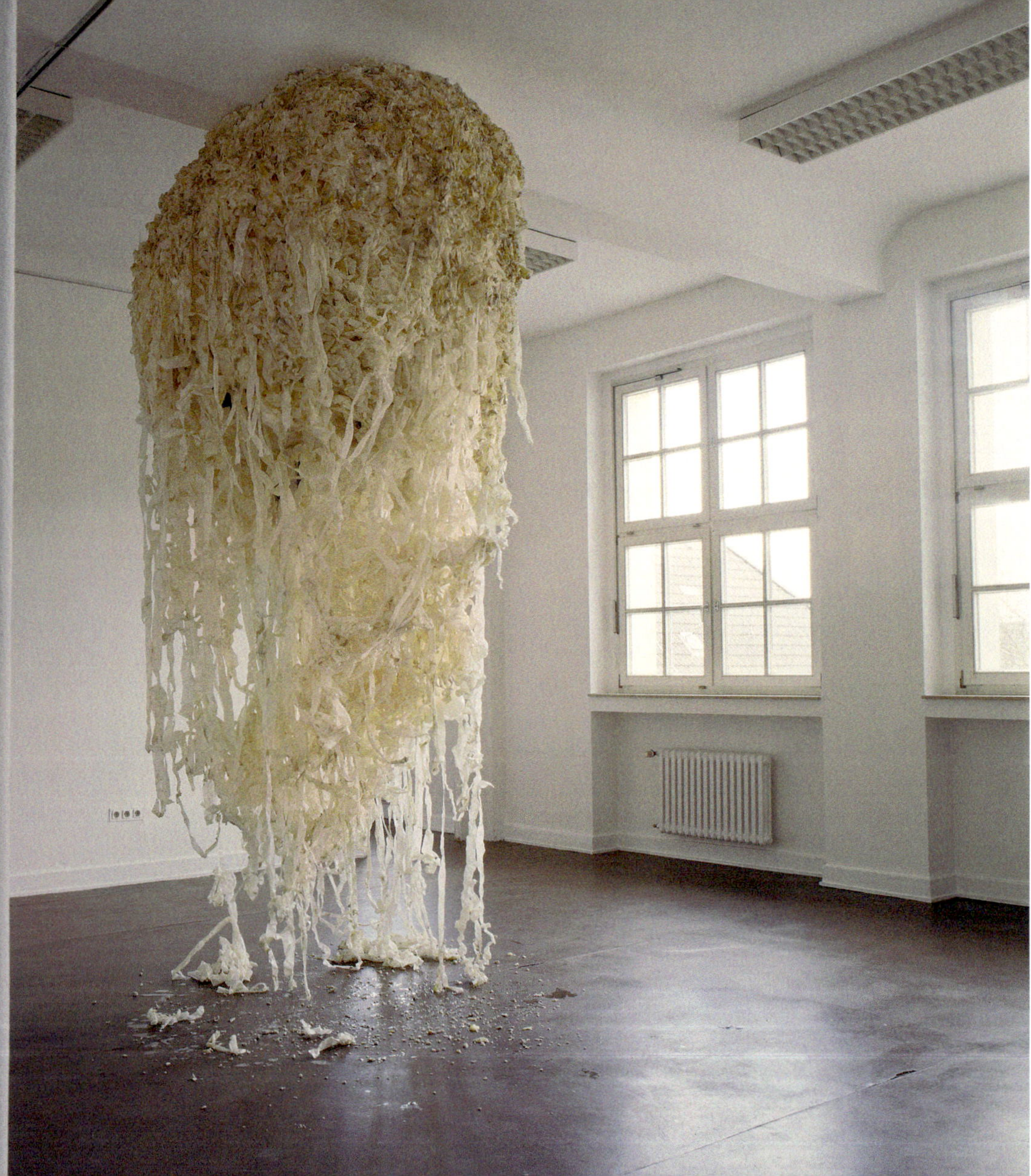


*Droopy*, 2008
Kreppband, Ballons,
Mayonaise
Masking tape, balloons,
mayonnaise
H: 3,4 m

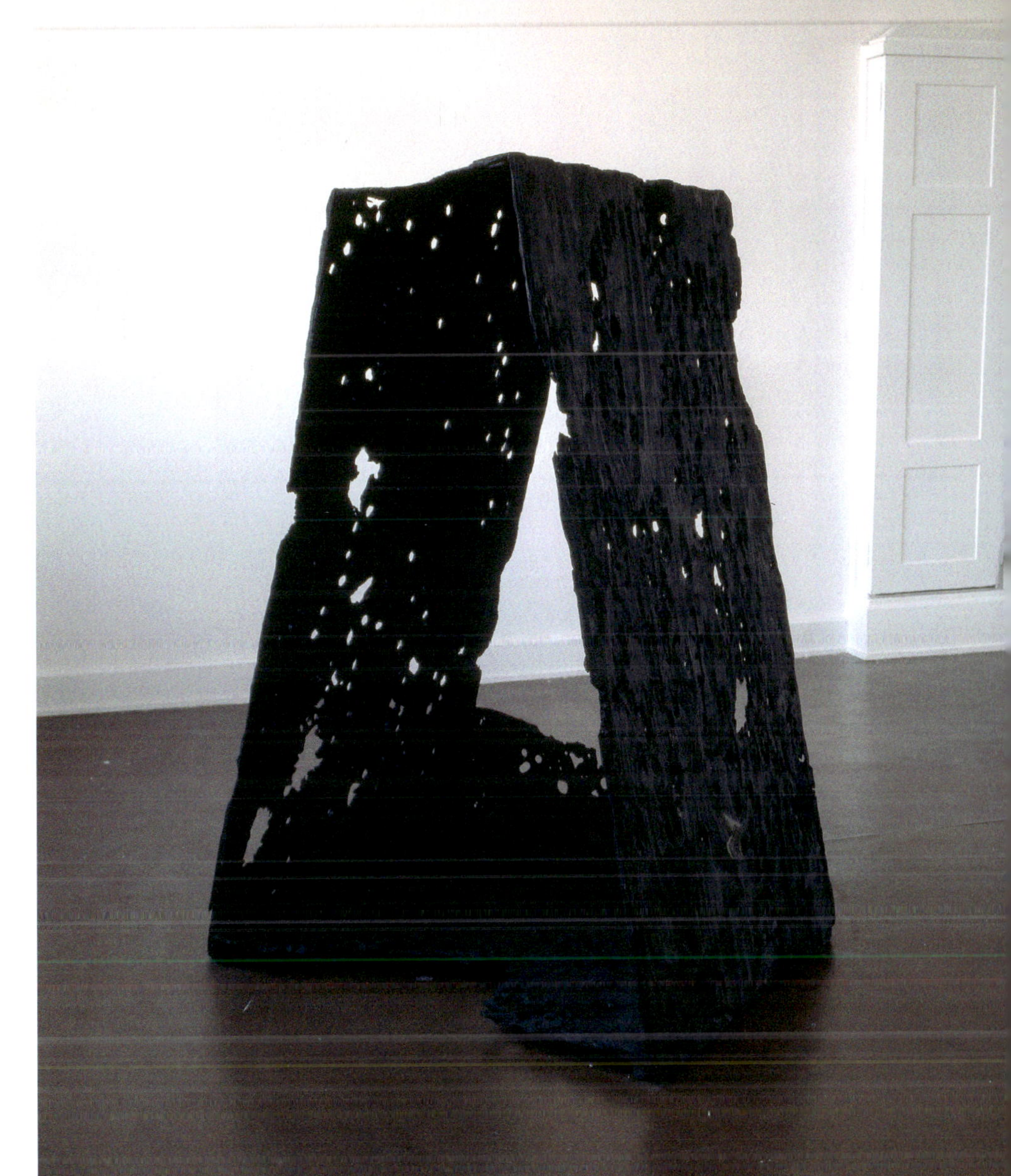

*Slice of a barricade,* 2008
Holz verbrannt
Burnt timber
H: 1,4 m

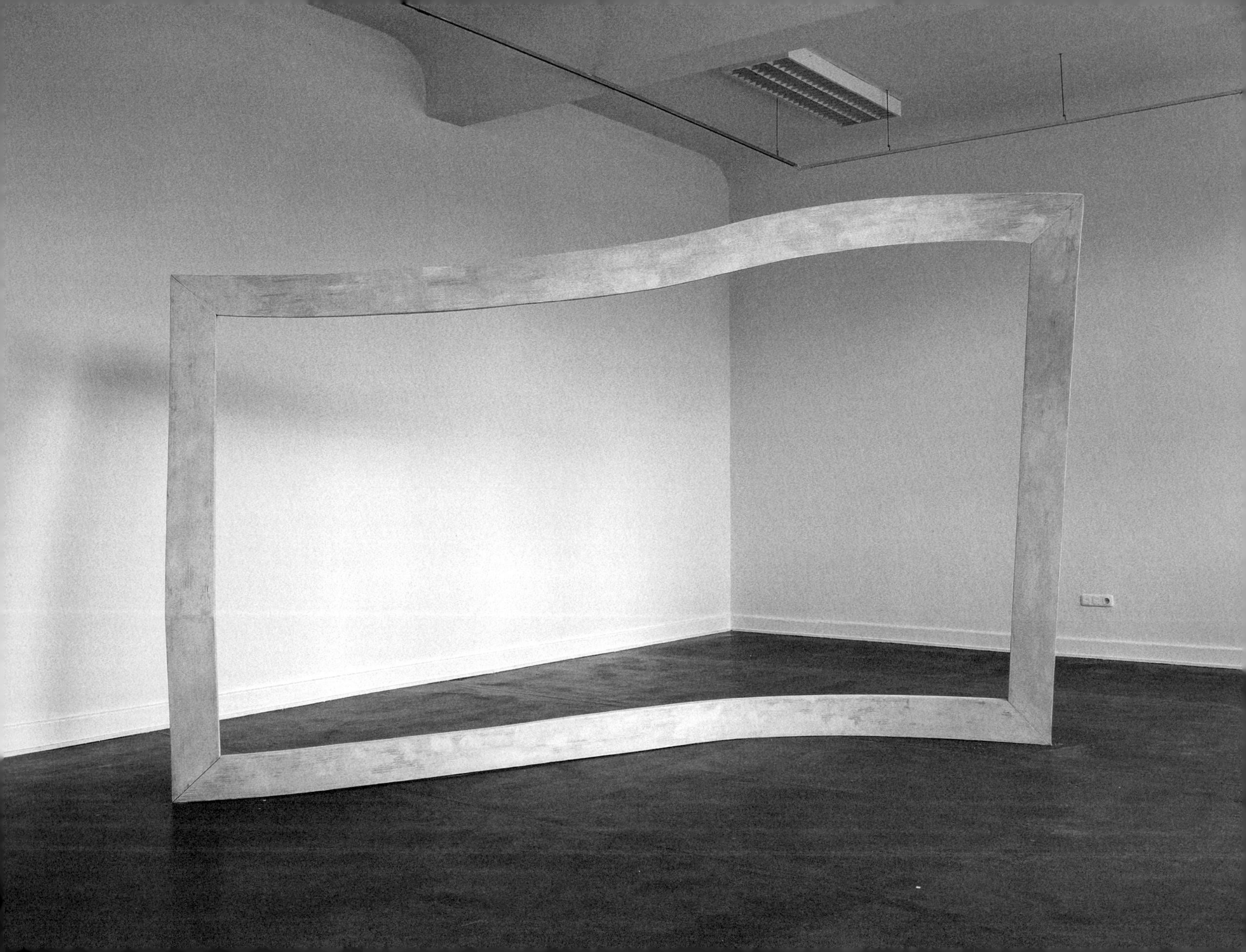

*Rahmen (Frame)*, 2008
Schichtholz, Spachtel,
Farbe
Plywood, filler, paint
L: 3,6 m

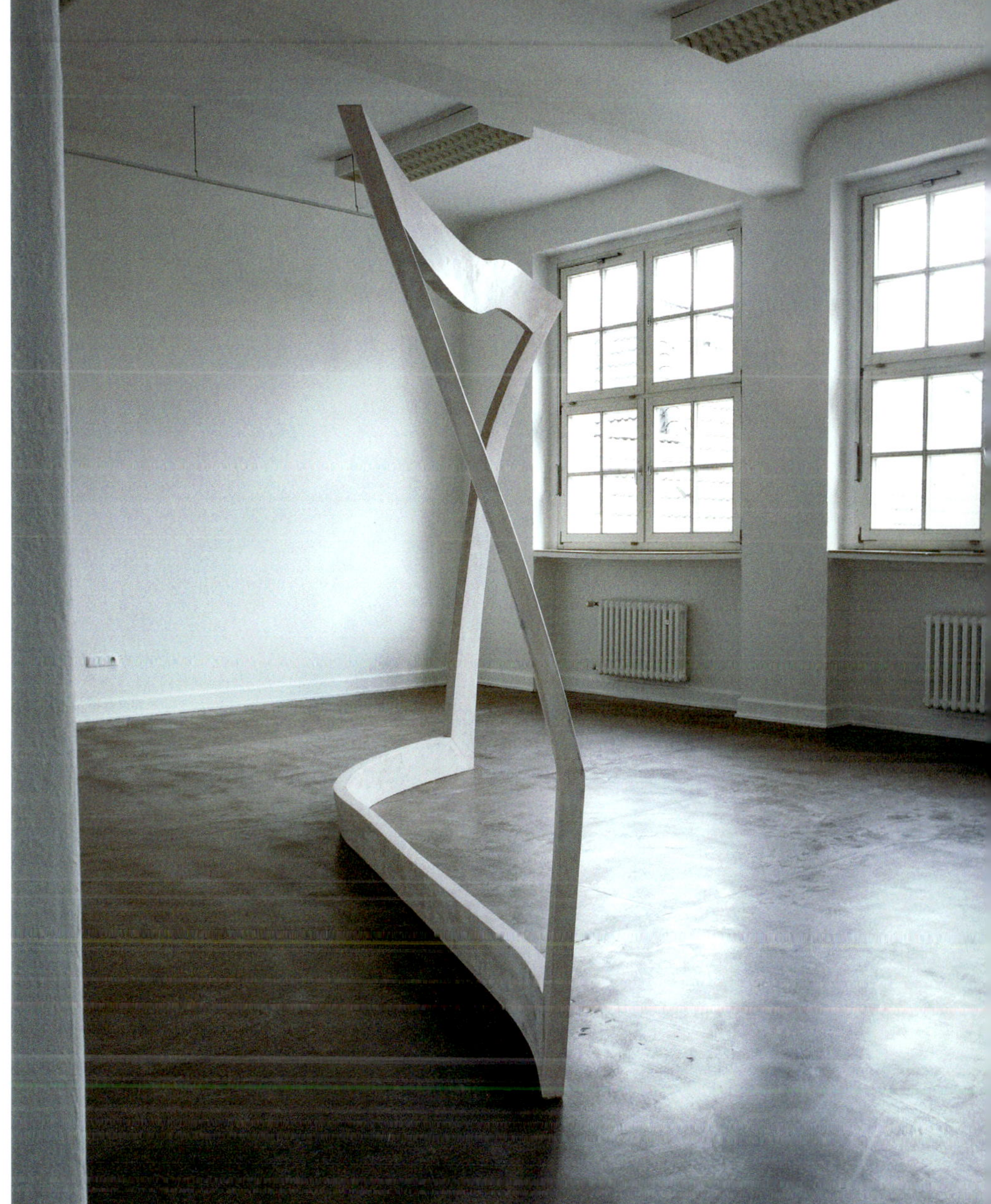

20.4.–8.6.2008

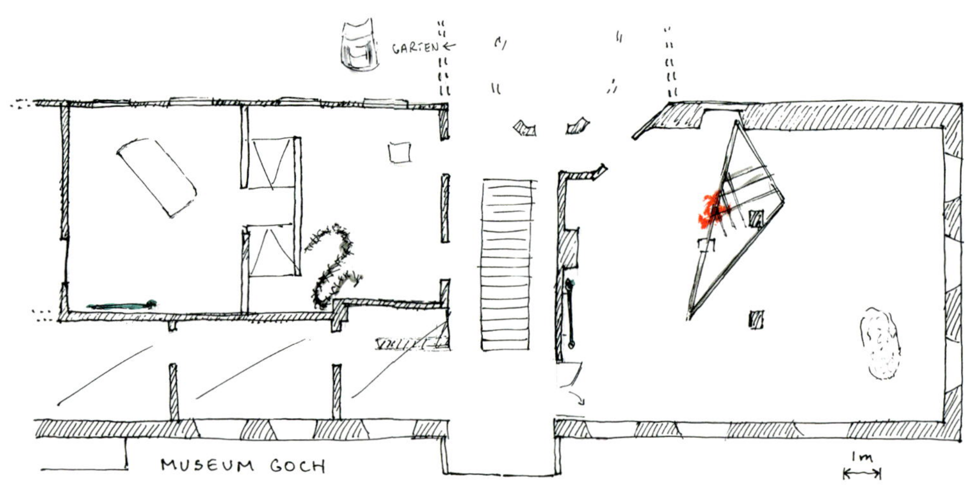


*Widget,* 2008
Stahl, Kordel, Zucker,
Sprühfarbe
Steel, cord, sugar,
spray paint
L: 5 m

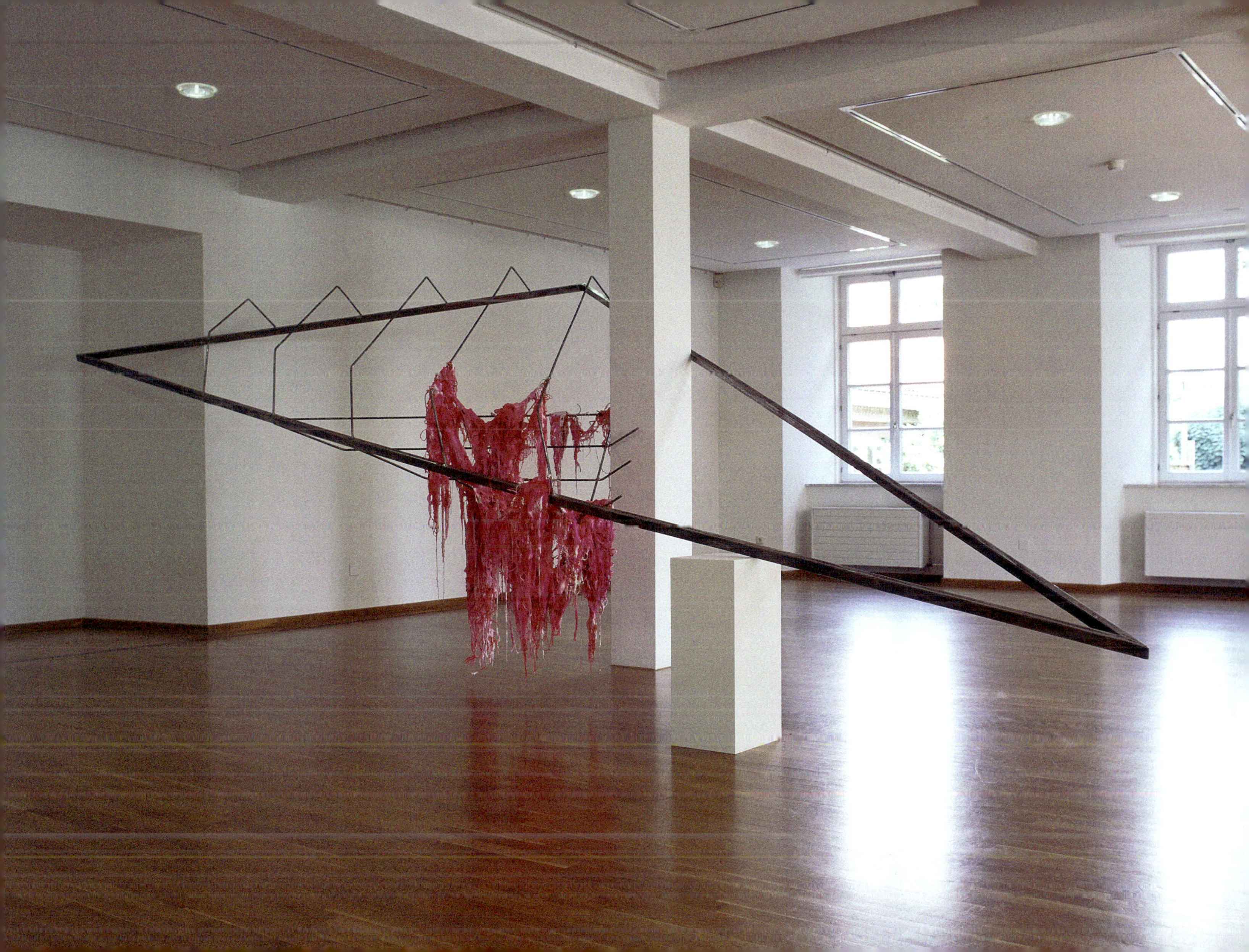

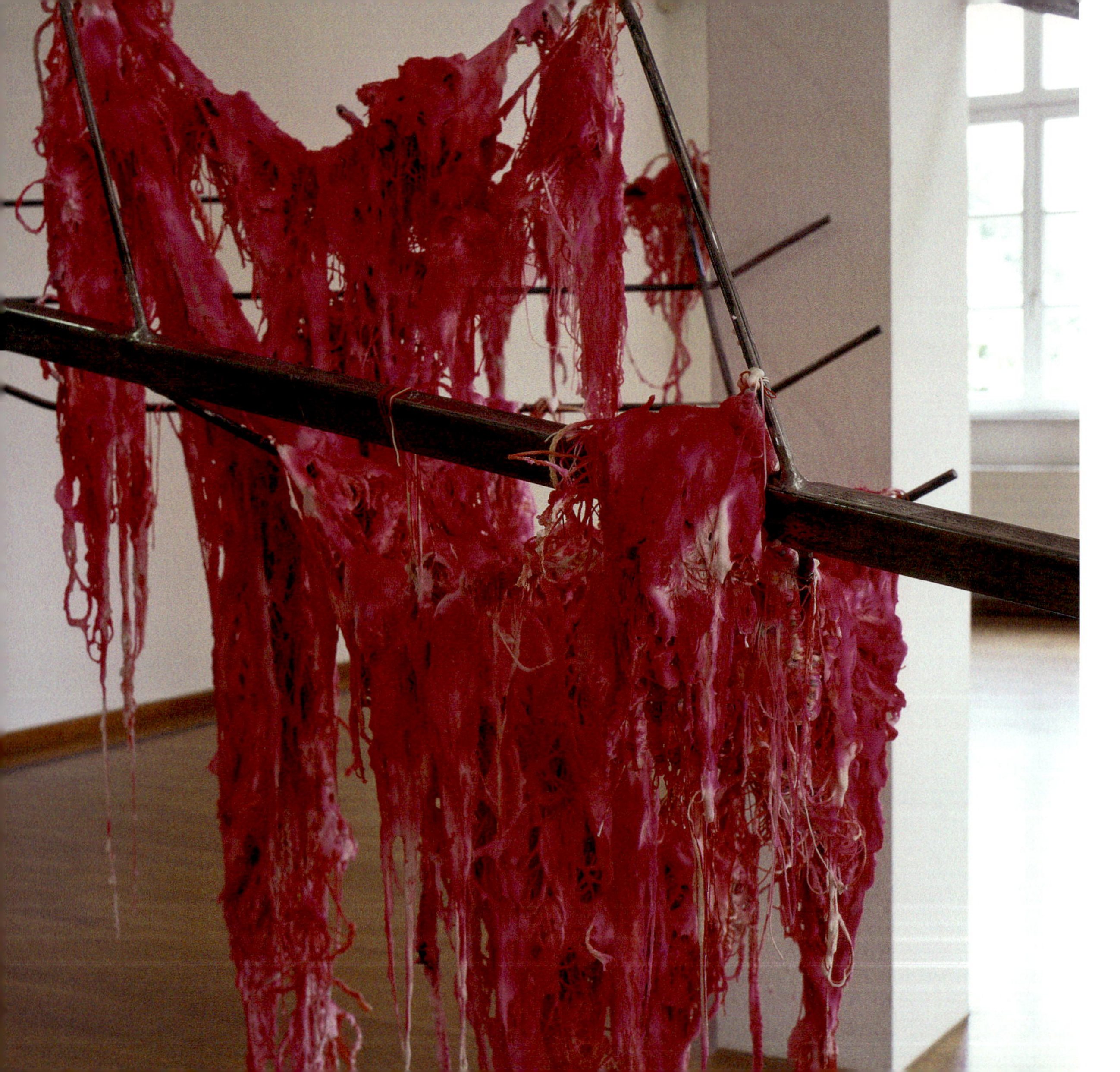

*Bonus,* 2008
Styropor, Bauschaum,
Acrylharz, Farbe
Polystyrene,
polyurethane foam,
acrylic resin, paint
L: 1,5 m

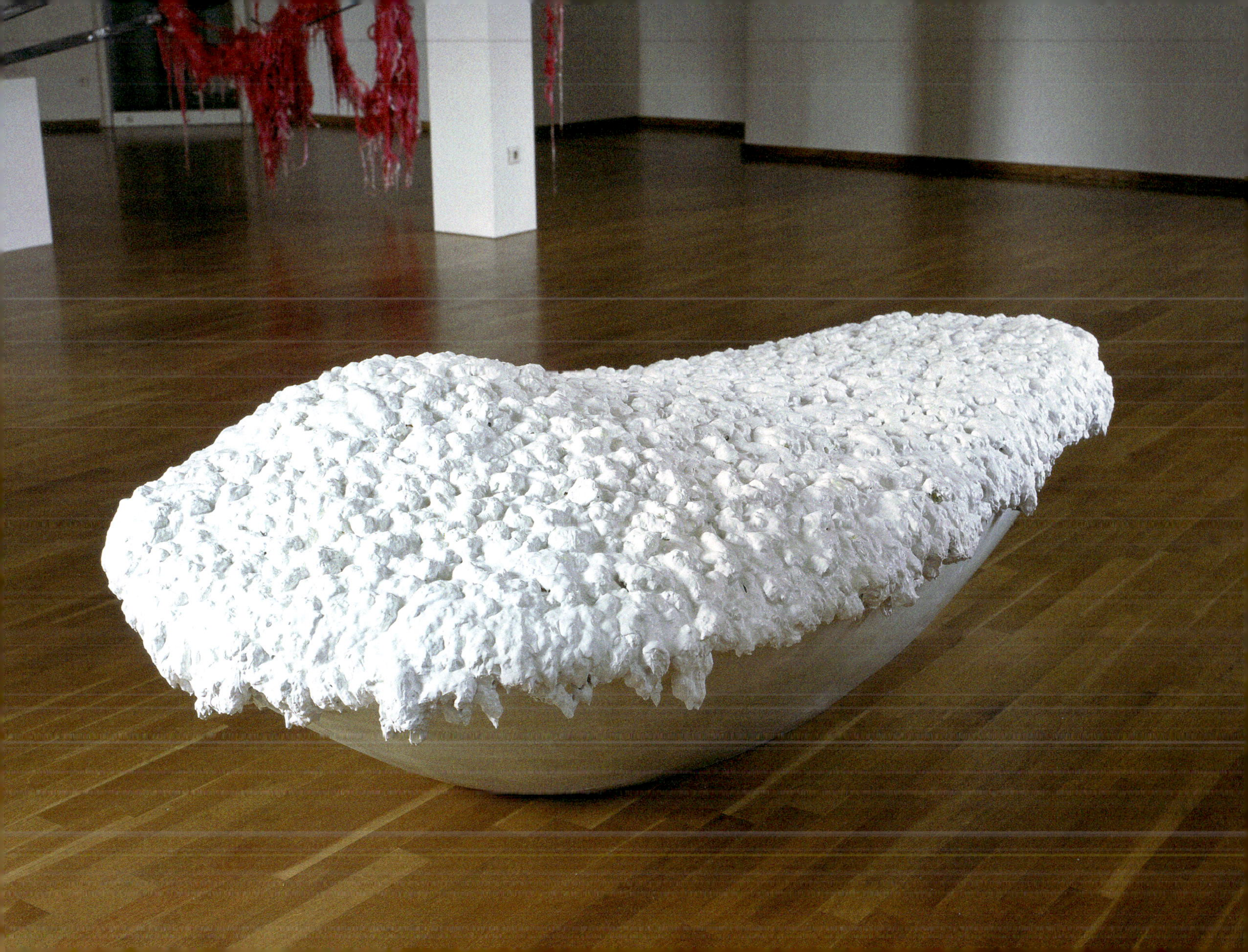

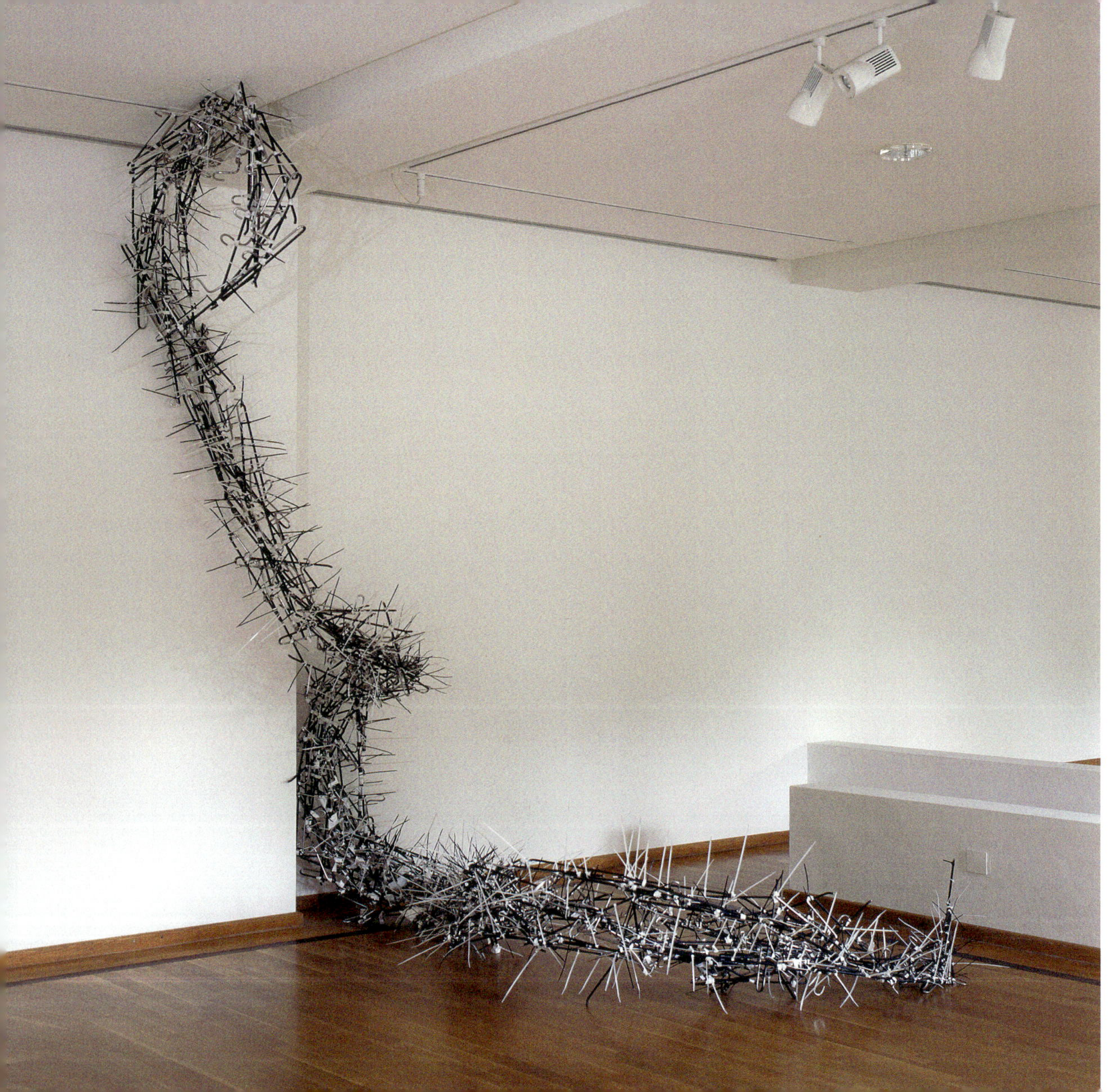


*Oxomoeno,* 2008
Hosenbügel, Kabelbinder,
Klebeband
Metal hangers, cable ties,
tape
H: 3 m

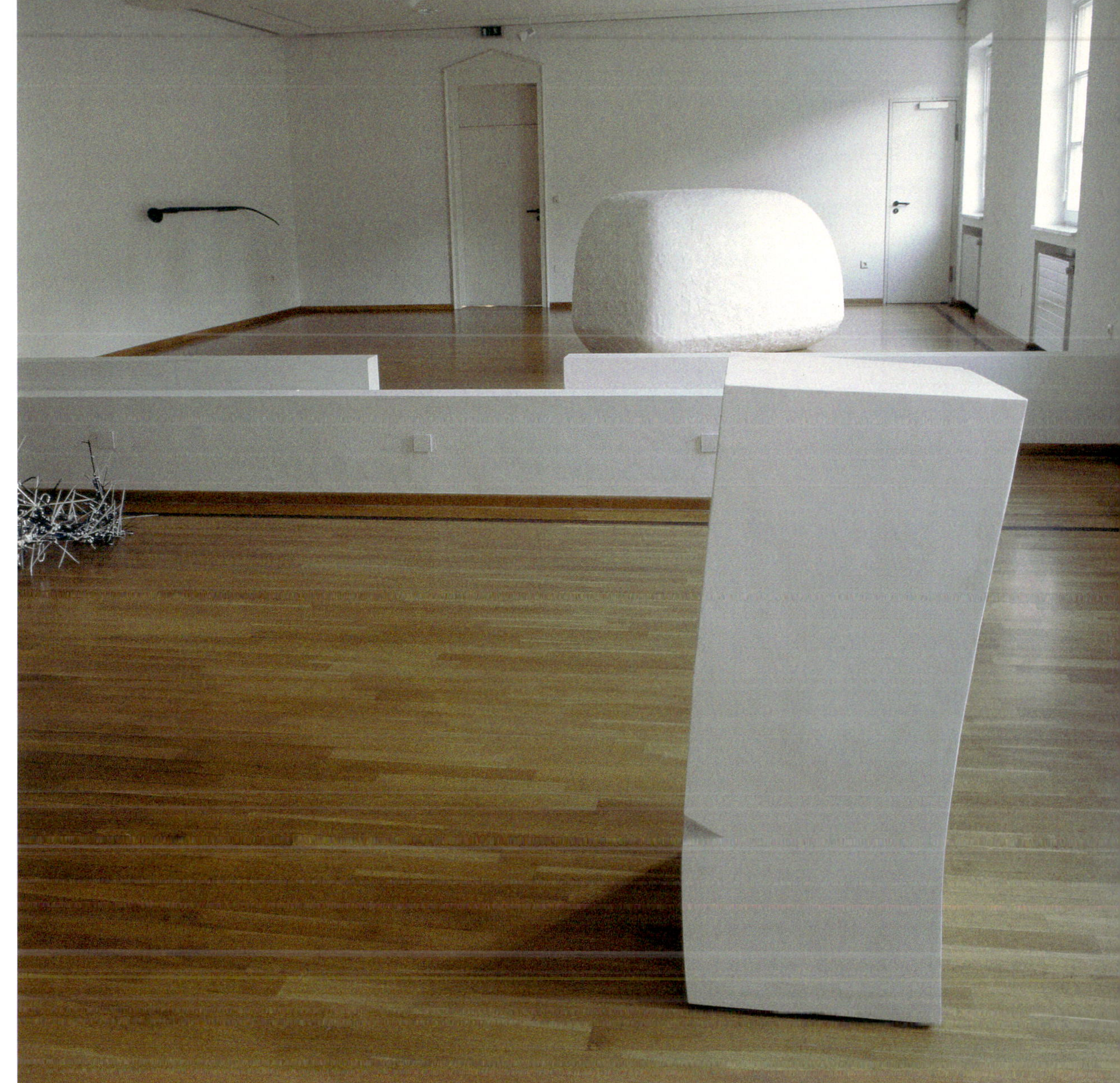

Wandarbeit | Wall
based work
*Probes,* 2002
Polyester, Spachtel,
Farbe, Lack
Polyester resin, filler,
paint, varnish
L: 2,2 m

*Gebogener Sockel
(Bended plinth),* 2008
Gips, Spachtel,
Styropor
Plaster, filler,
polystyrene
H: 1,2 m

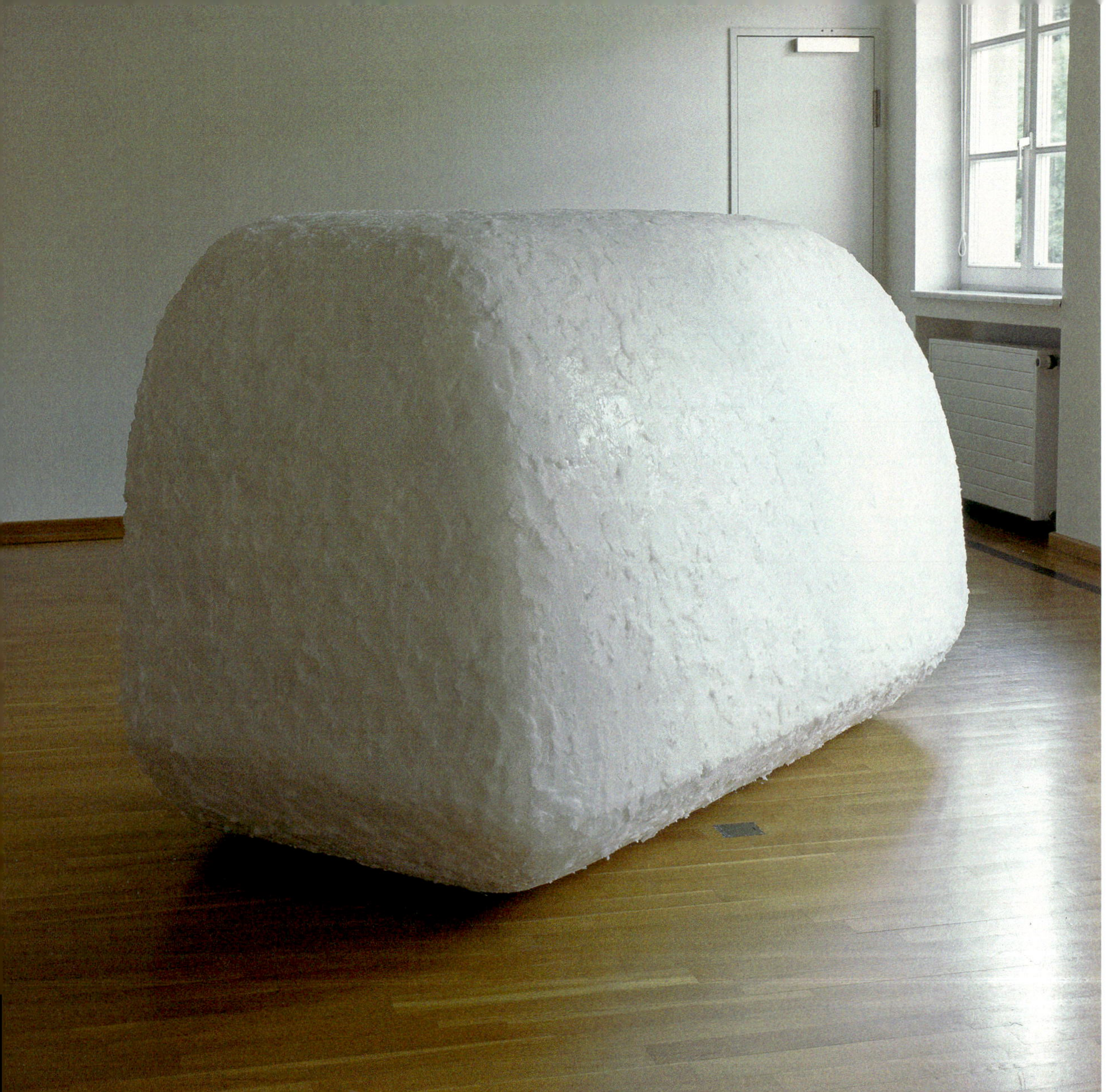

*Stückchen*, 2008
Wachs, Styropor
Wax, polystyrene
H: 1,5 m

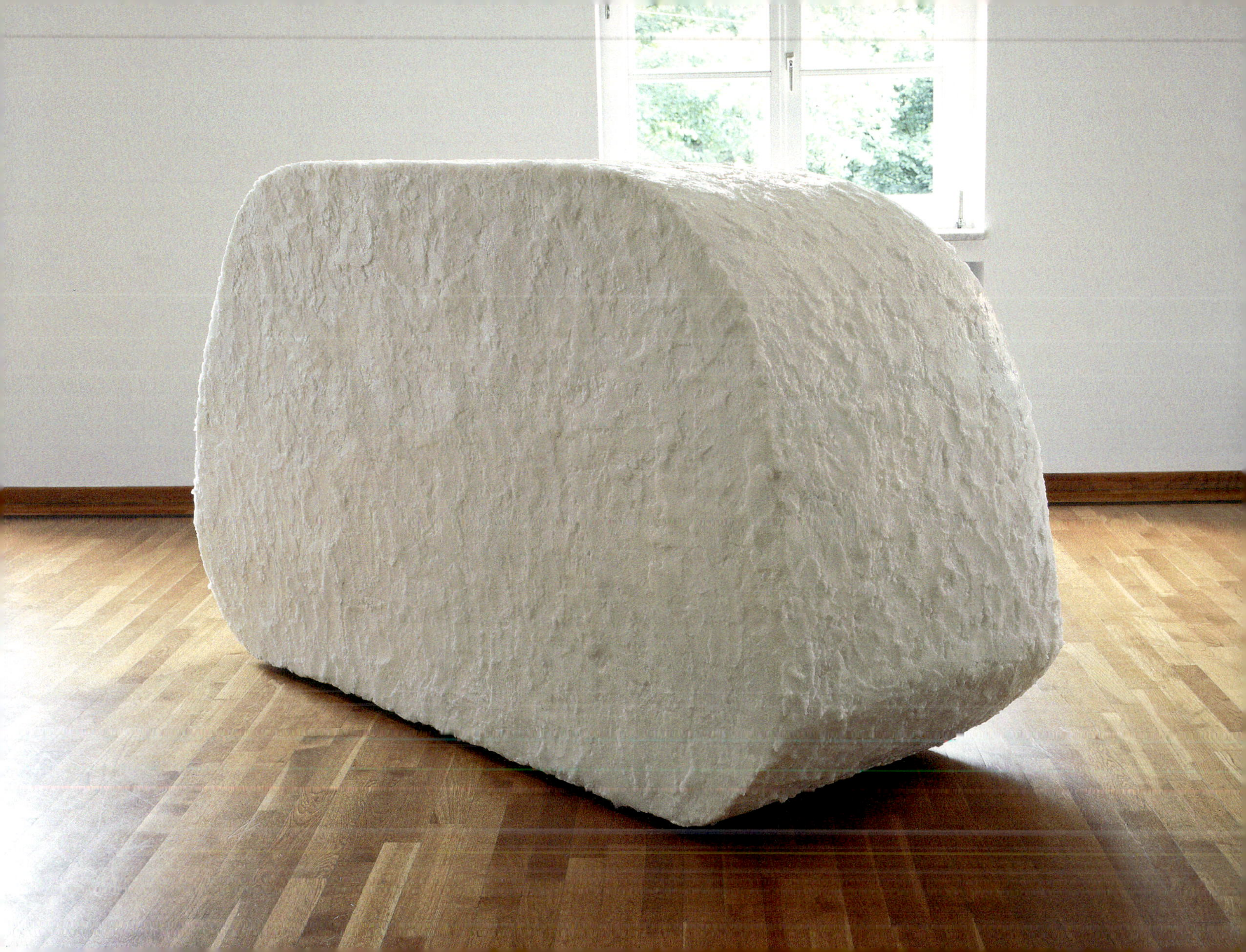

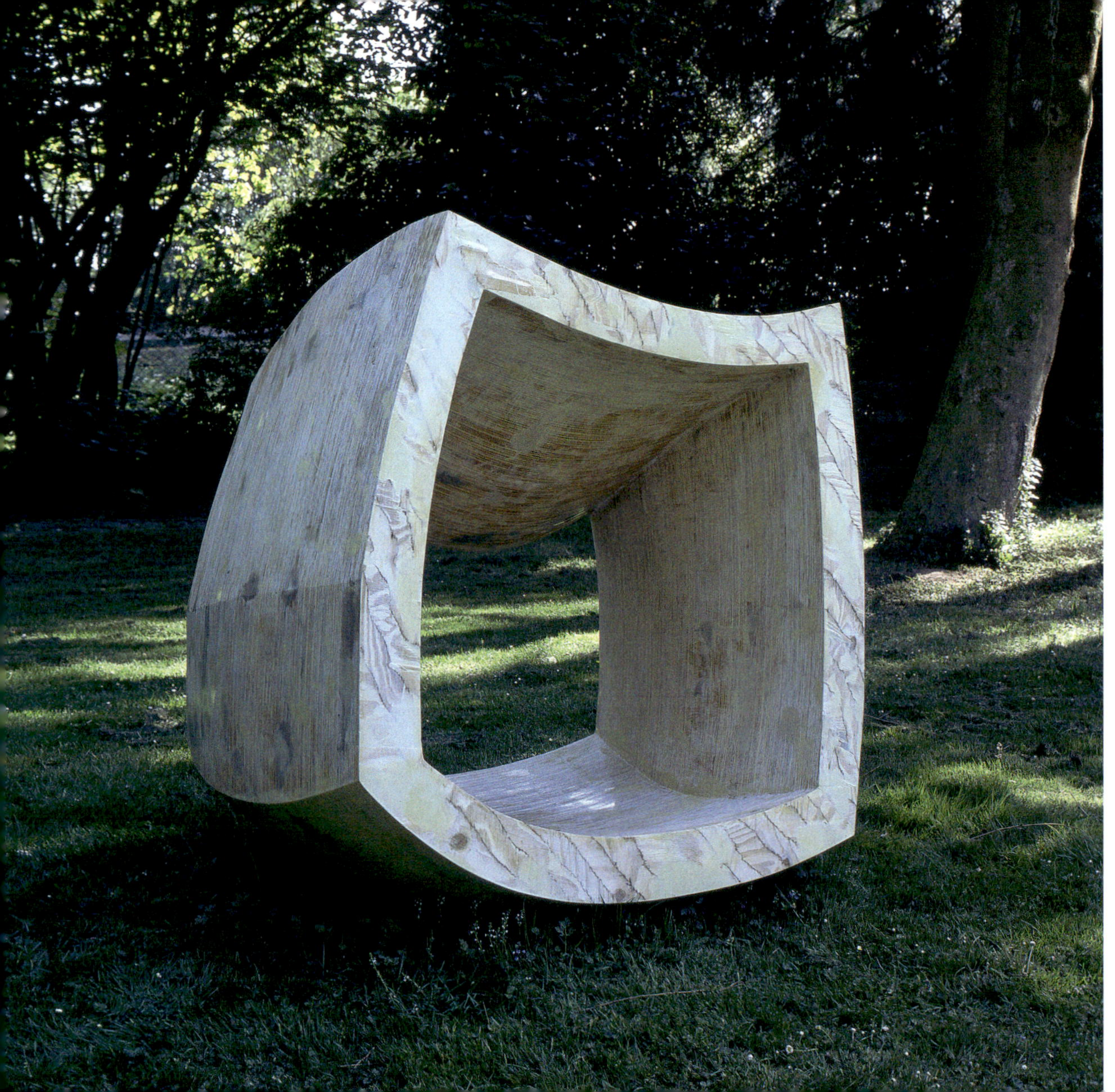

*Kleiner Tunnel,* 2008
Schichtholz, Spachtel,
Farbe
Plywood, filler, paint
H: 1,2 m

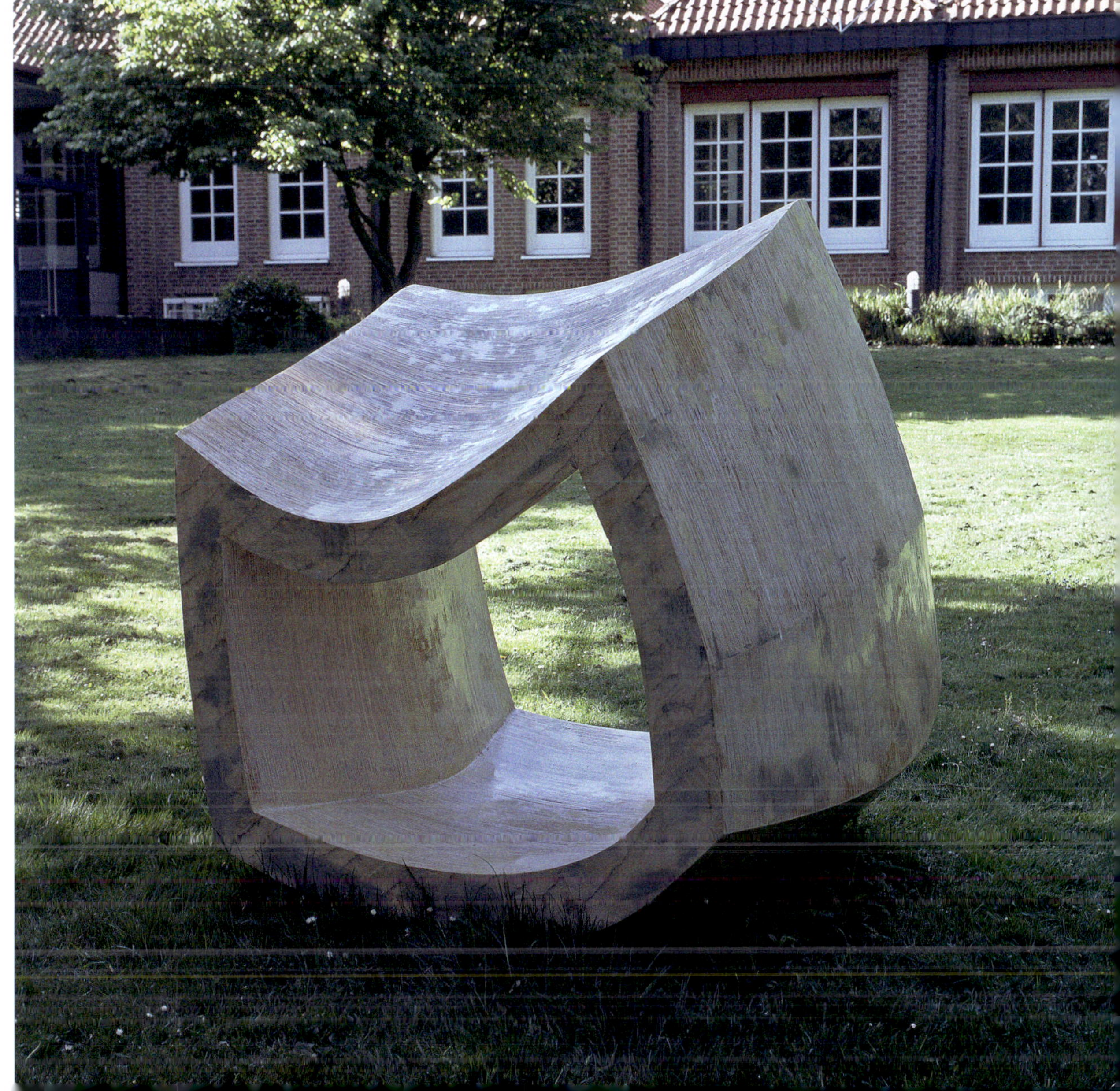

# Through a glass, darkly
# Kenny Schachter ROVE, London

26. 4.–24. 5. 2008

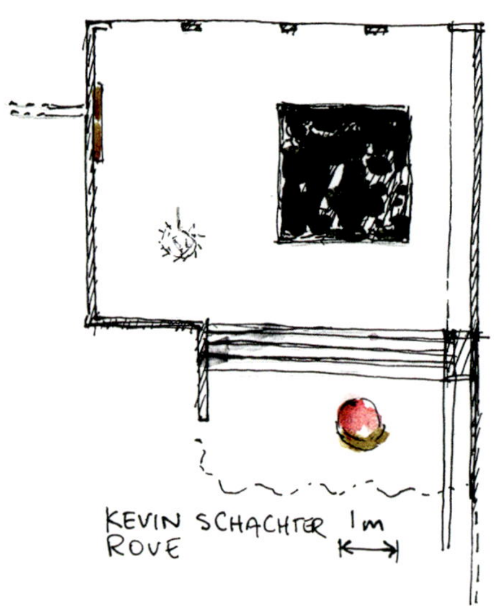



*Return (Schwarzes Quadrat |*
*Black Square),* 2008
Aufgeschlagener Fußboden,
Farbe, Lack
Crushed floor, paint,
varnish
B: 2,2 m

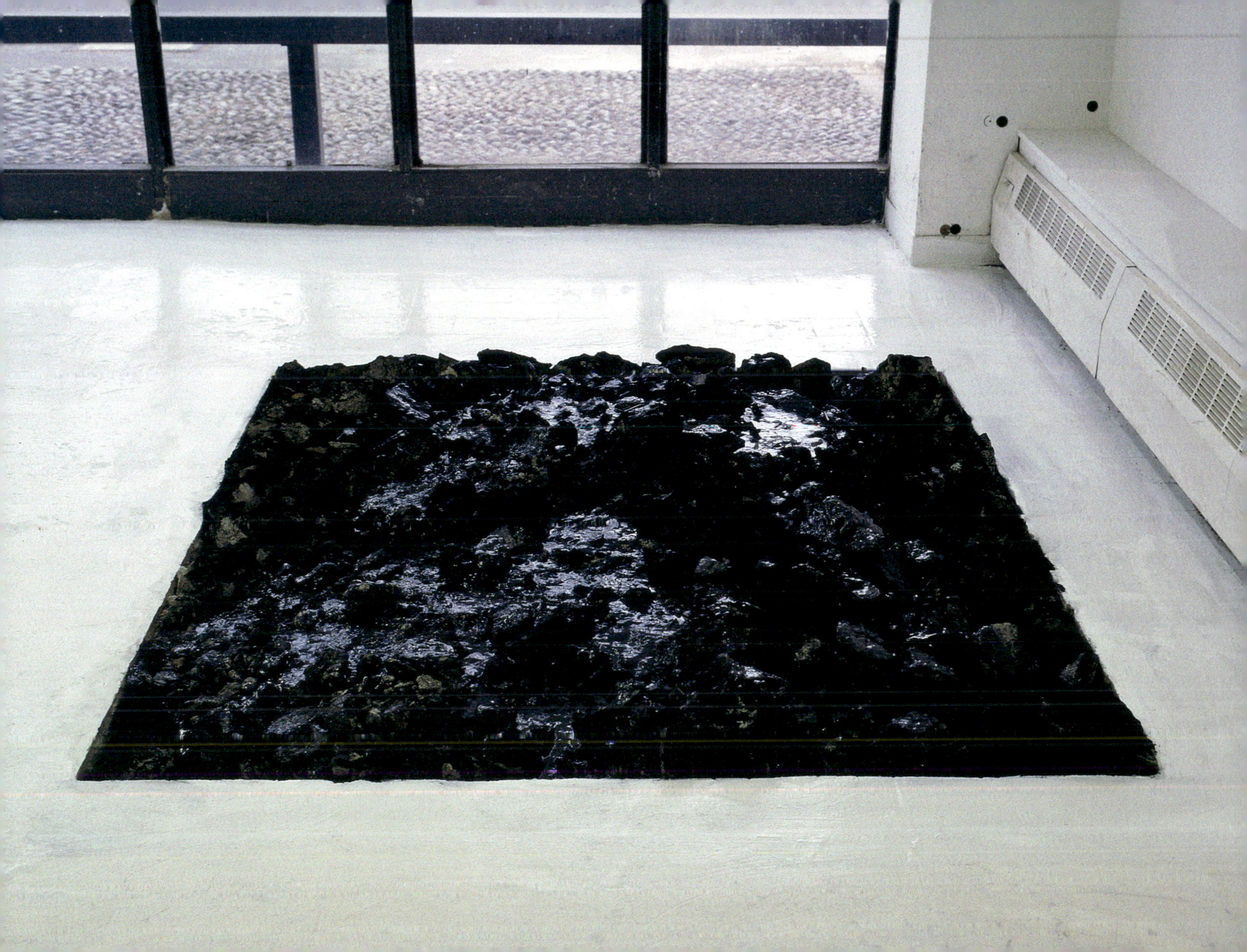

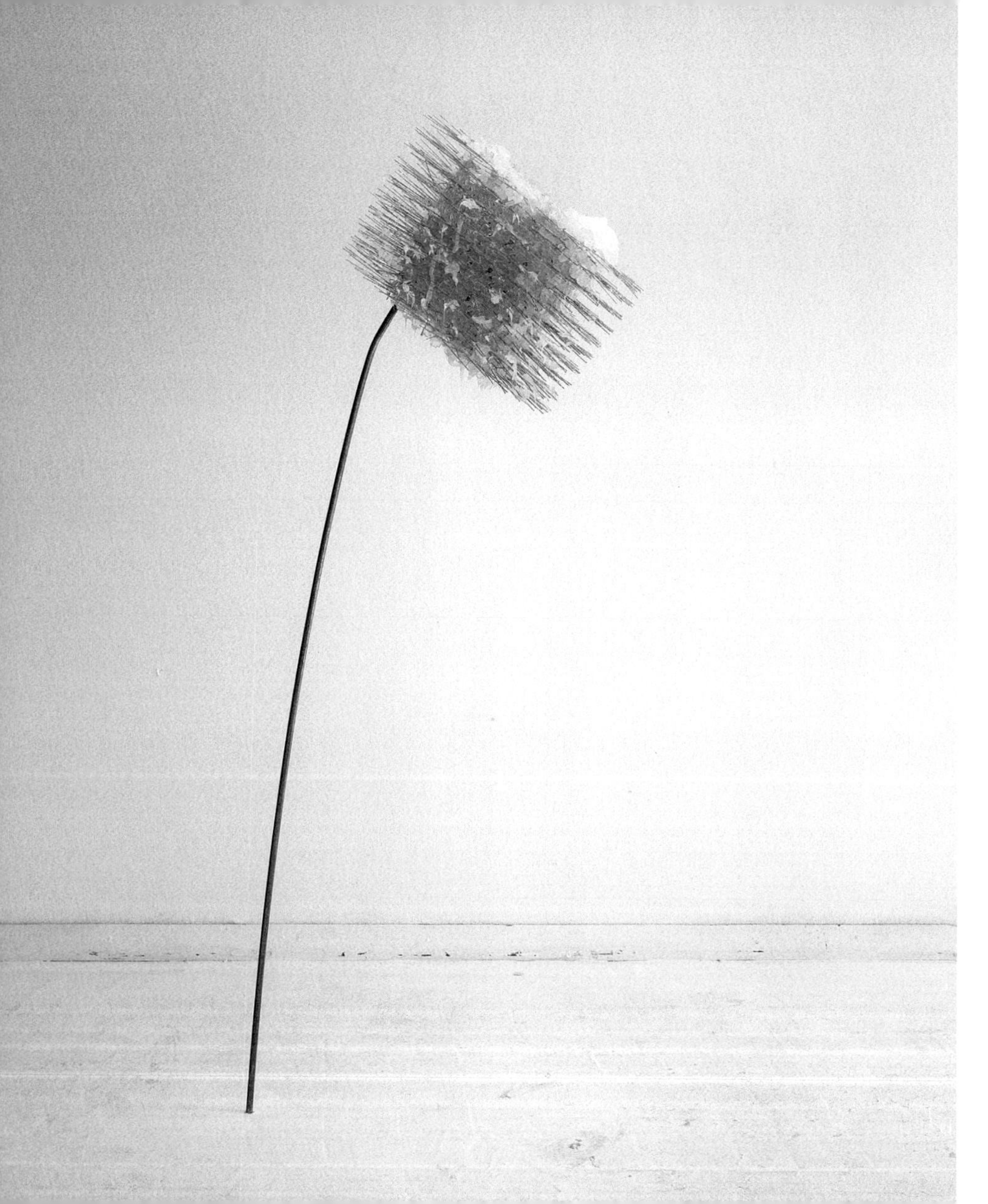

*No I can't,* 2008
Taubenabwehr, Silikon,
Stahlrohr
Pigeon spikes, silicone,
steel tube
H: 1,9 m

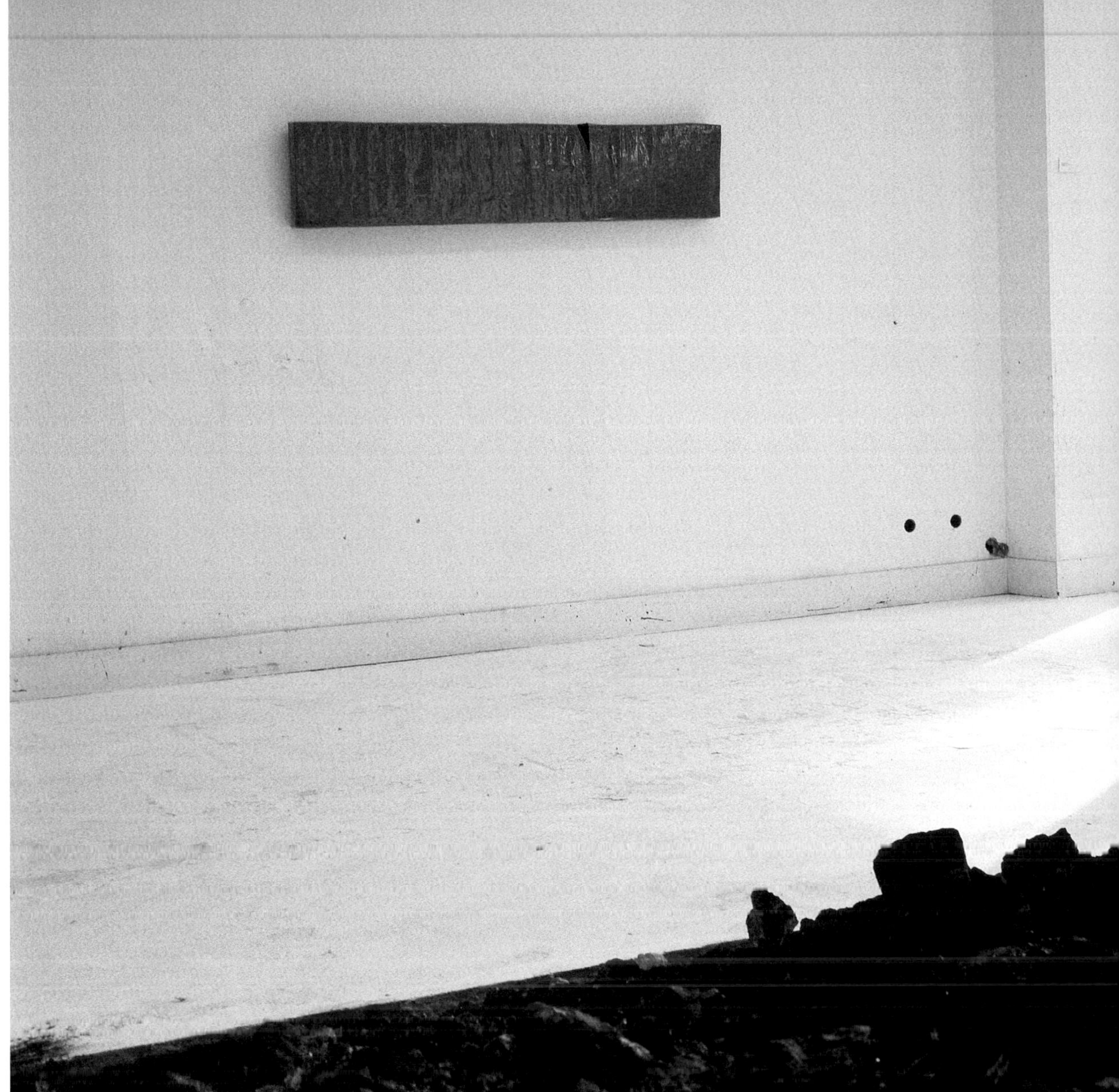

*Empty Board
(Leeres Brett)*, 2008
Klebeband
Tape
L: 1 m

# Wanderland
# Lustwarande 08
## NL-Tilburg

28.6.–28.9.2008

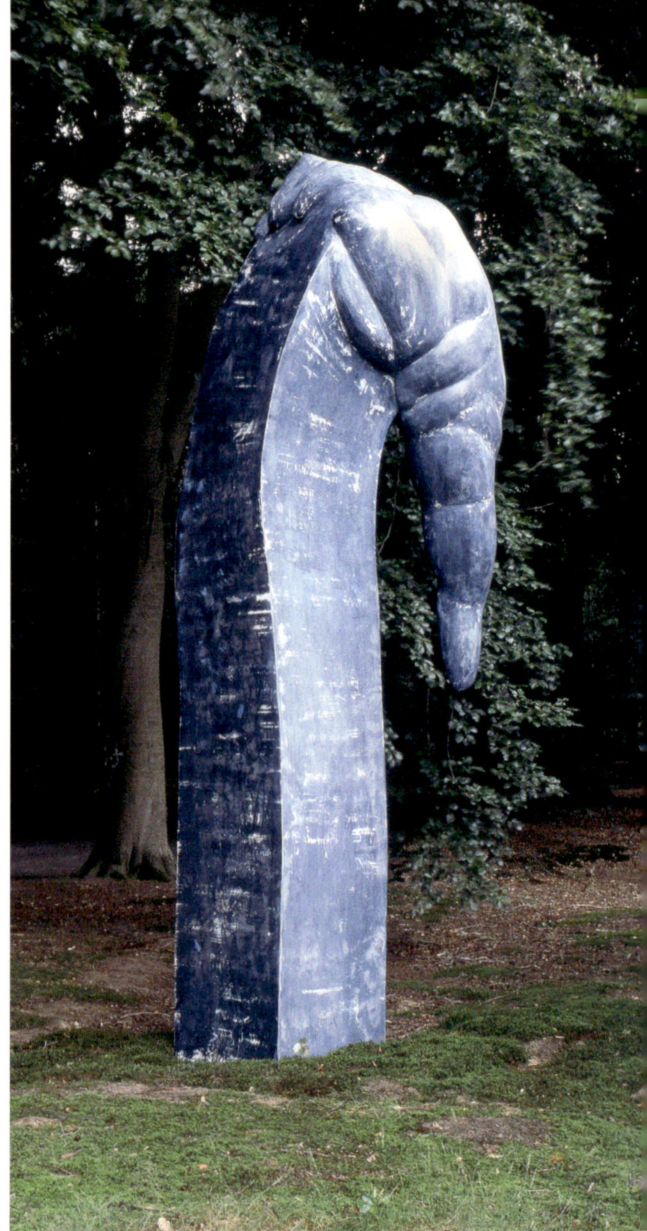

*Melpi*, 2008
Acrylharz, Styropor, Metall
arylic resin, polystyrene,
metal
H: 4,5 m

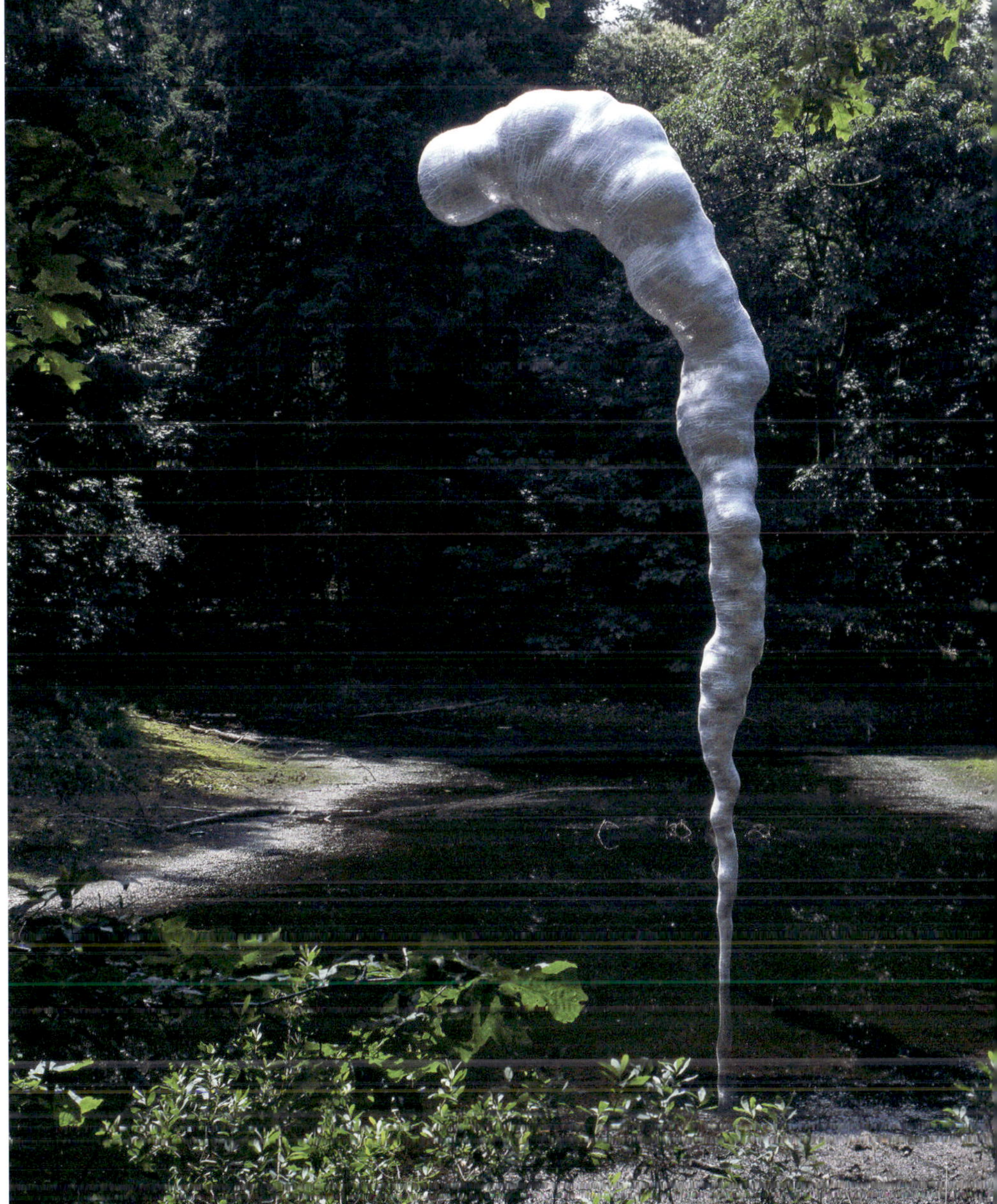

*Deemed*, 2008
Folie, Klebeband, Ballons,
Metallstab
Foil, tape, Balloons, metal
H: 7,5 m

# PawnShop Gallery, Los Angeles



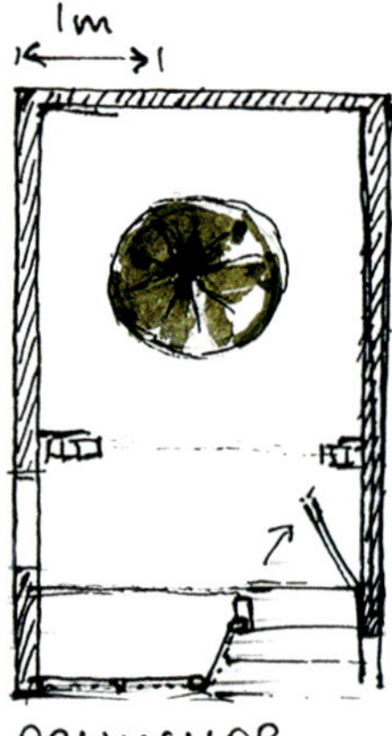



*Anus,* 2008
Beton
Concrete
ø 1,2 m

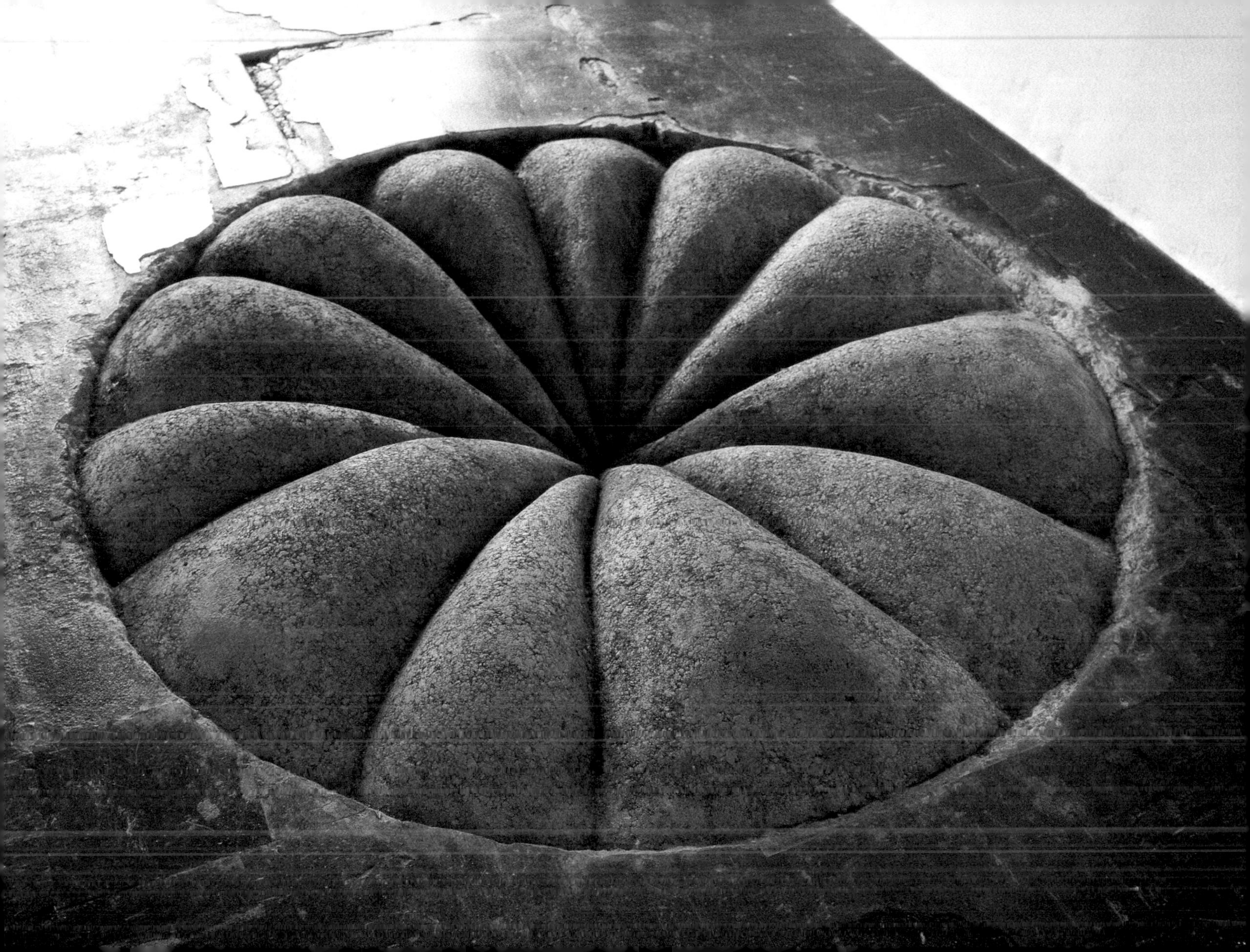

# Parkhaus
# Kunsthalle Düsseldorf

10. 8. – 21. 9. 2008

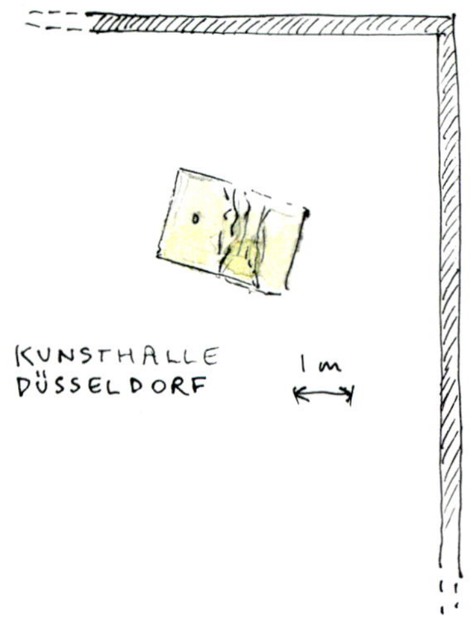

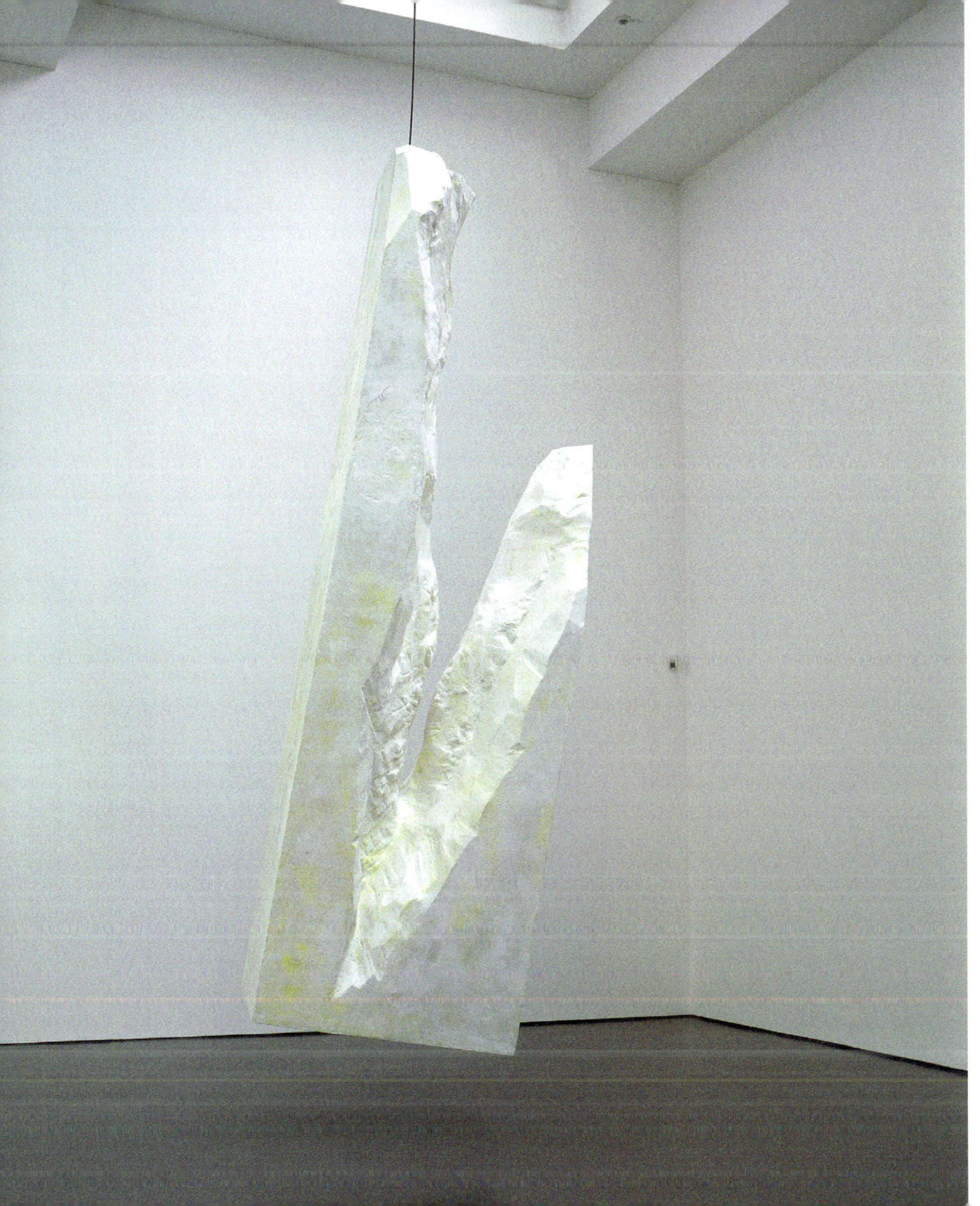

*Splice,* 2008
Wachs, Pigment,
Makulatur, Papier,
Styropor, Stange
Wax, pigment,
waste paper, paper,
polystyrene, rod
H: 5 m

# Dreimal da
# Zeitkunstgalerie, Kitzbühel

3.10.–21.11.2008

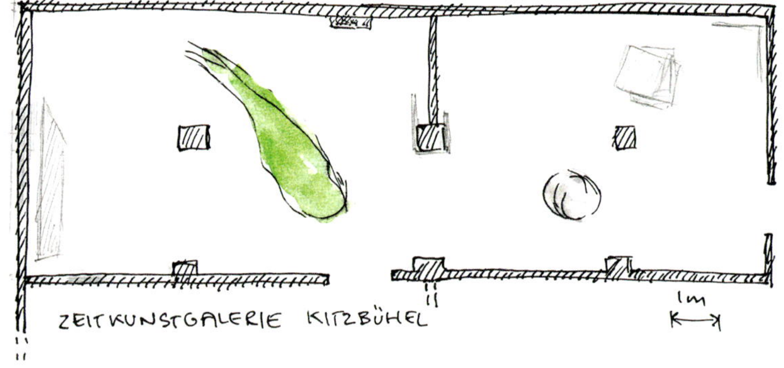

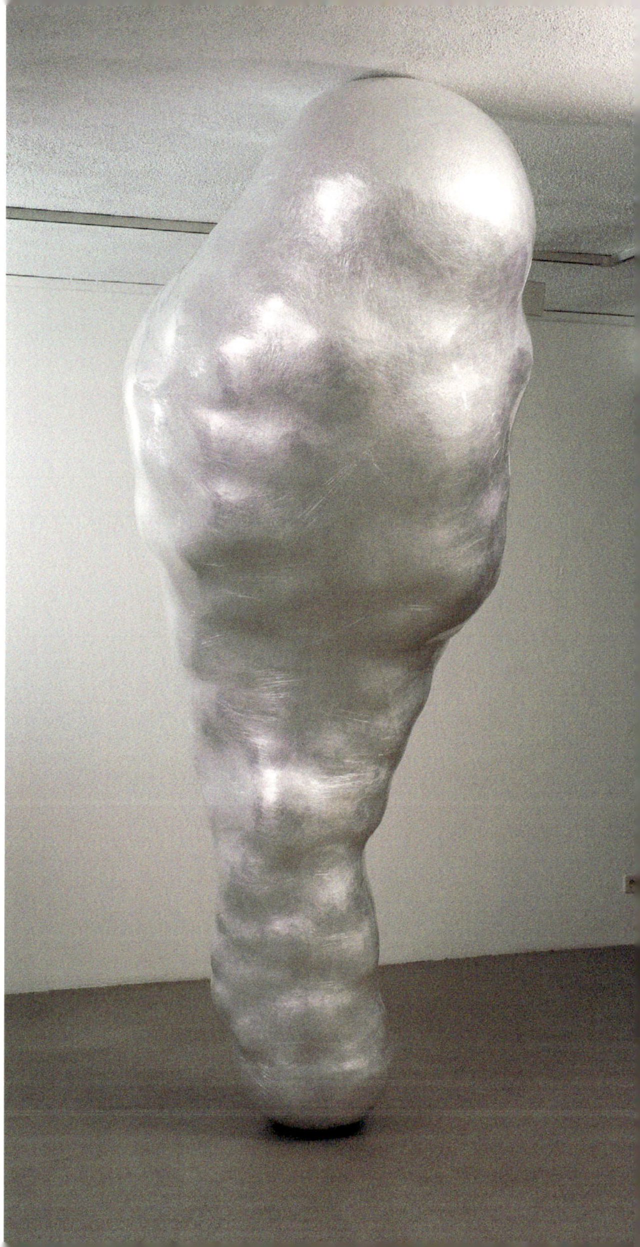

*Mind your head,* 2008
Folie, Ballons, Klebeband,
Metallrohr, Gips
Cling film, foil, balloons,
tape, metal pipe, plaster
H: 3,1 m

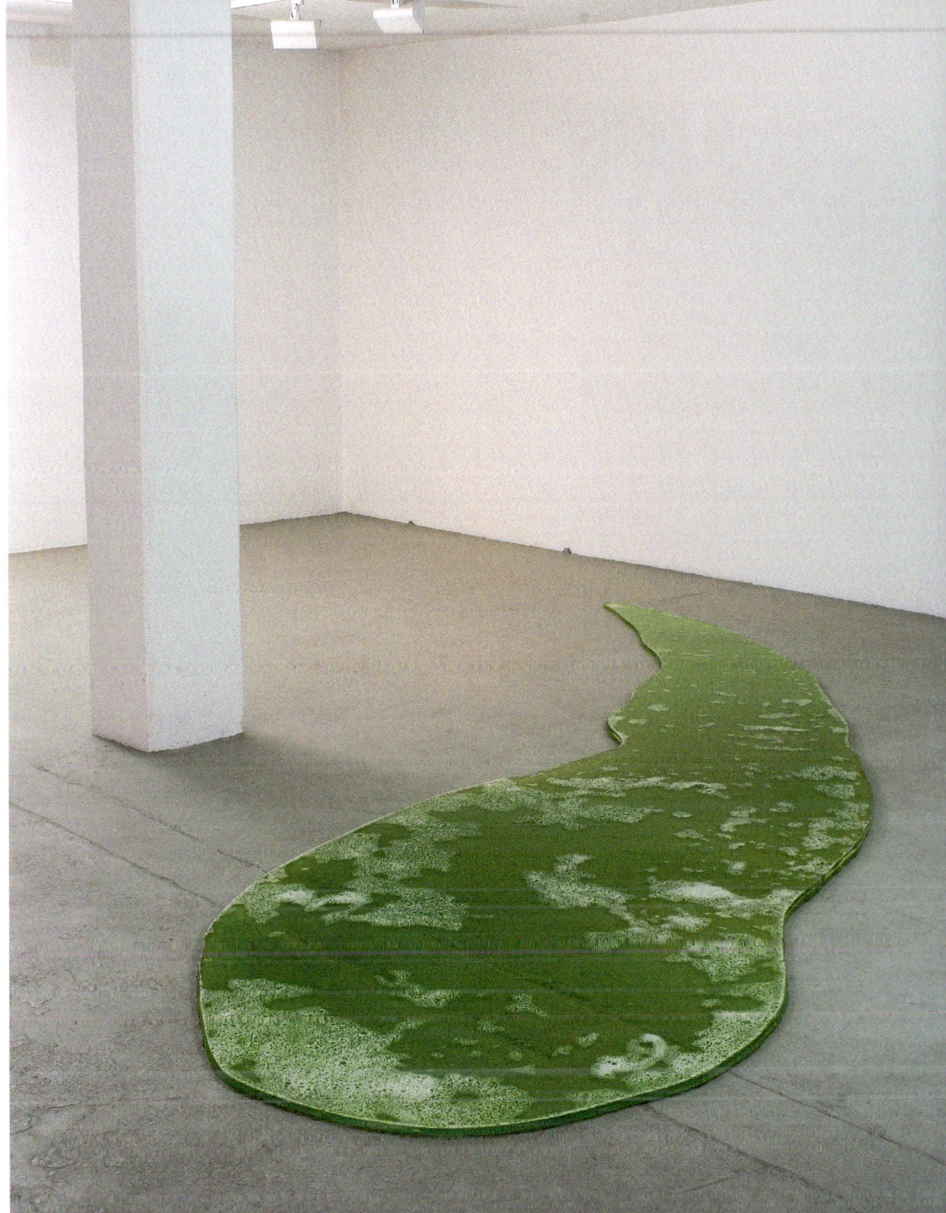

*Lache (Leek),* 2008
Gelatine, Glyzerin, Tusche
Gelatine, glycerine, ink
L: 4 m

# 90 Grad ist hart
# Simultanhalle, Köln

14.9.–11.10.2008

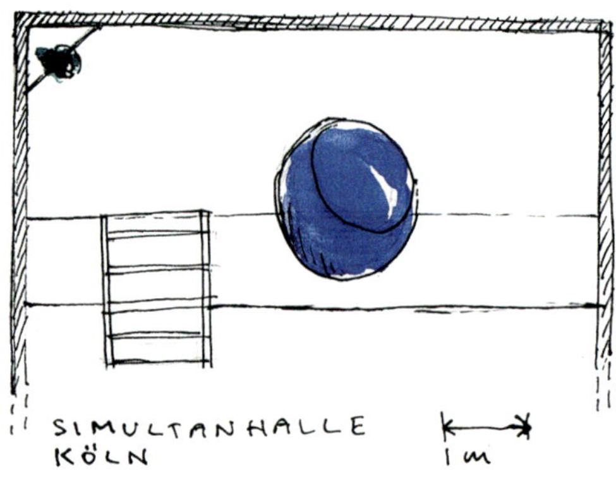



*Loopy vates,* 2008
Wellrohr, Silkon, Pigment,
Metallstange
Bendable pipe, silicone,
pigment, steel rod
L: 0,8 m

*Blauer Blobster,* 2008
Folie, Abfallsack,
Styropor, Holz
Foil, bin bag, polystyrene,
timber
H: 2,2 m

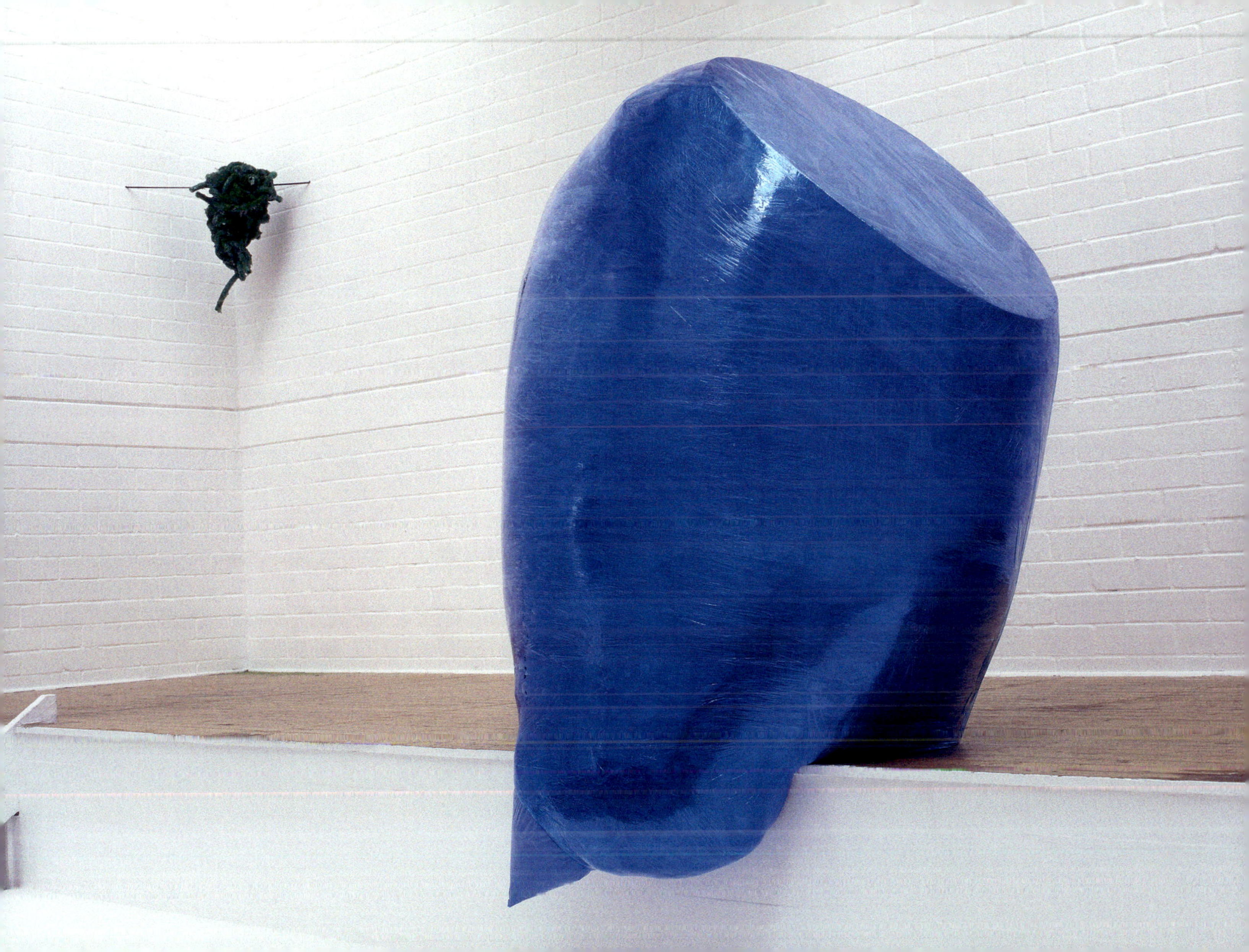

# Wollte könnte sollte
# Kunsthalle Bremerhaven

14. 9. – 2. 11. 2008

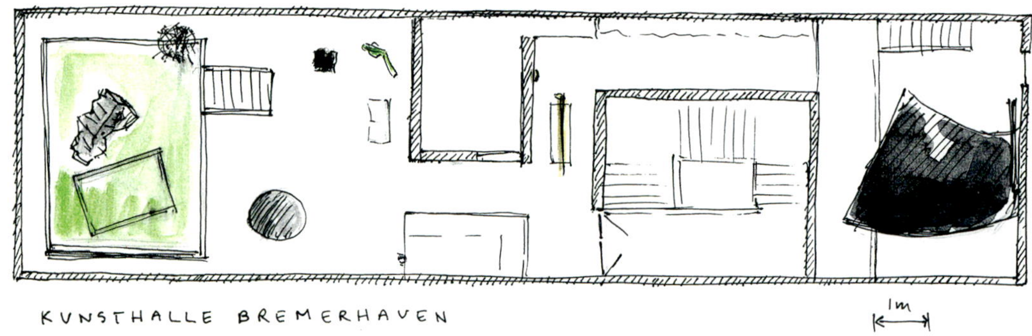





*Slope*, 2008
Teppich, Farbe, Holz
Carpet, paint, timber
B: 4,2 m

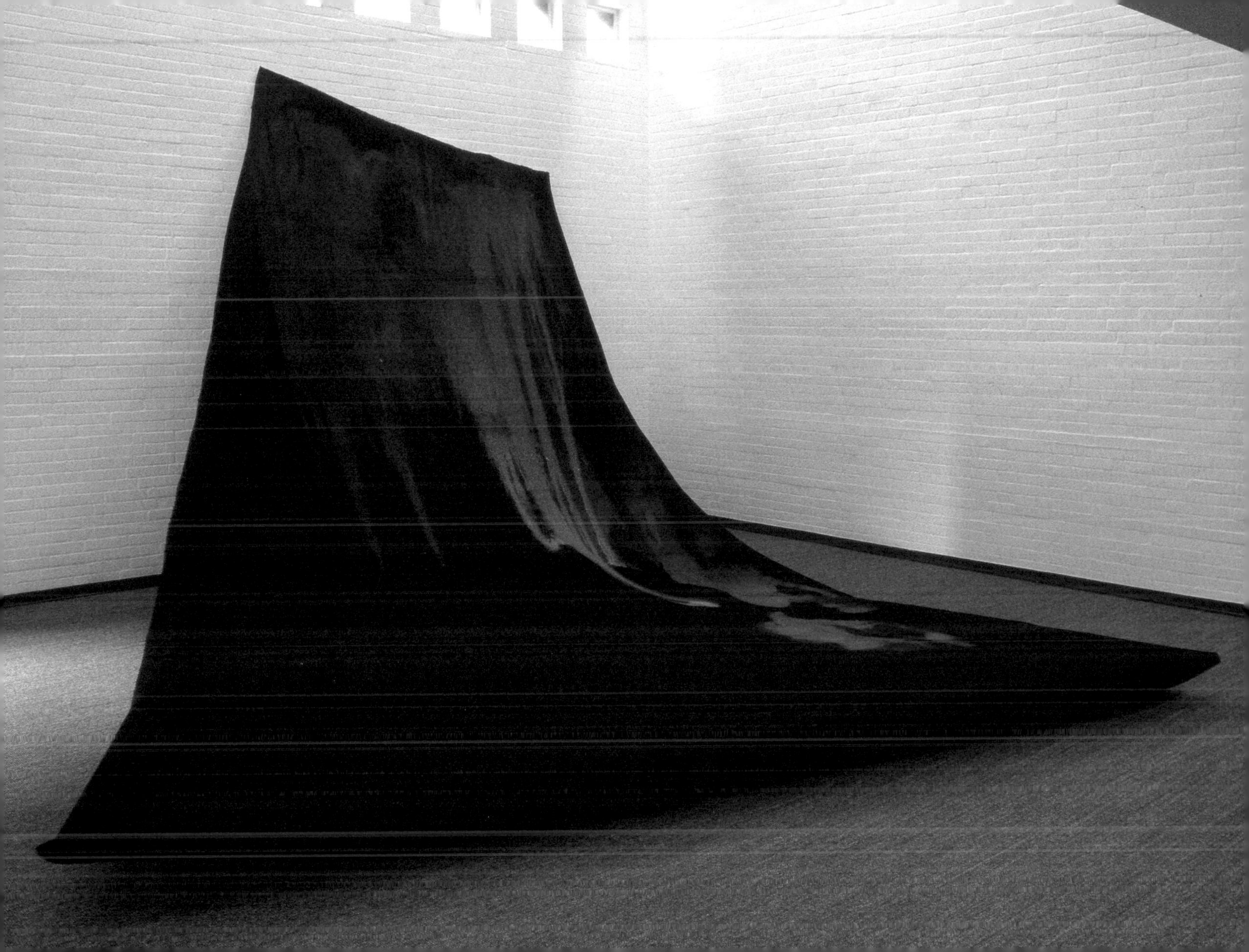

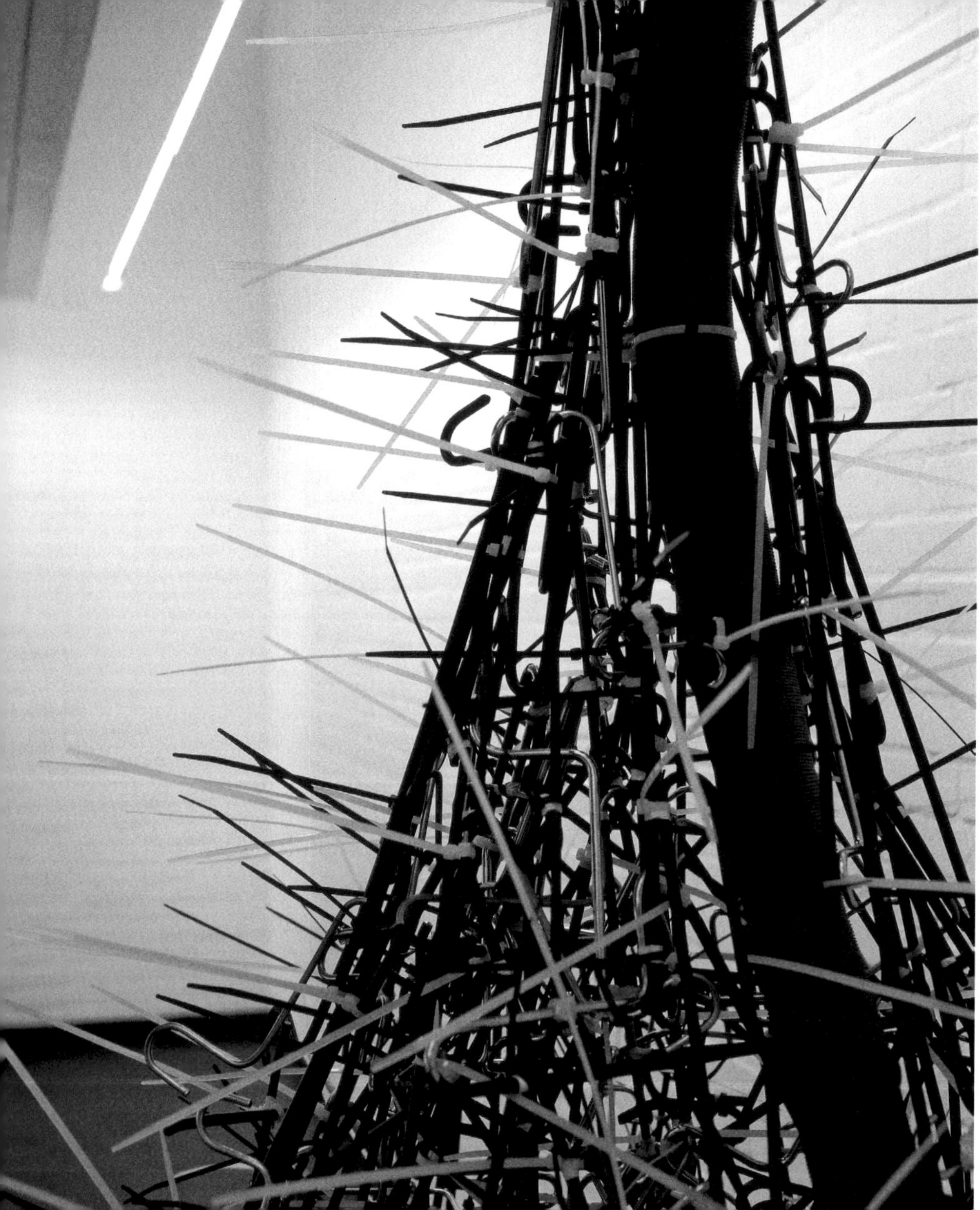

*Stropf* (Detail), 2008
Hosenbügel, Kabelbinder,
Klebeband, Wellrohr
Coat hangers, cable binders,
tape, bendable pipe
H: 2,2 m

*Ömmes*, 2008
Beton, Bauschaum,
Luftballon
Concrete, polyurethan
foam, ballon
H: 1,25 m

*Oozer*, 2008
Kleister, Spanplatte, Farbe
Wallpaper paste,
chipboard, paint
L: 2,5 m

Empore | Mezzanine level
*Decke auf grün (Duvet
on green)*, 2004
Papiermaché, Styropor,
Lack, grüner Teppich
Papermaché, polystyrene,
varnish, green carpet
L: 1,9 m
Teppich | Carpet L: 4,5 m

*Stropf*, 2008

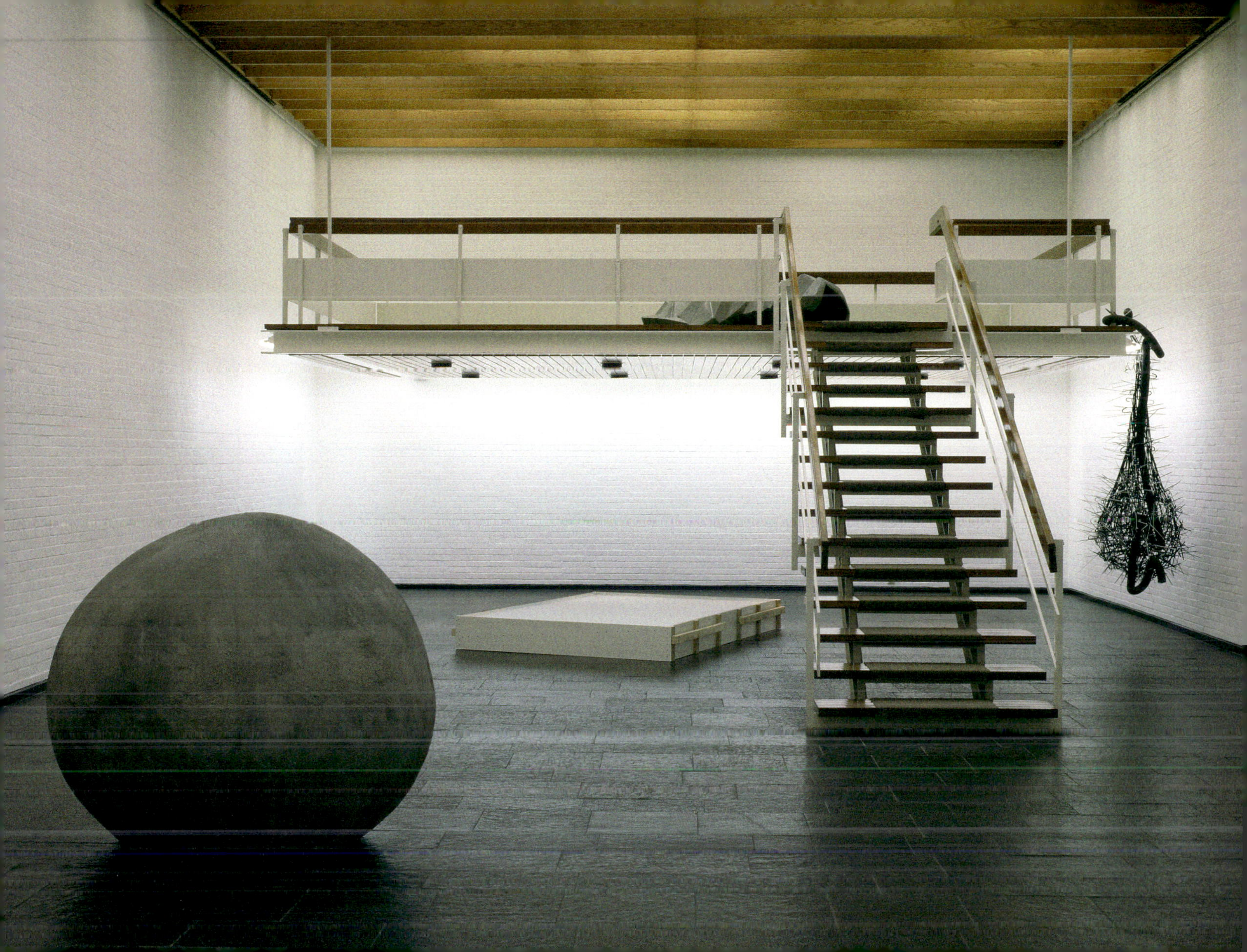

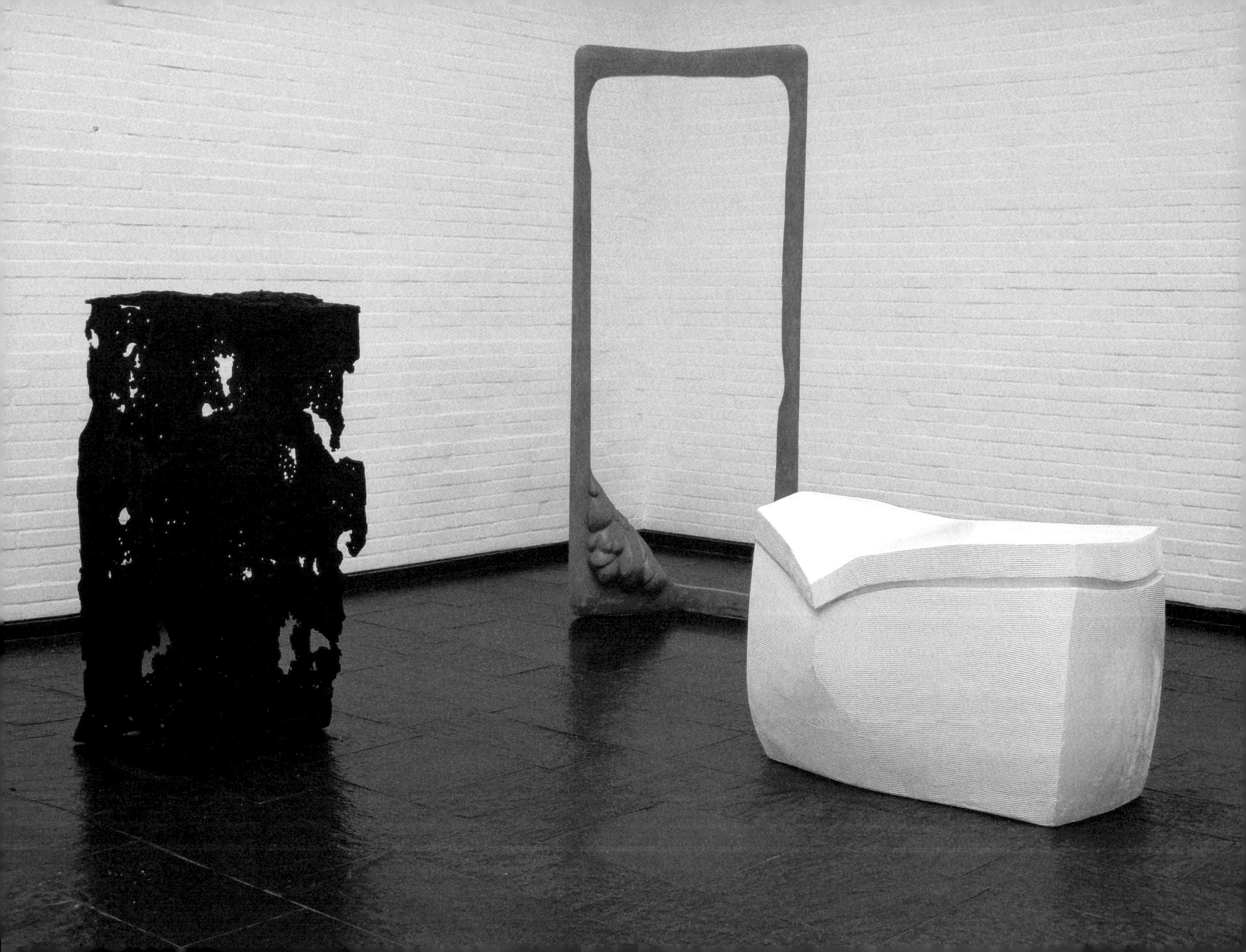

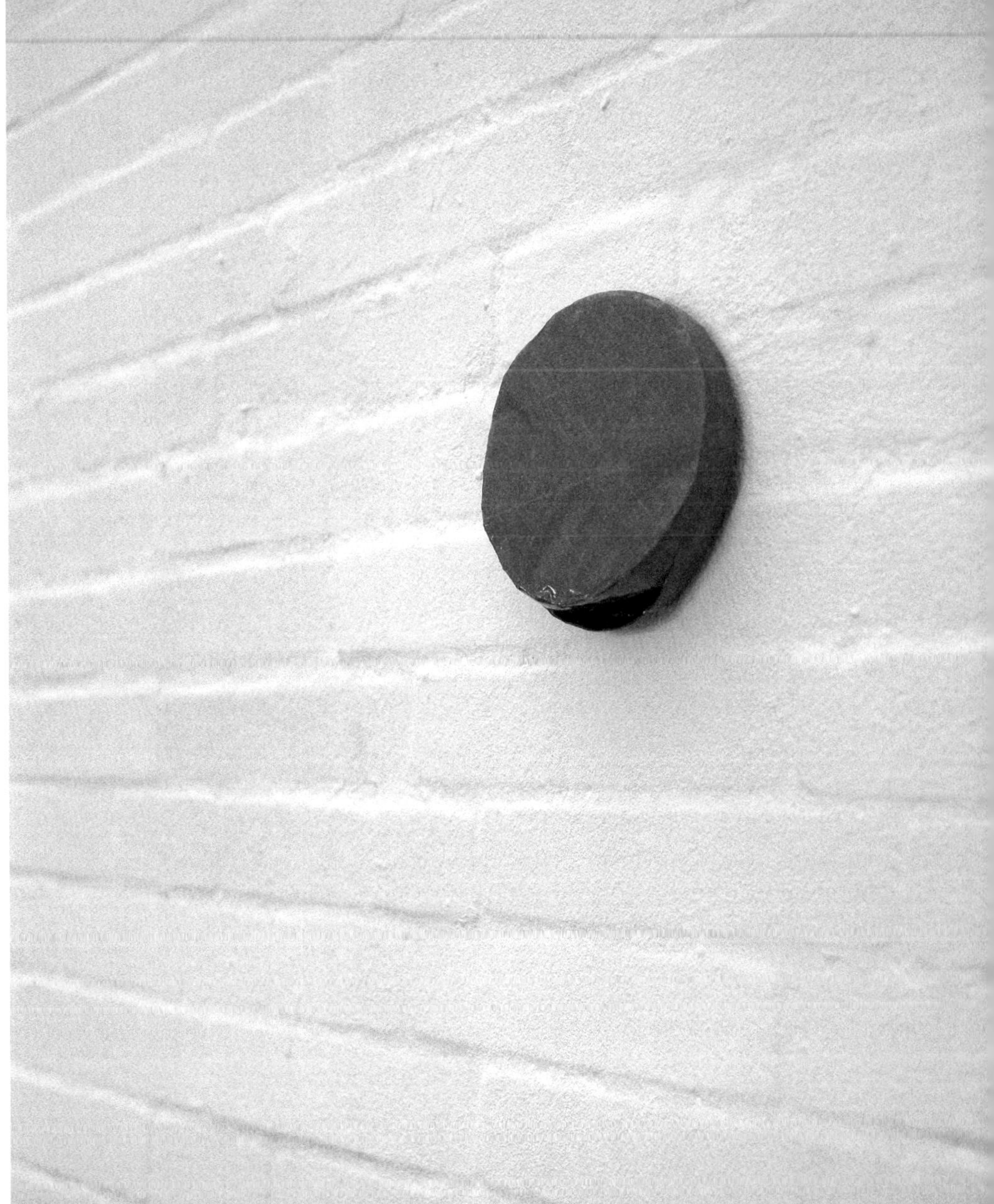

*Burpi*, 2008
Klebeband
Tape
ø 0,15 m

*Back in black*, 2008
Holz verbrannt
Burnt timber
H: 1,2 m

*Superduper*, 2008
Holz, Spachtel, Farbe
Timber, filler, paint
H: 1,9 m

*Truhe mit Delle
(Chest with dent)*, 2008
Gips, Lack, Styropor
Plaster, varnish,
polystyrene
L: 1,2 m

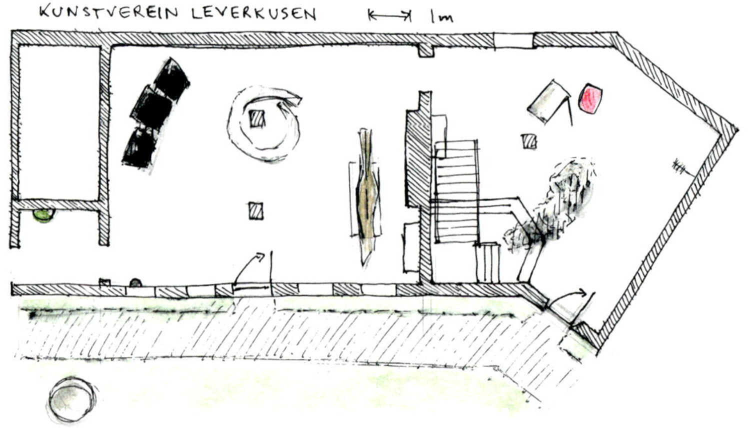


KUNSTVEREIN LEVERKUSEN
1m

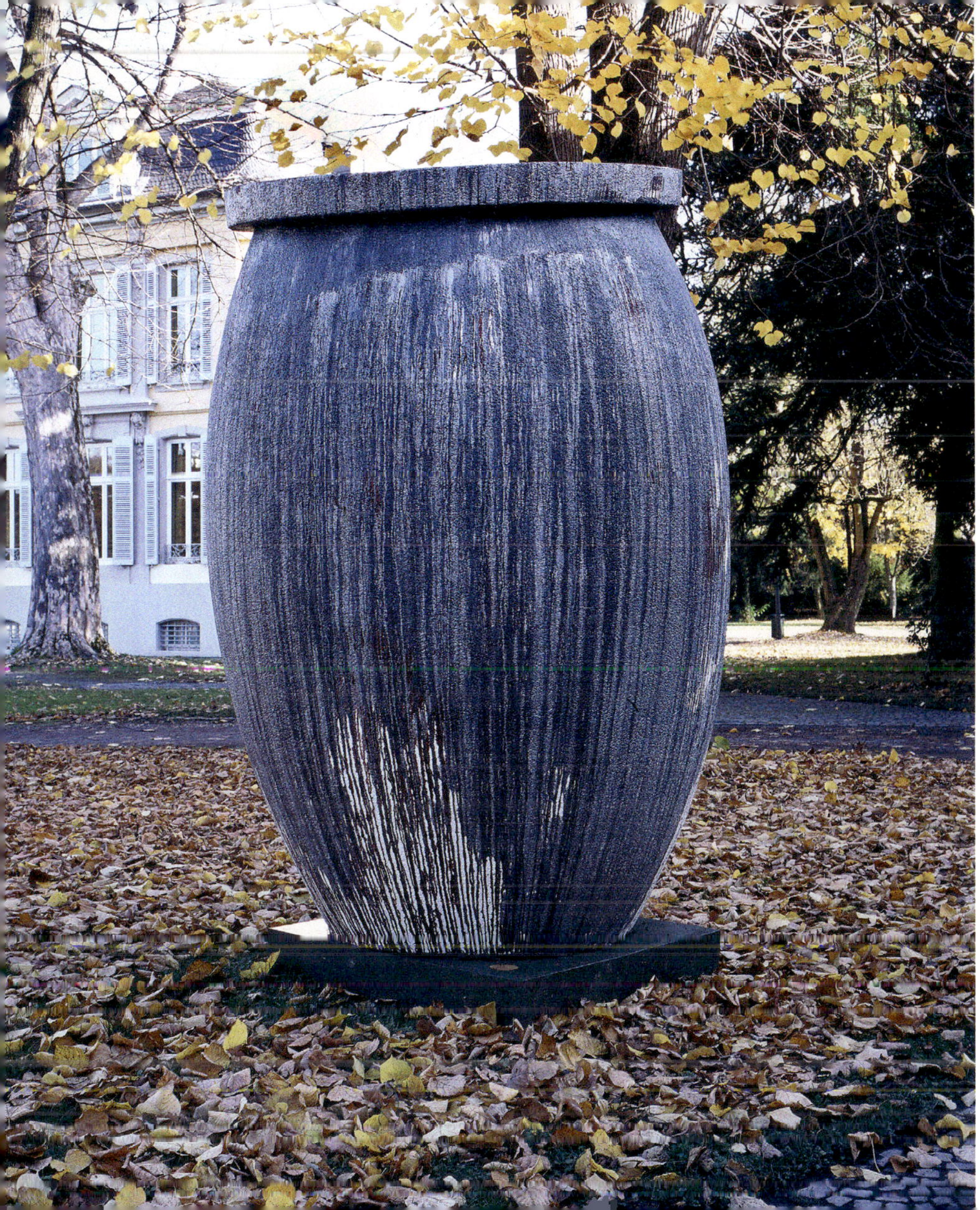

*Kruke*, 2008
Putz, Dispersion, Styropor
Wall plastering, paint,
polystyrene
H: 2,9 m
Sammlung | Collection
WEPA Apothekenbedarf,
Hillscheid

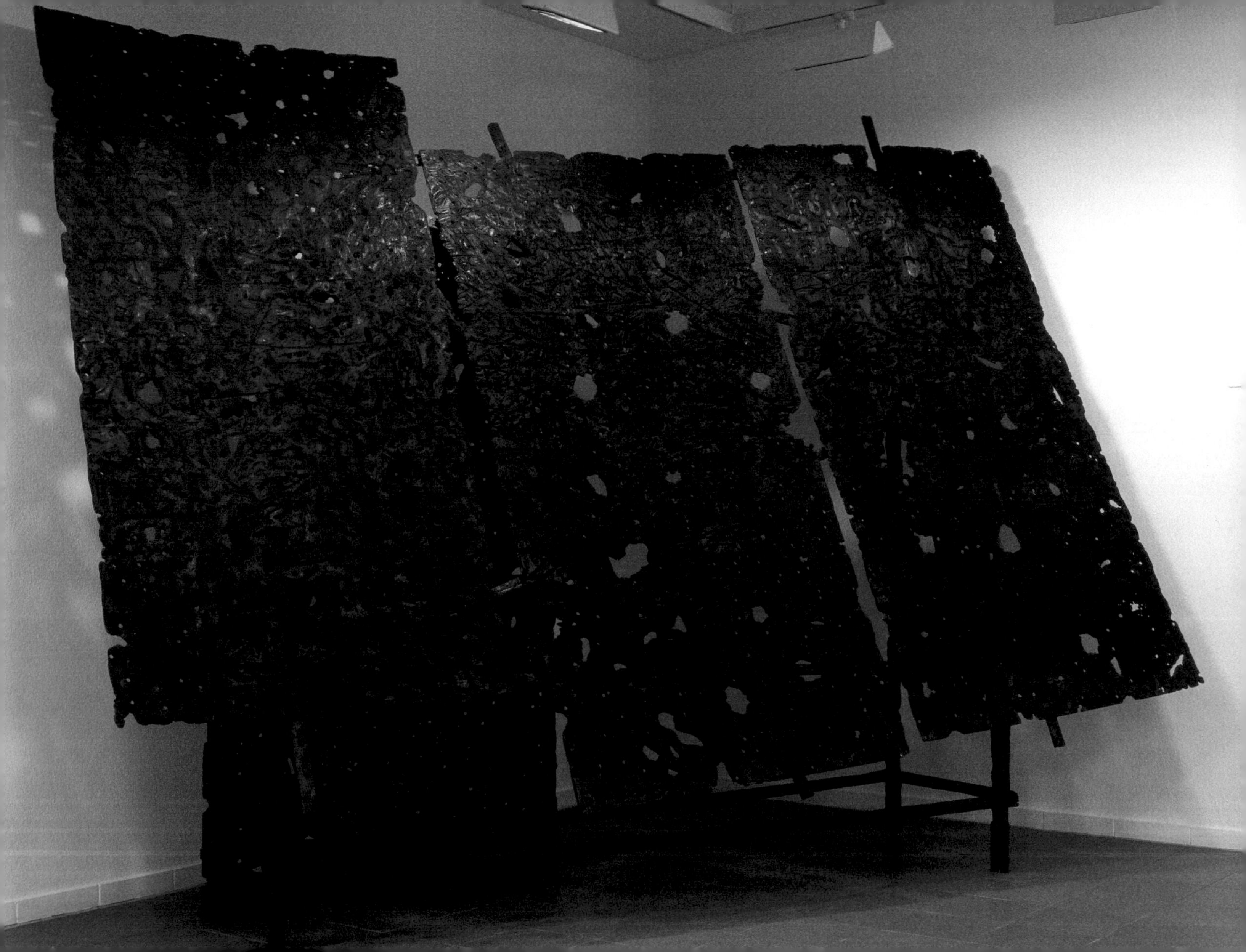

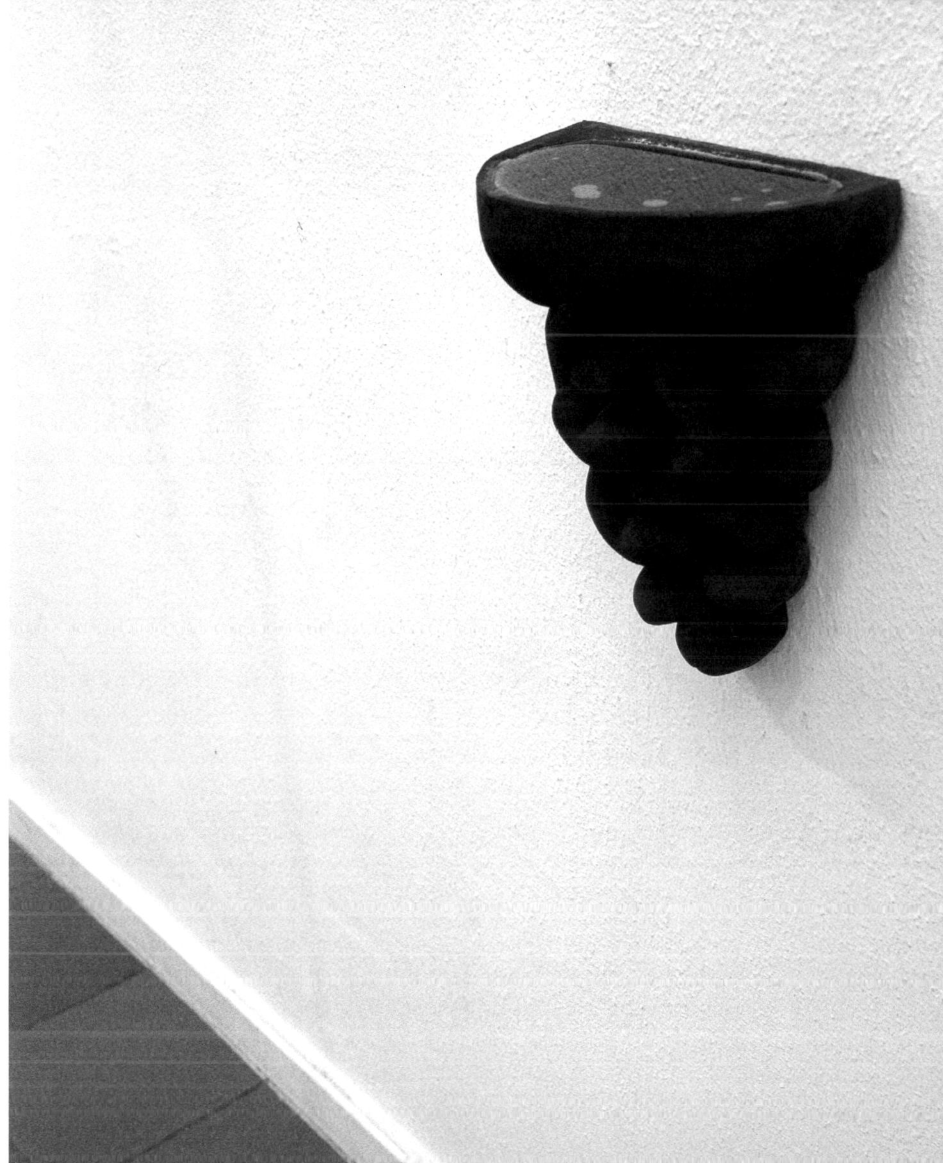

*Schwarzes Panel*
*(Black panel)*, 2008
Holz verbrannt
Burnt timber
H: 2,6 m

*Internals*
*(Colabecken)*, 2008
Beton, Pigment,
Armierung, Cola
Concrete,
pigment, rein-
forcement, coke
H: 0,6 m

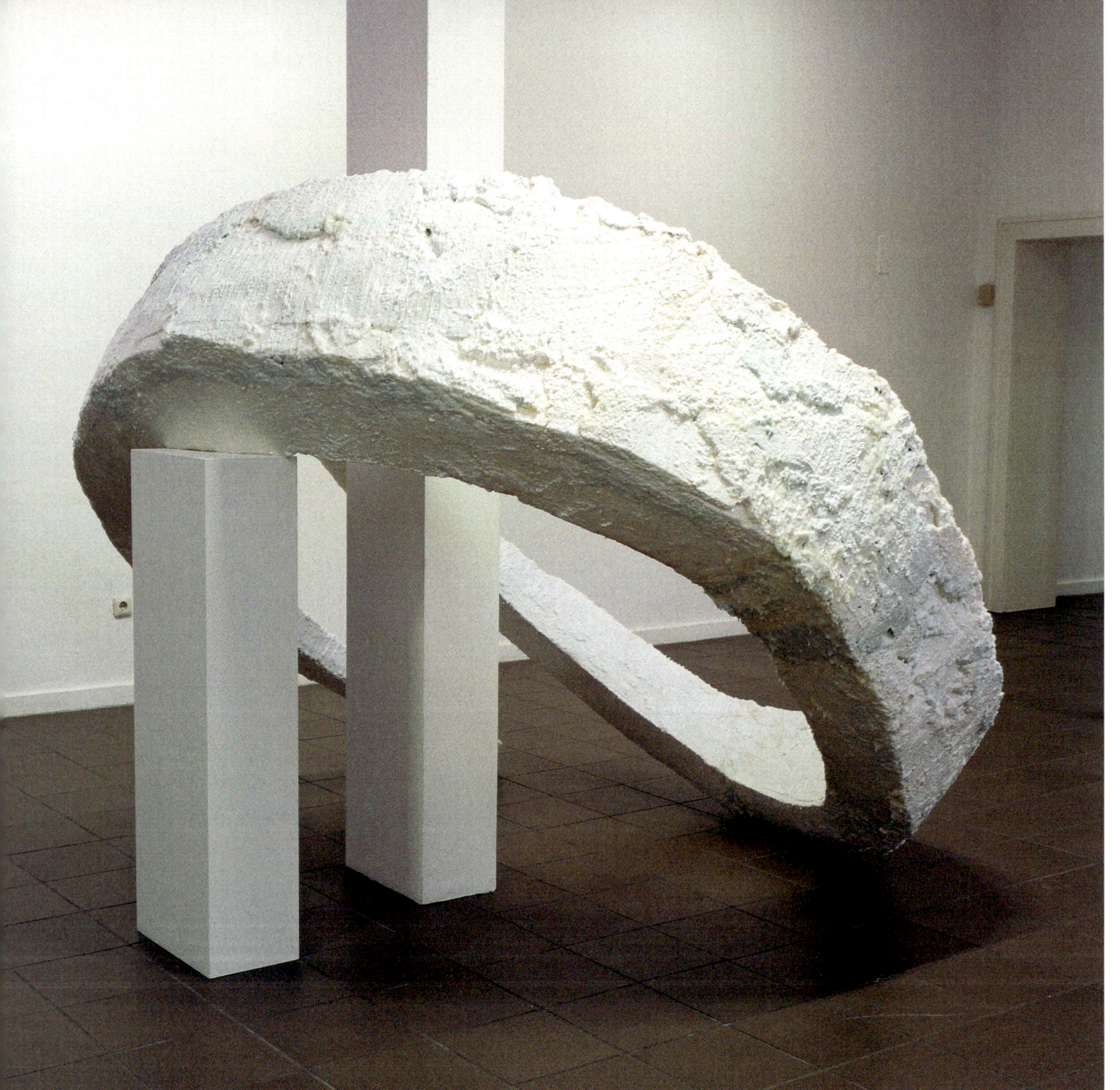

*Hoop*, 2008
Wachs, Bauschaum,
Styropor
Wax, polyurethan
foam, polystyrene
ø 1,9 m

*Streamer*, 2008
Holz, Spachtel,
Farbe, Lack
Timber, filler,
paint, varnish
L: 3,6 m

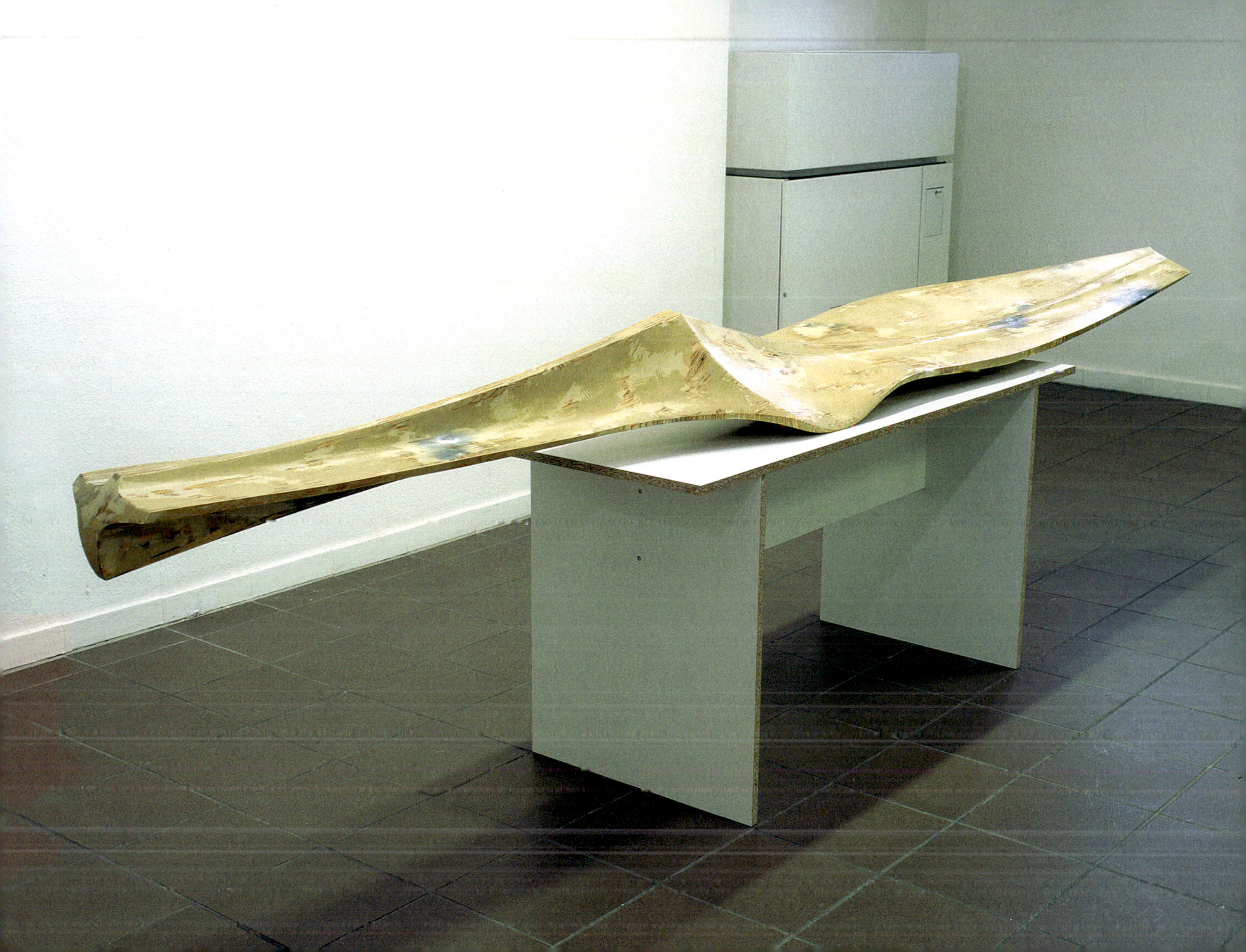

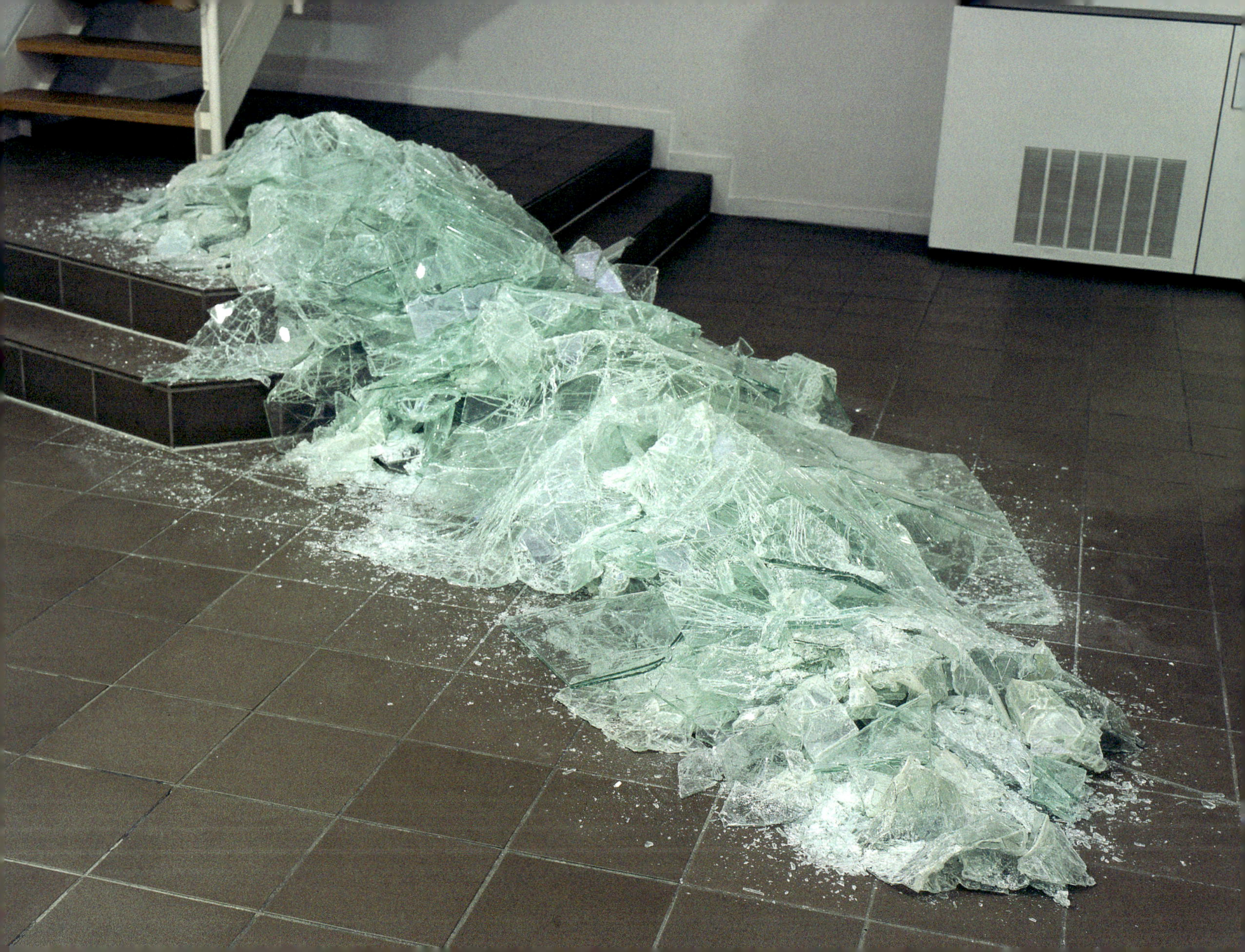

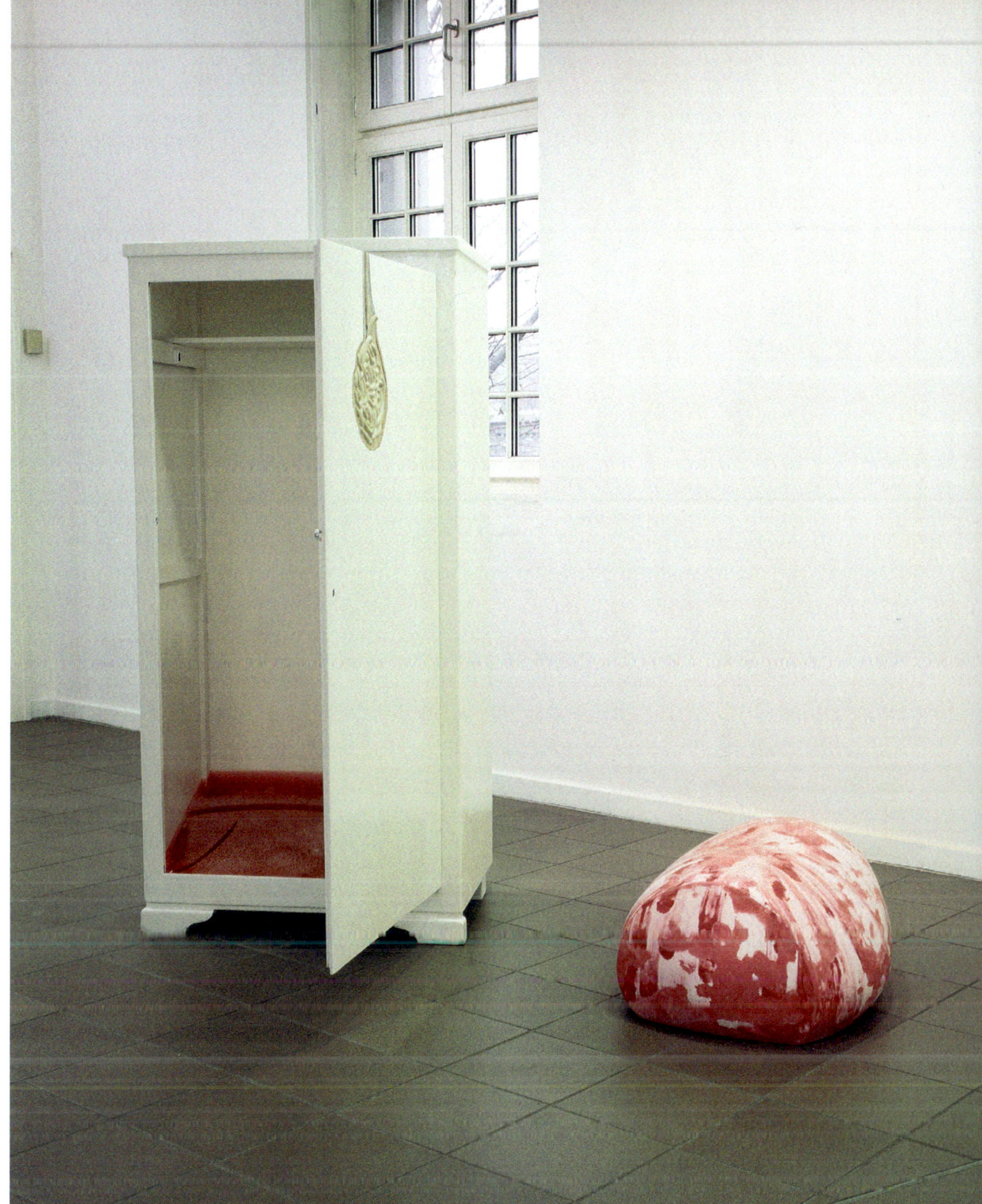

*Zunge (Tongue),* 2008
Verbundglas zerbrochen
Broken glass
L: 4 m

*Gulpy,* 2008
Schrank, Spachtel,
Lack, Gelatine,
Glyzerin, Pigment
Wardrobe, filler,
varnish, gelatine,
glycerine, pigment
H: 1,9 m

*Drop,* 2008
Acrylharz, Pigment
Acrylic resin, pigment
L: 0,8 m

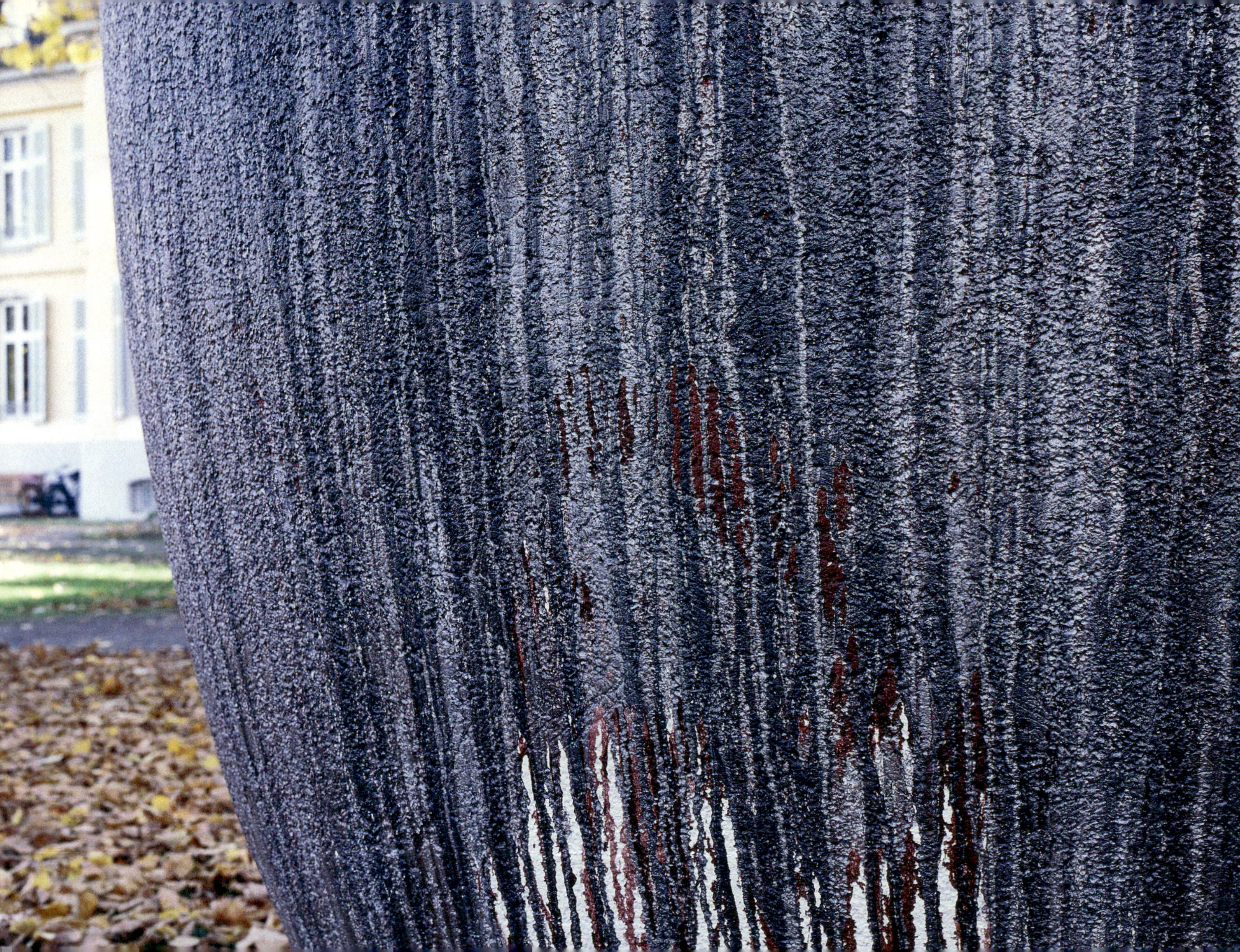

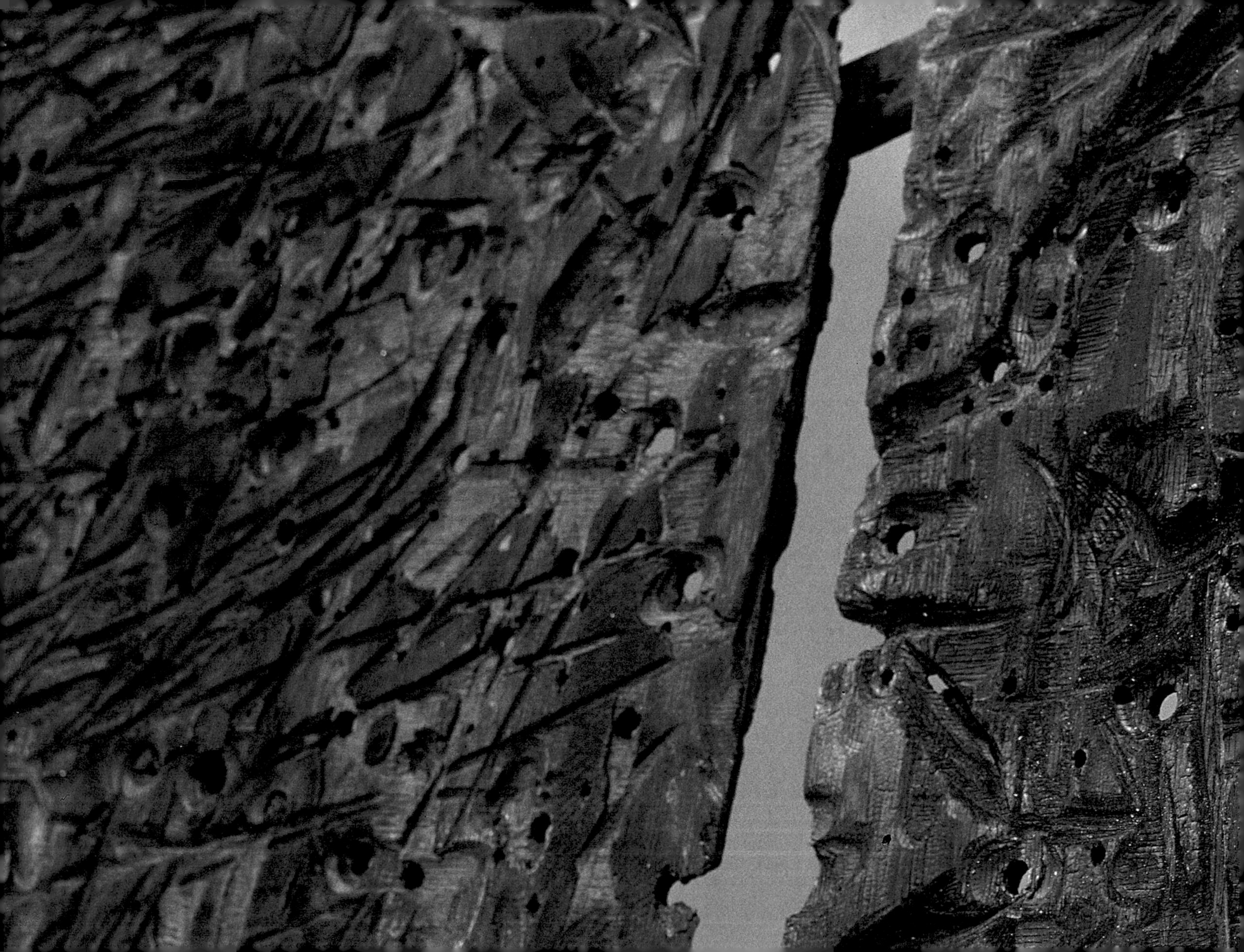

# Was, is, no more
# On the works of Gereon Krebber

SUSANNE WEDEWER

"A work of art is above all an adventure of the mind."

EUGENE IONESCO

*Superliminal,* the title of the exhibition at the Kunstverein Leverkusen, is – anticipating the inevitable question – an artificial word, made up by Gereon Krebber. "Super," as in "above," "superior," "great," but also "exaggerated." Part of the word "limit" is also there, indicating "limited" and therefore "exclusive" or "desirable." Krebber loves these mental games with the different possibilities that can arise out of the indeterminate, the unclearly defined – and also applies them to his sculptures.

Even if we try to determine the materiality of the sculptures by finding descriptions of their forms, using references to ordinary, familiar-looking objects, doubts about the correctness of our conclusions always creep in during what ought to be the clarification of perception. Frequently, the contradiction between the material – which we think we recognize through its function – and the sculpture that emerges from it is too irritating. Is it artificial or organic, hard or soft, solid or liquid? For example, Krebber takes glass and makes it "flow down" a staircase. Whole, frozen pieces are the marks of a track, fragmented, broken without being broken; they resemble ice floes, yet do not possess the drama of their dangerous, pointed fractures. Caspar David Friedrich's famous painting *The Sea of Ice* (1823–24), a work that was long known as *The Wreck of Hope,* comes to mind. Over time, very different interpretations of the painting's theme have emerged, ranging from the dangers of the polar region, to the divine in nature versus the temporality of humankind, all the way to political interpretations. For us, from the standpoint of the twenty-first century, however, it is not the interpretations of the painting's content, but essentially Friedrich's enduring depiction of ice that Krebber's installation awakens in our minds. And as far as the sculptor is concerned, his primary interest is also in the material, since he wants to sound out its various possibilities – in this case, the possibilities of laminated glass.

Krebber, born in 1973, often works with everyday objects, in his sculptures – employing their different material and spatial qualities, as well as their surface conditions. He also uses ordinary substances such as wood, concrete, Styrofoam, acrylic resin, or glass – burning it, charring it, filling it, plastering it, melting it – on a quest for the form that arises, for a moment, as if frozen, from the constantly unstable balance of what was, what is, and what is no longer.

The notion of the sculpture as an arrested moment of a process or change is not a new one.

1   JULIA HÖNER, "Komm,
wir machen mal 'ne Hänge-
probe," in: GEREON KREBBER,
*Slink,* published by Jochen
Heufelder, Fuhrwerkswaage
Kunstraum, Cologne 2007.
2   Conversation with
the artist, exhibition set-up
*Superliminal,* Kunstverein
Leverkusen 2008.
3   PAUL SUTINEN: „Carl
Andre – The Turner of Mat-
ter (1980)", in: Exhibition
catalogue *Carl Andre Sculptor 1996,* Krefeld, Wolfsburg
1996, p. 52.

After all, ever since Lessing at least, it has been considered sculpture's primary task to discover the right moment. Krebber knows about the history of his medium, about the works of Imi Knoebel, about the predecessors of Minimalism. Yet their "orthodox attitude," as he calls it, toward site-specificity does not interest him. For him, space – architecture and its structure – is simply one material among many. What does interest him, instead, is the interim state of a work – how it develops out of playing, experimenting, with materials. How far can I go, for example, in maltreating plywood with different tools and then with a flamethrower? When will the material cease to be serviceable?

Some of Krebber's sculptures teeter on the brink of total decay – and this is also something that differentiates his work from Minimal Art, an art period to which his work is soften compared. It means that, consistently, some of his works have to be "disposed of" after an exhibition, whether they are collapsing, or because they were made on site and cannot be removed in one piece without causing damage, or because they need to take other forms in other places.

However, marks of decay and traces of the process of creation are some of the elements of Krebber's work. As Julia Höner has already pointed out in her text on the work *Slink,* Krebber's sculptures speak "of temporality and usage, taking their own ability to be consumed by the art system to the point of absurdity." Krebber does not genuflect before the dogma of immutability, the uniqueness of a work of art. Rather, he uses some of his works as if they were letters that have to be constantly re-arranged, the space serving as the grammar that circumscribes the diction.

Installations – sometimes seemingly simple set-tings – are created either with a single main character that takes over the space, or, as is the case in Leverkusen, with an entire ensemble. Autonomous, independent, and yet interacting with each other, the space, the site ("In the case of some materials, doesn't it seem as if something went wrong at Bayer?", says Krebber), and the viewer. And this interplay works, even when, as Carl Andre put it in 1980, "Art (is) … not a form of communication. Art can, like electricity, assist in communication, but its basic nature has as little to do with communication as does the nature of electricity. Art is one of the ways to bear the things to which we can never be reconciled – death, for example." Krebber succeeds in this, especially on one particular level, which could almost be described by the famous phrase, the "lightness of being," if it were not for the doubt: the doubt about our perception, about the supposed essence of the things we perceive. And so, infected by Krebber's palpable curiosity, which is inherent in each of his works, we intellectually get involved with a game of the possible, having already become a physical form.

# Take a walk on the wild side
# Gereon Krebber in Essen

Uwe Schramm

Even for those practiced in viewing art, an encounter with Gereon Krebber's world of sculptural objects and ideas can be counted among those experiences that are as memorable as they are disturbing. In his shows, one meets with pieces of blue spaghetti hung up to dry over a free-standing metal frame, or a wobbly, bright orange wedge of gelatin snuggling up against a step, like an oversized gummy bear; or hollow forms resembling fonts are filled with Coca-Cola. Rolls made of plaster and Styrofoam recall frozen tiramisu; burgeoning, odd, cocoon-like constructs proliferate out of yellow cable conduits, and the floors of exhibition spaces are covered with puddles of a slippery, foamy substance, whose greenish, shimmering transparence evokes discomforting thoughts of human expectoration.

Krebber enthusiastically transgresses classic sculpture's dogma regarding material. In visualizing his artistic ideas he prefers to use unconventional materials, which are a severe test for some viewers' understanding of art. Yet Krebber's inventiveness in selecting his materials seems inexhaustible. The artist's ability to create articulate sculpture is formed by his use of trash bags, adhesive tape, toothpaste, adhesive dots, sugar, silicon, gelatin, clothes hangers, concrete, glycerin, cable ties, plastic sheets, balloons, and other organic

and artificial materials that impressively demonstrate the entire spectrum of ordinary, everyday materials available.

Krebber's use of unusual materials, however, is not simply self-serving. The artist wants us to forget pure rationality as the standard method of perceiving the world, so that we will instead be confronted with sensory experiences that will take us back to the complexity of human life.

By employing certain materials and their many associations, Krebber allows memories of entities from the everyday world we perceive to proliferate. They disturb, irritate, and make one question one's view of the world. Krebber plays with physical growths consisting of a variety of mental associations that are deliberately intended to disturb one's sense of "good taste." They touch the viewer, like things or creatures from another world, and the closer they come to one's own experience of reality, or the more they derive their forms from it, the more intense their effect.

The sense of perturbation and disturbance created by Krebber's works is caused by the fact that the artist, through the presence of his sculptures, deliberately aims to address parts of the human body that are part of its survival mechanism, but which are normally taboo subjects for discussion. Thus, in his sculptures, he humorously stages the excretion process or its results, for instance, using visual or even olfactory stimuli that immediately trigger our learned responses of disgust or decorous denial. At the same time, however, the lucent materiality of his installations lures the viewer to take a closer look, so that it seems impossible to avoid the emotional conflict arising from equal amounts of fascination and revulsion.

In subversive ways, Krebber's sculptures seek or find comparisons and analog connections to the human body, in terms of both physicality and biochemistry. The processes of breaking taboos, causing provocation, and posing questions determines two things that are always connected to the articulate presence of Krebber's sculptures: the number of contradictions, and to what extent the viewer will emotionally react.

### When life begins

After Krebber decided to exhibit at the Kunsthaus Essen, he visited the space to check out the possibilities of the provided location. Quickly, he outlined his first ideas for a show. With impressive confidence and precision, Krebber grasped the tension of the space, its architectural particulars, and the uniquely underlying atmosphere of the site.

Krebber went through all of the rooms, measuring walls, door openings, and window niches with his own body and outspread arms. For the biggest room – with its pillars and a continuous row of windows – he decided that something large, which would fragment the room's dimensions, should be created. A soft, round, longish form, similar to a snake or a worm would be gently twined around the angular pillars and extend over the entire length of the space. Its elegant twists and turns would force visitors to make their way carefully around the growths and stumps lying on the ground.

In addition to this physical, sensory experience, an aspect of visual surprise would be caused by the confrontation with Krebber's selected materials. To achieve this aspect, Krebber did not resort to the usual sculptural materials for the realization of his spectacular intervention in the space. Instead, he chose items that would normally be found in a regular supermarket. First, layer after layer of aluminum foil and then brilliant green plastic sheets were wrapped around a simple wooden structure, creating a strange, organic-looking form that completely hid the original structure from view. Space, architecture, and sculptural shape suddenly formed an inseparable unit, whose special visual presence seemed to cause the room to vibrate, conveying a sense of flow that abrogated the usual perceptual constants.

Krebber gently undermines our preconceived view of the world and preconception of things, but in a way that is very determined and highly effective. This applies especially to the perception of the architecture; Krebber's intervention literally gives the room a new face, and hence, a surprisingly palpable appearance.

As an optical counterpart to *vymbo,* as Krebber called the line in the space that had turned into a thing, *droopy* was meant to surround the visitor, not only with an unusual material form, but also with an unmistakable smell. Starting with the notion that his sculptures should not be limited to their physical and visual presence, but that they could naturally be perceived through the other senses, Krebber created a strange looking object that would hang from the ceiling and whose corporeal form and smell would dominate the entire room. *Droopy's* core is made up of a number of inflated balloons held together by countless meters of adhesive tape. All of the balloons were covered with sausage-like shapes made out of adhesive tape, some of which hung down to the floor. Krebber meticulously painted this bladder-like form with a mixture of yellowish-white mayonnaise and glue, which slowly and tantalizingly dripped onto the floor in some places. The whole thing looked like a jellyfish whose tentacles reached into the space, or a cocoon in which a new, unfamiliar life form seemed to be incubating.

Visitors to the exhibition reacted with decided ambivalence. They hovered between fascination and disgust, curiosity and revulsion, between the irresistible urge to touch the "nest," and their respect for the obvious independent existence of the materials, which practically forbade anyone to get any closer.

*Droopy* is an impressive visualization of the artist's fascination for working with materials that cause effects and reactions from visitors, which he himself can not really control. This meant that his work on this figure was a kind of experiment, with somewhat unpredictable results. It sheds some light on Krebber's desire to take some controlled risk in his work with the unknown and the uncontrollable, in order to create new and exciting experiences for himself and the viewer. In his artistic concept, the material is involved in an automatic, continual performance, which results in the metamorphosis of his objects.

Thus, *droopy* also changed shape over the course of the exhibition. The air leaked out of the balloons, so that more and more bits of twisted adhesive tape fell to the floor. Gradually, its color turned more yellow. Like an organic life form, Krebber's sculpture seemed to be alive, seemed to move and change. Every once in a while the noise made by the materials hitting the ground echoed through the rooms. A delicate lake of yellowish, liquid slime was formed beneath the object, which gradually began to give off an unpleasant stench.

### Killing me softly

It is precisely these dominant material qualities in his sculptures that allow one to perceive the artist's overall intention of finding new ways of working with classic themes of sculpture. Krebber's unconventional artistic procedures aim to counteract the sculptor's traditional tasks – which are based on concepts such as lightness and heaviness, mass and void, transparence and opacity, balance, stability, and linearity – in order to level the way for more expressive potential. The desire for provocation is also part and parcel of his work. Krebber deliberately creates a sense of disquiet and discomfort, intentionally walking a fine line between attraction and revulsion, fascination and rejection – annoyances included.

"I had the idea," Krebber once said in an interview, "of declaring war on the viewer. Literally saying, 'Hey. I want to kill you.'"

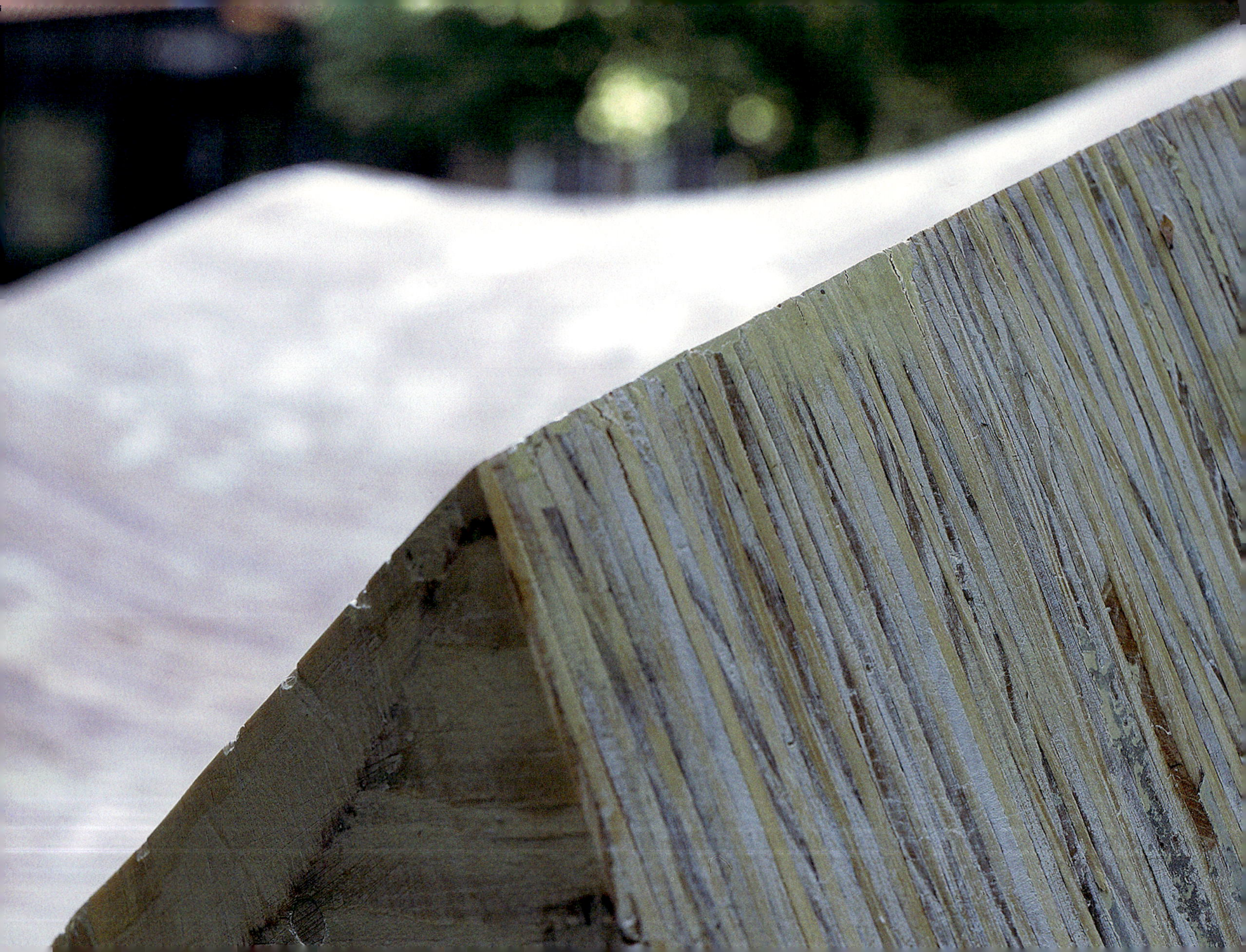

# Sorrysorrysosorry
# Gereon Krebber's Apology

STEPHAN MANN

Gereon Krebber has created two corresponding works precisely for the space at the Museum Goch. In the gallery on the left, *Oxomoeno,* a caterpillar-like structure, snakes across the floor and up the wall to the ceiling. Its "head" at a slight angle, the exotic animal twists around several times, looking down from the ceiling at the visitor. Something apparently like an animal lures the visitor into the space, encouraging him to come closer. Yet there is nothing soft about the surface of the thing – rather, it is prickly, unapproachable, equipped with countless points and injurious barbs.

The visitor retreats and is left alone to wonder what it is he sees before him, yet he also has a desire for a palpable sense of direction. If he is brave, he will come to realize that the object is a construct of hangers and cable ties. Meticulously glued and twisted together, the artificial animal slithers through the space.

In the room opposite, Widget reacts to this situation. Krebber pushes a pointed, triangular form made of steel toward visitors entering the space. When the viewer enters the large hall, with its clearly segmented windows and two central pillars, he feels as if he is looking at a relict from the old days. Stranded in the museum, the ship-like object becomes an exhibition piece. It seems to float, invisibly fastened to the wall, placed on a pedestal that echoes the form of the two pillars in the middle of the room. With great ease and confidence, the mythical relict dominates the space. Here, too, Krebber toys with the curiosity of visitors. They approach a steel form, which looks as if something like seaweed has accidentally become entangled in it. The unusually, aggressively red construct made of a tangled mishmash of items dangles downward. Again, it is only after careful examination that the visitor realizes what sort of materials Krebber is working with here. As he did previously in his work *Wireframe* (2007), shown in Breda, the Netherlands, Krebber has molded sugar, twine, glue, and candles into a mass of items sprayed with brilliant red paint. However, unlike *Wireframe, Widget,* as Krebber also calls the Goch installation, reaches into the space and allows the visitor to become an active partner in the work.

Through its size alone, *Widget* fractures the space. It is constructed around one of the two pillars, so that the careful observer will notice that it must have been assembled in the room. Yet it is not only the proportions of the work that fragment the space: Its pointed form introduces a great dynamic into the usually peaceful architecture of the room.

Both *Oxomoeno* and *Widget* play with the viewer's sensibilities. The sight of the works makes him feel very uncertain. Krebber evokes a cornucopia of associative thoughts in us. At first, there is the uncertainty about the materials used. "But it really looks as if ..." was one of the phrases most frequently heard during the run of the show. Viewers are disturbed and bewildered, and the artist leaves them alone with this experience. Even the titles of the objects do not help. They are also simply associations thought up by the artist, and do not provide any hints about the interpretation of the works. "Oxomoeno is, first of all, a very freely associated series of sounds, which I wanted to use to describe the caterpillar thing. ... Oxomoeno starts as an onomatopoetic assembly of open 'o's and crossed 'x's – the way that the hangers cross and create a looping 'o.' In terms of content, it is a mix between Mötörhead (a funny band name burdened with umlauts), mono (meaning individual), and oxymorons (a rhetorical figure of speech that contradicts itself, like 'black snow'). I like contradictions: slithery, yet prickly, etc.," Krebber says about this work.

There is no interpretation involved in Krebber's work. Rather, the visitor must resort to his own emotions and senses. He sees, smells, even feels the works, and then creates the images in them that will bring him closer to the secret of the works. He will wait in vain for certainty, for explanations. Krebber works with the ability of the viewer to remember. It does not matter in which direction the visitor moves; the interpretation remains his alone.

Seen in this way, Krebber is a sensory-oriented artist, through and through. His plans are very precise and specific, but the last phase of the creative process lies entirely in his hands – which have been captured in the moment.

Krebber's objects are both installations and autonomous sculptures at the same time. On one hand, they are conceived and constructed for a specific space, as they are in the exhibition at the Museum Goch. They are made to adapt to a particular architectonic setting. On the other hand, the works exist independently, on their own. They are so arbitrary that they can maintain their own against any sort of structure, and isolated, they could also fit into other settings.

Krebber likes to give his works space. He knows that they will have to be circumnavigated, that the visitor wants to become a part of them and needs enough room to be able to perceive them with his senses. The installation at the Goch is also distinguished by a lucid arrangement of other sculptures.

All of these works are based on the idea of the trompe l'oeil, the deceptive image or the disturbing game played with perception. Regardless of whether it is a foaming bathtub or a white block of ice, which Krebber playfully calls *Stückchen,* or *Little Piece,* he always confronts the visitor with a range of well-known images and associations, which he is ultimately left to question on his own, as he carefully examines the object. It looks as if – and yet, it isn't, is it? For the playfulness, the irony that Krebber uses to deceive the visitor, the artist apologizes in our exhibition, giving it the title *sorrysorrysosorry.* What more could one want?

Even the pedestal, that clear and functional element found in every museum, whose only purpose

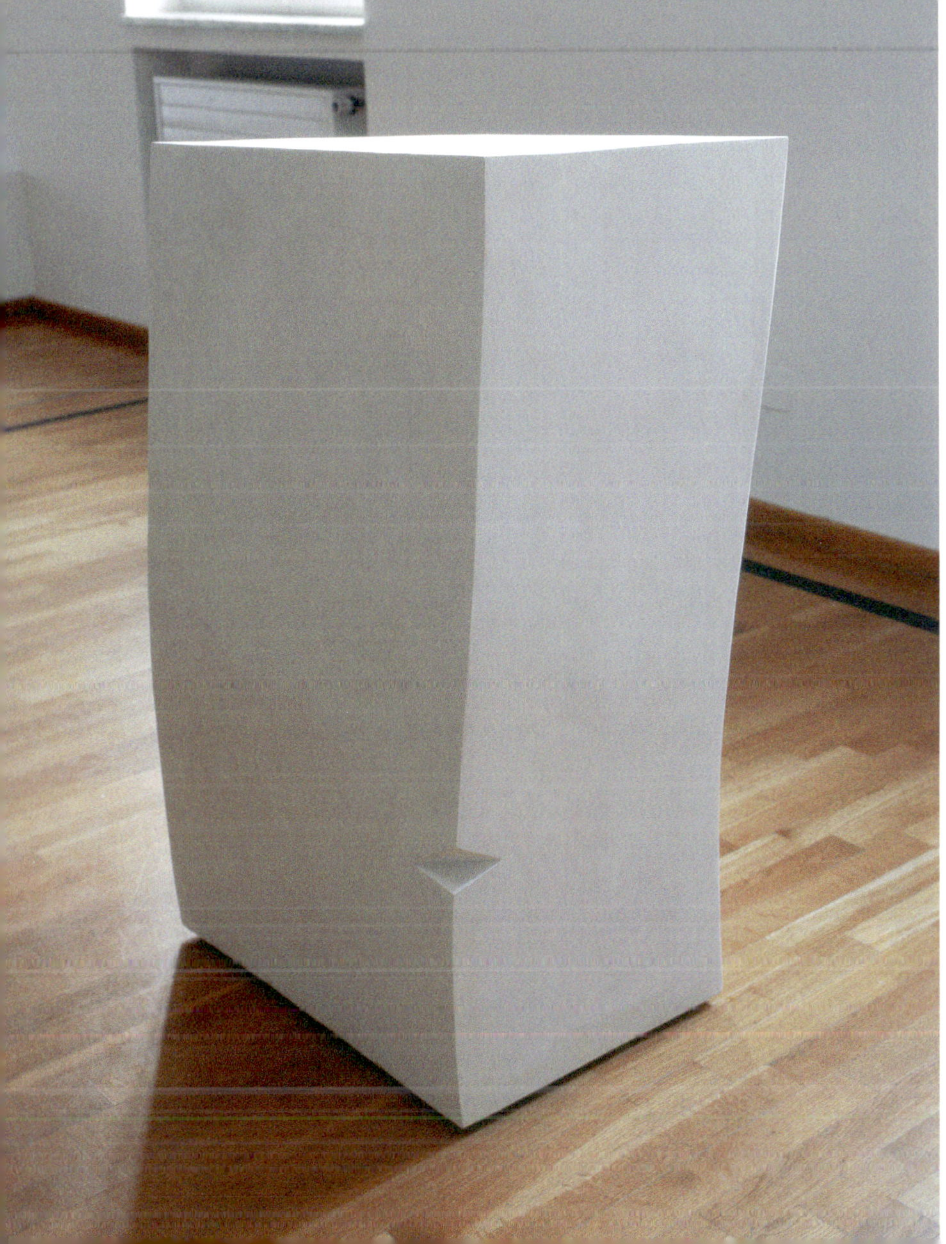

is to display a precious object to the best possible effect, becomes, in Krebber's hands, an uncertain piece of museum technology. *Gebogener Sockel (Bended plinth)* is scratched along the edges, with an uneven surface, even its material does not turn out to be what it seems: plaster and paint. Out of an apparently solid pedestal is made an object of great fragility. For this, the artist apologizes: "Sorrysorrysosorry."

Despite their seriousness, these works can be read with much humor. They play with the familiar, taking it to a new artistic reality. Krebber's installations celebrate appearances. And, as is so often the case, they turn out to be nothing more than a game. To achieve this, Krebber shrinks from nothing. Any sort of material is good to work with, even the popular sugar necklaces.

Gereon Krebber seduces us again and again. He uncovers the surface and, in so doing, reveals the superficiality of the present time.

*Sorrysorrysosorry,*
Museum Goch, 2008:
*Gebogener Sockel
(Bended plinth)*

Gereon Krebber
Geboren 1973 in Oberhausen, lebt/arbeitet in Köln
Born 1973 in Oberhausen, lives/works in Cologne

**Studium | Education**

2000–2002 Royal College of Art, London, MA Fine Art Sculpture
1995–2000 Kunstakademie Düsseldorf, Prof. Tony Cragg und | and Prof. Hubert Kiecol

**Einzelausstellungen | Solo exhibitions**

2009
*Let the pigs pay*, Galerie Christian Lethert, Köln
*Boards with bumps*, Number 35, New York

2008
*Superliminal*, Kunstverein Leverkusen
*Wollte könnte sollte*, Kunsthalle Bremerhaven
PawnShop Gallery, Los Angeles
*Sorrysorrysosorry*, Museum Goch
*Frischzelle_08*, Kunstmuseum Stuttgart
*Droopy*, Kunsthaus Essen

2007
*Slink*, Fuhrwerkswaage Kunstraum, Köln
*Slurp*, Stiftung DKM, Duisburg
*Leichter getan als gesagt*, Galerie Jarmuschek & Partner, Berlin
*All that is solid melts into air*, Kunsthalle Wilhelmshaven

2006
*Loopy loo loopy lie*, Galerie Ferdinand-Ude, Gelsenkirchen
*Too far fetched*, MMIII Kunstverein Mönchengladbach
*Can't hold back*, marksblond Projekte, Bern

2005
*Kringel*, Josef-Albers-Museum Quadrat, Bottrop
*Jelly beam*, Henry Peacock Gallery, London

2004
*Squeezed*, Laden, Düsseldorf
*Wolke zwei*, Förderpreis der Stadt Gelsenkirchen | Gelsenkirchen Award, Kommunale Galerie Gelsenkirchen

2003
*Upstairs*, Henry Peacock Gallery, London

2002
*blorp*, Galerie Ferdinand-Ude, Gelsenkirchen

2001
*Peacock baits*, Henry Peacock Gallery, London

1999
Hof Heisterkamp, Kirchellen

**Gruppenausstellungen | Group exhibitions**

2008
*Parkhaus*, Kunsthalle Düsseldorf
*Wanderland*, Lustwarande, Tilburg
Kevin Kavanagh Gallery, Dublin

2007
*Dreizueins*, Kunsthalle Recklinghausen
*Eye Love Candy*, KOP Stichting, Breda
*Triband*, KunstKlub Berlin

2006
*Double take*, mit | with Luka Fineisen, Parkhaus im Malkastenpark, Düsseldorf
Saar Ferngas Kunstpreis, Pfalzgalerie Kaiserslautern
*From life*, Royal Academy Summer Show, London
*Pleasuring the black sun*, mit | with Markus Vater, Zingerpresents, Tilburg

2005
*Poseidon Adventure*, Sadlers Well, London
*Myyourtheirspitalfields*, Skulpturenprogramm | Sculpture program Spitalfields, London
*Siege*, Parkhaus | Car park Commercial Road, London
*Nordwestkunst*, Kunsthalle Wilhelmshaven

2004
*Zombie*, Galerie Ferdinand-Ude, Gelsenkirchen
*bloodshot brighteyed*, Galerie Neurotitan, Berlin
*Hier und jetzt*, Gustav-Lübke-Museum Hamm
*Praxis*, mit | with Martina Jenne, Galerie Ferdinand-Ude, Gelsenkirchen
*domestic (f)utility*, New Art Centre, Salisbury
*Bottrop 25ers*, Quadrat Bottrop

2003
*hydrophobia*, Henry Peacock Gallery, London
*Trendwände*, Kunstraum Düsseldorf
*bloodshot brighteyed*, Tea building, London

2002
*Soap on the rope*, mit | with Noah Sherwood, Atrium Gallery, London
*Vier zu vier*, Kunstverein Gelsenkirchen

2001
*Kunstpreis Junger Westen*, Kunsthalle Recklinghausen
*Ernst-Klusen-Preis*, Städtische Galerie Viersen
*Junge Kunst im Ruhrgebiet*, Gladbeck

2000
*Mandelbaums Wunderöl*, Johannesstraße, Köln / Haus des Lehrers, Berlin

1999
*Junge Kunst im Ruhrgebiet*, Gladbeck

1998
*für pathos*, mit | with Björn Dahlem, Kunstakademie Düsseldorf

Index

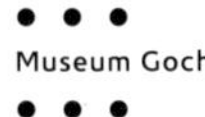



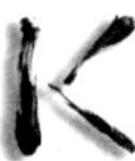



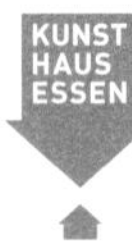




Diese Publikation erscheint anlässlich der Ausstellungen |
This catalogue is published on the occasion of the exhibitions
*Gereon Krebber – Sorrysorrysosorry*, Museum Goch
*Droopy*, Kunsthaus Essen
*Superliminal*, Kunstverein Leverkusen
Herausgeber | Editor
Museum Goch in Kooperation mit den beteiligten Museen |
in cooperation with the participating museums
Ausstellungsförderung | Exhibition sponsoring
Stiftung Kunstfonds Bonn, Sparkasse Essen,
Kulturbüro der Stadt Essen
Katalogförderung | Catalogue sponsoring
Kunststiftung NRW, dimensional GmbH, Köln
Texte | Texts
Stephan Mann, Uwe Schramm, Susanne Wedewer
Übersetzungen | Translations
Allison Plath-Moseley
Fotografie | Photographs
Gereon Krebber
Gestaltung | Design
Andreas Koch, Bielefeld
Detailaufnahmen | Details
Umschlag | Cover: *Widget,* Vorsatz, vorn | Endpaper, front:
*Bonus,* S.|p. 2: *Slink,* S.|p. 3: *Bürste,* S.|p. 4: *Blauer
Blobster,* S.|p. 6: *Zunge (Tongue),* S.|pp. 22/23: *Oxomoeno,*
S.|p. 114: *Kleiner Tunnel,* Vorsatz, hinten | Endpaper, back:
*Schwarzes Panel (Black panel)*
Printed, published and distributed by
Kerber Verlag, Bielefeld
Windelsbleicher Straße 166–170
33659 Bielefeld, Germany
Telefon  +49(0)521 9 50 08-10
Fax       +49(0)521 9 50 08-88
info@kerberverlag.com, www.kerberverlag.com
Kerber, US Distribution
D.A.P., Distributed Art Publisher Inc.
155 Sixth Avenue 2nd Floor
New York, N.Y. 10013
Phone  +1(0)212 6 27-19 99
Fax       +1(0)212 6 27-94 84

Persönlicher Dank | Personal thanks
Klaus Becké, Daryl Brown, Renzo Cavallin, Hilary Crisp,
Katja Davar, Chris Driessen, Annabel Emson, Stephan
Engelke, Steffen Fischer, Gelita Deutschland, Carsten
Helmke, Jochen Heufelder, Julia Höner, Graham Hudson,
ISP Biochema Schwaben, Andreas Jacobi, Martina
Jenne, Dirk Krämer, Familie Krebber, Christian Lethert,
Klaus Maas, Jacqui McIntosh, Heidi van Mierlo, Anna
Mirbach, Karl-Heinz Rummeny, Peter Schloß, Lukas
Schmenger, Klaus Schmitt, Natascha Schmitten, André
Schnitzler, Hans-Jürgen Schwalm, Philip Seibel, Daniel
Spanke, Sebastian Strahl, Tazalika te Reh, Ferdinand
Ullrich, Viola Weigel und den Autoren | and the authors





Die Deutsche Nationalbibliothek verzeichnet diese
Publikation in der Deutschen Nationalbibliografie; detail-
lierte bibliografische Daten sind im Internet über
http://dnb.ddb.de abrufbar. | The Deutsche National-
bibliothek holds a record of this publication in the
Deutsche Nationalbibliografie; detailed bibliographical
data can be found under: http://dnb.ddb.de.





ISBN 978-3-86678-250-1

Printed in Germany